I0446010

The
History
of Art
IN ONE SENTENCE

500 YEARS
OF ART
(BUT FUNNY)

The History of Art

IN ONE SENTENCE

Verity Babbs

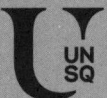

For me, at 17.

Contents

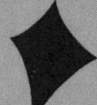
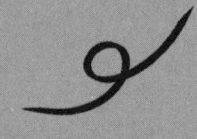
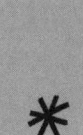
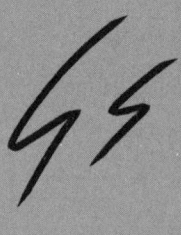

Introduction

WHAT IS THIS BOOK?

The History of Art in One Sentence is a quick guide to some of the major art movements, styles, groups and schools in Britain, Europe and the US over the past 500 years.

WHO IS IT FOR?

It's for anyone who wants to engage with art history but isn't quite sure where to start.

HOW IS IT STRUCTURED?

Each chapter of this roughly chronological book features ten questions, plus three key artists and three key artworks, each covered in a single sentence, to give you a taste for the art movement and its core characters.

WHO WROTE IT?

Me, Verity Babbs – I'm an art historian and comedian.

WHY WAS IT WRITTEN?

Art history is great – full of laughs and relatable bits, and while there are certainly plenty of art history books around, many of them want you to have a PhD-level of knowledge just to get past the cover.

WILL IT COVER EVERYTHING?

Absolutely not; this book focuses solely on art in the West, and even then it doesn't mention everything or everyone – it's not commenting on which art is most important, it's just a little guide with some funny bits.

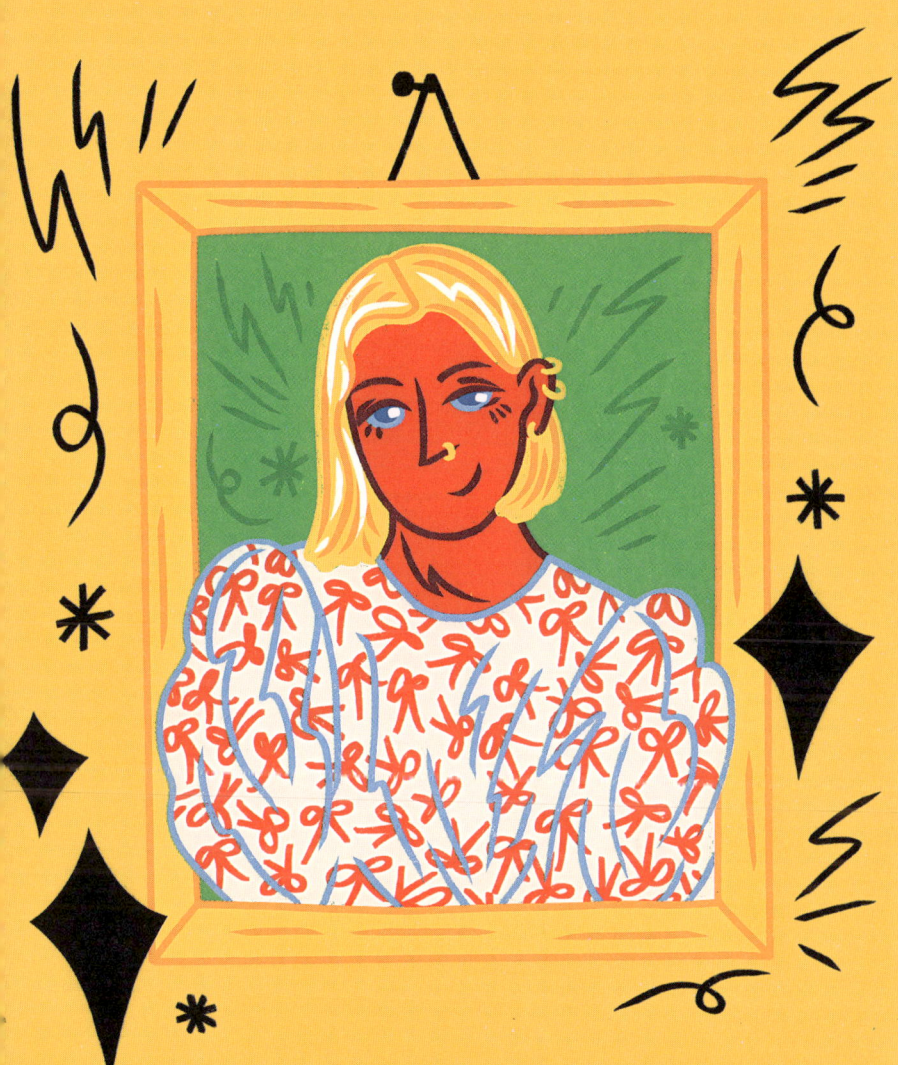

600

WHY DID YOU CHOOSE THESE FIFTY MOVEMENTS?

Being included in this book isn't an indication of the significance of the movement, but rather reflects the number of times I thought, 'Ooh, that's interesting/funny/odd!' during my research, or how regularly they come up on *University Challenge*.

WHY JUST FROM THE WEST?

Western art history is what I studied, and living in the West, it's the art I've had the most exposure to and feel the most confident in lightly taking the piss out of throughout this book.

WHY DO WE START AT THE RENAISSANCE?

The Renaissance is often seen as a new beginning for art so it seemed a good place to start, plus I really wanted to talk about Michelangelo's bosoms.

WHY AREN'T SOME MAJOR ARTISTS INCLUDED IN THE 'KEY ARTISTS' BIT?

In order to include as many artists as possible in each chapter, I've tried not to repeat them, so not being a 'Key Artist' doesn't reflect an artist's unkey-ness – sometimes they're included in a question instead, or not – it's a short book.

HOW TIGHT IS THE CATEGORISATION?

Art history isn't neat: many artists worked under multiple labels (or none) and with multiple groups (and the start and end points are almost always hard to rigidly define), so just because someone pops up in one chapter of this book, it doesn't mean they weren't also doing interesting stuff in other areas.

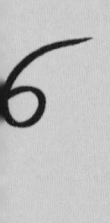
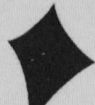

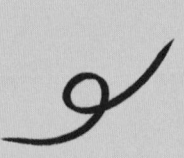
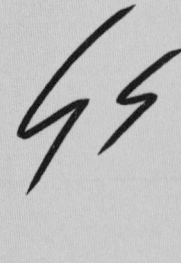

WHY ARE SOME PEOPLE LISTED AS 'ARTIST' BUT OTHERS AS 'PAINTER' OR 'SCULPTOR'?

I've tried to categorise artists (they're all artists) under the type of work they're best known for, and when I've used 'artist' it's because they were known for working in a variety of disciplines.

COOL, SO I IMAGINE EVERYONE INCLUDED IS A GOODIE?

Plenty of the artists and institutions mentioned in this book were unpleasant characters at best and serious criminals at worst, which I don't always cover – so please don't take this book to be an endorsement of, well… anyone or anything really.

WILL I BE AN ART GENIUS BY THE END?

No (sorry), but you might feel a little less lost next time you're in a museum, and may be more helpful to your pub quiz team.

DO I NEED TO KNOW ANYTHING IN ADVANCE?

No – let's go.

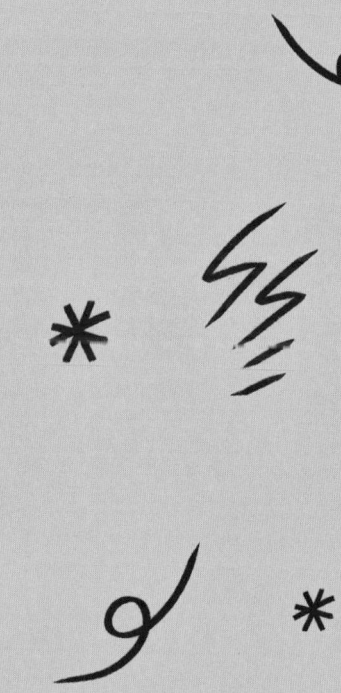

It was a period in Italy in
which artists emphasised
compositional harmony
(things looking nice and
balanced), idealised figures
(people looking beautiful)
and anatomical accuracy
(everyone's bits fitting right).

Italian
Renaissance
1300s-1500s

ITALY

WHY A 'RENAISSANCE'?

The Renaissance – named by the French historian Jules Michelet in 1858 – comes from the French term for 'rebirth', as it was seen as a period of cultural, economic and political renewal following the Middle Ages, harking back to the glory days of ancient times.

WHAT DID RENAISSANCE ARTISTS PAINT?

There were lots of biblical scenes, as most artwork was being commissioned by and for the Church, but artists were also getting hooked on humanism – a philosophy that spotlighted the human experience – so they also painted great thinkers and figures from the ancient past.

WHAT WAS A GUILD?

If you were an artist in Renaissance Europe, you had to be registered to a craft guild – a formal collective that kept the number of registered artists low to keep prices in check, protected its members' financial interests and ensured artworks' quality.

NICE, HOW DID YOU GET IN?

You had to present the guild with a 'masterpiece' – a really good piece of work that, if accepted, earned you the title of Master and entitled you to join the guild, run your own workshop and have your own apprentices.

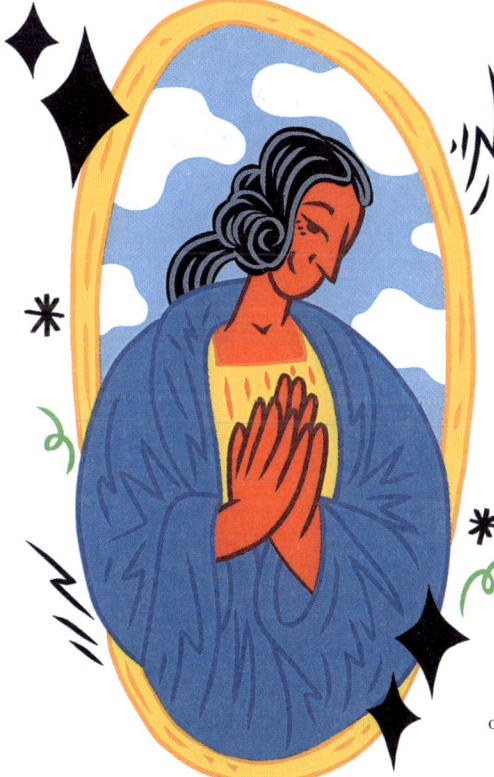

WHO WERE THE MEDICI?

They were a powerful banking and political family who ruled Florence pretty much consistently between the early fifteenth and the early eighteenth centuries – popping out a whopping four popes in the space of 100 years – and who spent a lot of money sponsoring the arts and paying for major architectural projects.

WHY HAS EVERYONE IN RENAISSANCE PORTRAITS GOT SUCH GREAT SKIN?

Sfumato was a popular technique that involved artists blending colours very gradually and softly, creating a smooth, airbrushed effect (jealous).

WHY IS THE VIRGIN MARY ALWAYS IN BLUE?

The blue pigment lapis lazuli (which came from just one mine in Afghanistan, ages away from Italy) was so rare and expensive that its use was strictly controlled by the Church, and deemed suitable only for a really significant figure like Mary.

WHY DOES THE BABY JESUS LOOK LIKE A CREEPY OLD MAN?

In paintings, Jesus often has off-puttingly strong control of his neck for a newborn, but this comes from the 'Homunculus Christ' concept, which held that Jesus wasn't like any old weak baby (he's Jesus, for Christ's sake!), but rather was born as a tiny version of a grown man.

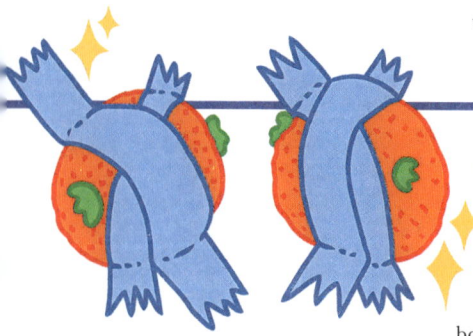

WHAT'S UP WITH MICHELANGELO'S BOSOMS?

Michelangelo's sculpture *Night* is known for its wonky boobies that look a bit like oranges sellotaped on at the end; one explanation for this is that the masculine body in the Renaissance was considered the highest beauty standard, so the most beautiful women were the ones who sort of looked like blokes.

3 KEY ARTISTS

Donatello (c.1386-1466)

Florentine sculptor, queer and specifically hired hunky assistants; kept his money in a basket hanging from his roof on a rope, so friends could take what they needed, but (shockingly?) not massively wealthy by the end of his life.

Titian (c.1488-1576)

Venetian painter and big celeb in his lifetime (even the Holy Roman Emperor picked up Titian's brush when he dropped it); very nice hair colour named after him.

Raphael (1483-1520)

Painter and architect from Urbino, hard worker but easily distracted by his willy (so much so that one patron had to convince Raphael's girlfriend to move near to the palace the artist was painting in, to save time on his commute).

3 KEY ARTWORKS

Sandro Botticelli, *The Birth of Venus* (1482-1485)

The image of the birth of the Roman goddess of love, emerging from a wind-blown scallop shell, is more glamorous than the story of her conception, when her father, the sky-god Uranus, had his tackle cut off, which then fell into and fertilised the sea.

Leonardo da Vinci, *The Last Supper* (1494-1498)

There are multiple interpretations of *The Last Supper*, including that the hands of the Apostles spell out a musical tune, and that each of the figures represents a Zodiac sign (with Judas as a typical, moody Scorpio – duh).

Michelangelo, *Sistine Chapel Ceiling* (1508-1512)

Michelangelo actually didn't want this painting gig, refusing the offer from Pope Julius II the first time around because he preferred sculpting to painting (oh to be multi-talented, you bastard!).

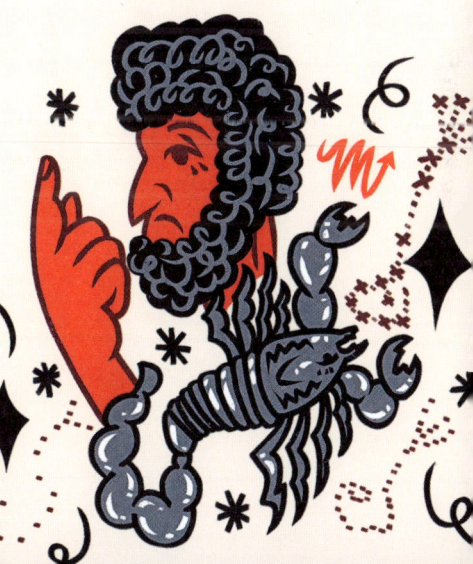

WHAT WAS THE NORTHERN RENAISSANCE?

Pretty much what it sounds like: it was a counterpart to the Italian Renaissance, happening north of the Italian Alps.

Northern Renaissance

1400s–1600s

NORTHERN EUROPE

HOW DID IT SPREAD FROM ITALY?

Renaissance ideas and designs were shared through Europe via trade routes out of Italy, by the newly-acquired ability to mass-produce literature and also by Italian artists who had been invited by royals and aristocrats to visit Northern European courts.

HOW DID IT DIFFER FROM THE ITALIAN RENAISSANCE?

Artists tended to tackle more secular themes than in Italy and didn't shy away from grittier, even uglier subjects; they often included hidden meanings which meant that some artworks were also a good laugh.

WHAT WAS THE PROTESTANT REFORMATION?

In the sixteenth century, people began to question the authority, rules, and even the artistic tastes of the Catholic Church; these protestors became known (somewhat unimaginatively) as Protestants.

WHAT WERE THE ARTISTS INSPIRED BY?

In addition to the stuff coming out of Italy, the Northern Renaissance was inspired by local medieval and Gothic art and architecture, which was characterised by an attention to small details and generally being a bit pointy.

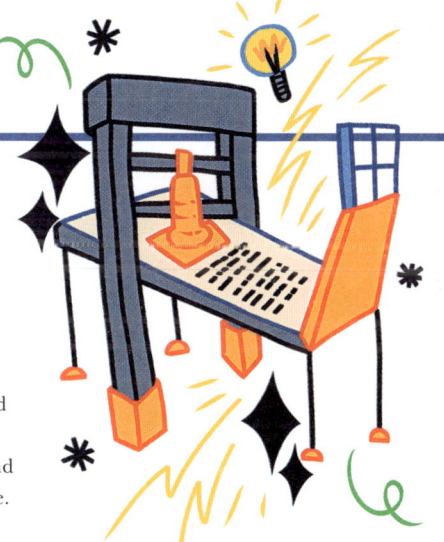

WHY WAS THE PRINTING PRESS SUCH A BIG DEAL?

Around 1440 (when movable type was already old news in China and Korea), the German goldsmith Johannes Gutenberg invented his printing press, meaning books could now be published (comparatively) quickly, spreading information – and images – on an unprecedented scale.

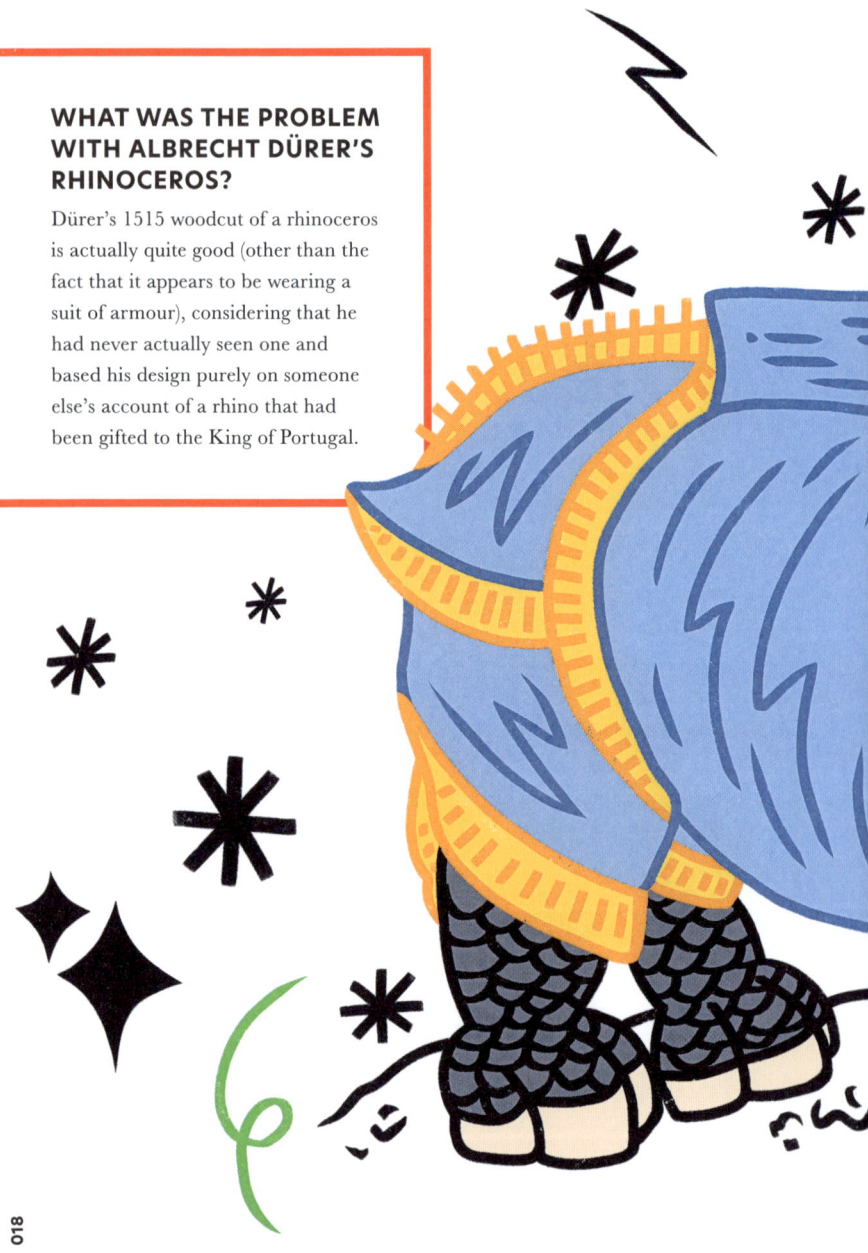

WHAT WAS THE PROBLEM WITH ALBRECHT DÜRER'S RHINOCEROS?

Dürer's 1515 woodcut of a rhinoceros is actually quite good (other than the fact that it appears to be wearing a suit of armour), considering that he had never actually seen one and based his design purely on someone else's account of a rhino that had been gifted to the King of Portugal.

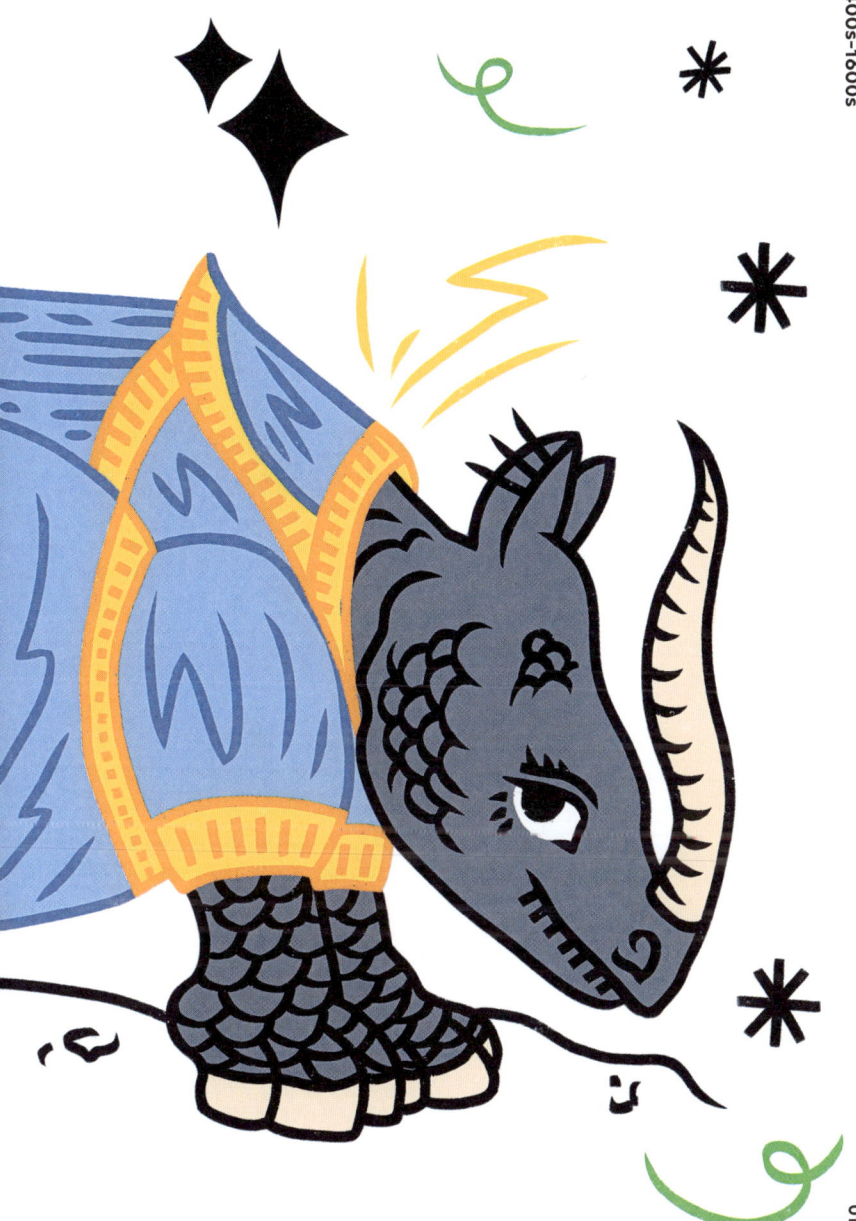

DOES EGG TEMPERA SMELL?

Until around 1500, a major painting medium was egg tempera – where egg is used to bind coloured pigments to create paint – but the paintings don't smell eggy because it dries odourlessly (phew!) and was often mixed with nice-smelling stuff like Jesus' favourite birthday present, myrhh.

DOES RESTORING MASTERPIECES ALWAYS IMPROVE THEM?

The Ghent Altarpiece, created by Jan and Hubert van Eyck (isn't it nice when brothers get along?) shocked many in 2020 when a key character, the Lamb of God, was restored; the original turned out to have super-spooky human eyes and appears to be blowing you a horrible kiss.

WHAT ARE SOME OF THE BEST DUTCH PROVERBS?

In Pieter Bruegel the Elder's 1559 busy painting *Netherlandish Proverbs*, each figure represents a Dutch saying, including a man squatting out of a window onto a globe ('to crap on the world' – to hate everything), someone weeing out of a window ('to piss against the moon' – to waste your time), and two people pooing at the same privy ('they both crap through the same hole' – they're great pals).

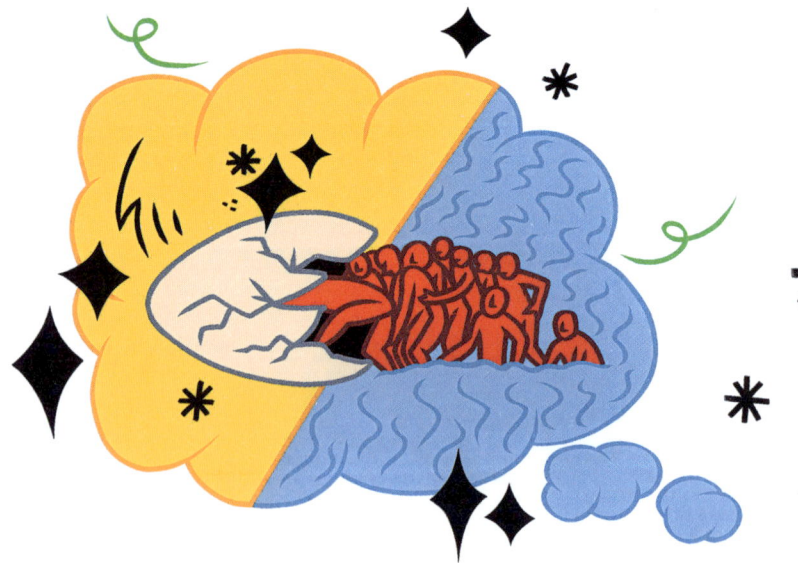

3 KEY ARTISTS

Albrecht Dürer (1471–1528)
German artist, big on prints and well-travelled by fifteenth-century standards.

Pieter Bruegel the Elder (c.1525–1569)
Dutch painter, better known than Pieter Bruegel the Younger (you can't beat the original); 'Elder' feels misleading, given that he was under forty-five when he died.

Catharina van Hemessen (c.1528–after 1566)
Flemish painter, first lady artist in the region to whom paintings are officially attributed; mostly created portraits and self-portraits, which were rare in the sixteenth century.

3 KEY ARTWORKS

Jan van Eyck, *The Arnolfini Portrait* (1434)
One of the world's most mysterious paintings, because there isn't definitive proof of who is being portrayed or why, and also why is he wearing that massively hot outfit when it's clearly lovely out?

Hieronymus Bosch, *Garden of Earthly Delights* (c.1490–1510)
A triptych (three-panelled picture) filled with mad shit, including enormous berries, a man being eaten by a large bird while smoke and birds fly out of his bum, and loads of people running into a massive egg.

Hans Holbein, *The Ambassadors* (1533)
In his portrait of a bishop and the French Ambassador to England, Hans Holbein (famous for his portraits of Henry VIII) hid a skull on the rug, which can only be seen properly when viewed from the side; this device is a *memento mori* – a reminder of death.

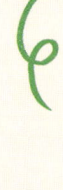

WHAT WAS MANNERISM?

Mannerism turned its back on the idealised, harmonious compositions of the Italian Renaissance (see page 12) and instead created artworks with a lack of symmetry, emotional use of colour and dramatic, theatrical poses.

Mannerism
1500s–1600s

ITALY (AGAIN)

WHAT GOT IT STARTED?

Mannerism kicked off in 1527 with the Sack of Rome, when Holy Roman Empire troops stormed the city to rebel against Pope Clement VII; its decimation marked the end of the prosperity of the Renaissance.

WHAT WAS IT INSPIRED BY?

Mannerist artists looked for ways to take art further than it had gone during the Renaissance, wanting not only to show how the world really looks but also to add tension and emotion to their compositions.

WHY THE NAME?

Artists working in this style had no clue that they were in the 'Mannerist club' – in fact, the term (from the Italian *maniera*, meaning 'style') wasn't even applied to this movement until the early twentieth century.

WHAT WAS *TERRIBILITÀ*?

Terribilità is a term often used to describe Mannerist paintings; no, not meaning that they were terrible, but rather that they inspired a sense of great emotional intensity or awe, which the artists got pretty serious about.

WHAT WAS THE FIG LEAF CAMPAIGN?

It was launched in 1563 by the Catholic Church's Council of Trent (like the UN of priests), to combat 'lascivious' nudity in art, ensuring that figures in new artworks wouldn't have their bits on show and adding cover-ups to existing work to make them more 'modest'.

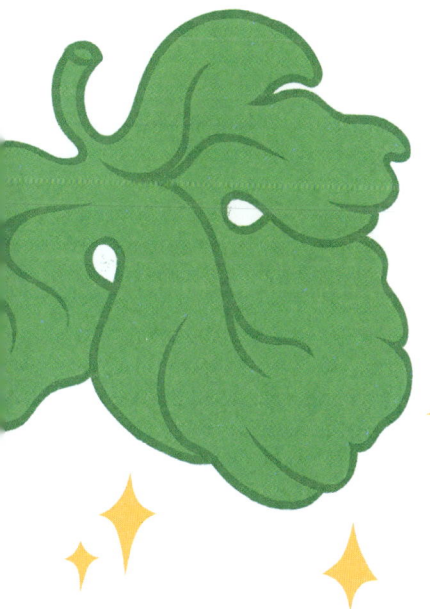

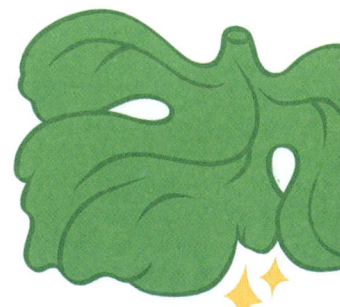

HOW DID A 1550 BOOK PREDICT CELEB CULTURE?

Artist and architect Giorgio Vasari's *Lives of the Most Excellent Painters, Sculptors, and Architects* was one of the first major biographical art history books, setting up a tradition for us to consider the artist's story and lifestyle when we're thinking about their artwork.

WHAT WAS EL GRECO'S PRESCRIPTION?

In 1914, the ophthalmologist Germán Beritens claimed that El Greco's characteristically long, stretched human figures were the result of the artist having astigmatism, but if El Greco was seeing figures as stretched-out, surely he would have seen his canvases that way too, so his eyes were probably fine.

WHAT WOULD BE A BAD GIFT FOR THE KING OF FRANCE?

It's not clear exactly what *An Allegory with Venus and Cupid* (c.1545) by Agnolo Bronzino shows, but one theory is that the figure holding their head in agony in the background is a representation of syphilis, which would have been harsh given that the painting was a gift for the French King Francis I – and syphilis was nicknamed the 'French disease' in Italy.

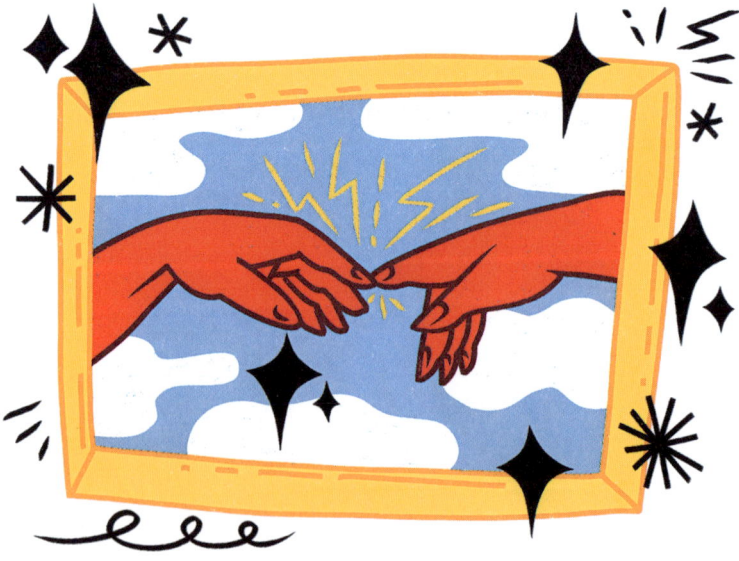

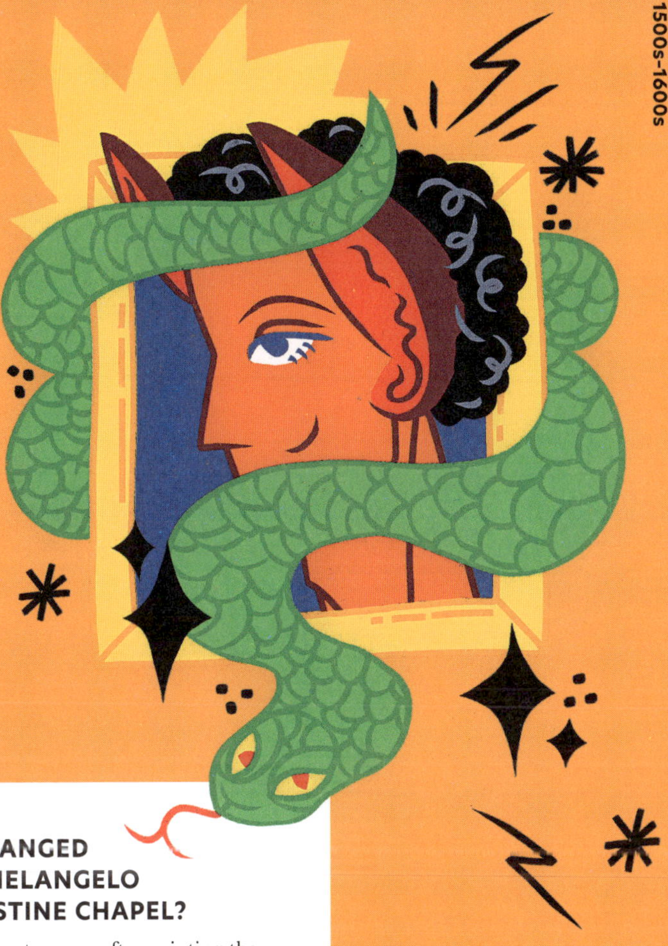

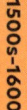

WHAT CHANGED
FOR MICHELANGELO
IN THE SISTINE CHAPEL?

More than twenty years after painting the
chapel ceiling, Michelangelo was asked
back to create a new fresco, but when his
new Mannerist style was criticised by Papal
Master of Ceremonies Biagio da Cesena,
he added a final detail; a portrait of
da Cesena with donkey ears, being bitten
on the dick by a snake.

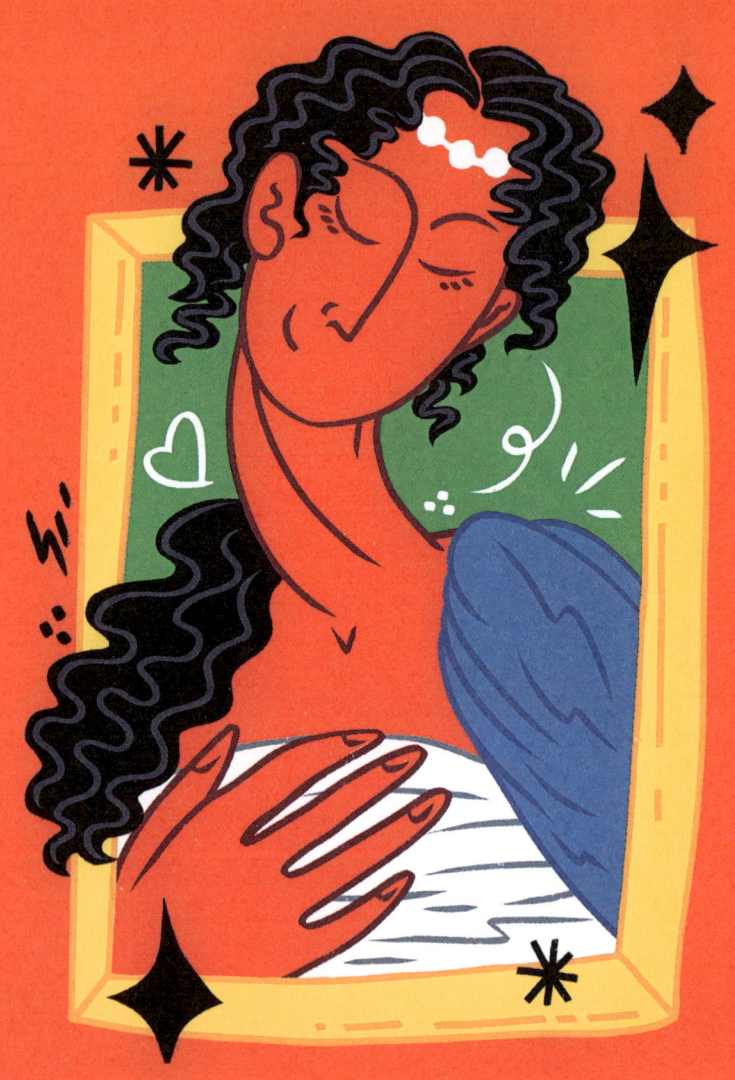

3 KEY ARTISTS

Tintoretto (1518-1594)

Italian painter who had the very cool nickname *Il Furioso* because of how energetic his paintings were, but for some reason went with his other nickname, meaning 'little dyer', after the fact that his dad was a cloth-dyer.

Giuseppe Arcimboldo (c.1526-1593)

Italian painter, known for his portraits composed of images of vegetables and household objects; often seen as a Surrealist born 400 years too early (see page 194).

El Greco (1541-1614)

Greek painter, offered to repaint the Sistine Chapel because he didn't think Michelangelo was much good; born Doménikos Theotokópoulos but called El Greco meaning 'the Greek' because… well, he was Greek.

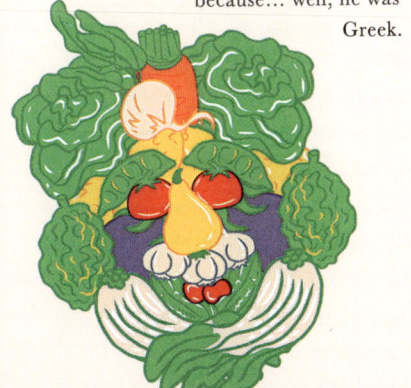

3 KEY ARTWORKS

Parmigianino, *The Madonna with the Long Neck* (c.1534-1540)

This portrait is typically Mannerist in the way it prioritises emotion and theatrical beauty over accurate perspective (look at the size of that neck… and the size of that baby!).

Lavinia Fontana, *Self Portrait at the Virginal with a Servant* (1577)

Considered Western Europe's first professional female painter, Fontana painted this self-portrait as part of her dowry; to seal the deal with her fiancé's family, the inscription promises that she is **definitely** a virgin.

Joachim Wtewael, *Perseus and Andromeda* (1611)

This painting shows massively whitewashed Ethiopian princess Andromeda tied against a rock to be eaten by a sea monster as punishment from the gods for her parents bragging about how fit she is.

WHAT WAS THE DUTCH GOLDEN AGE?

It was a period of huge prosperity for the Netherlands when it became one of the world's leading military, trading, academic and cultural powers.

The Dutch Golden Age

1580s–1670s

NETHERLANDS

WHY A GOLDEN AGE?

Well, times were golden (for the Dutch, that is – not for the people and countries they were busy colonising).

WHERE DID ALL THEIR MONEY COME FROM?

The Netherlands wasn't a resource-rich country itself, but trade conducted by the Dutch East India Company (dealing in spices, cotton and tea) and the Dutch West India Company (most profitable in the trafficking of enslaved people) brought huge wealth to the country, and made Amsterdam one of the world's most powerful cities.

AND HOW DOES ALL THAT RELATE TO ART, 'ART HISTORIAN'?

The money sloshing about in the country and the developments in industry created a new middle class, whose members were happy to splash their cash on artworks that would prove their status.

WHAT NEW TECHNIQUES WERE DEVELOPED DURING THIS TIME?

Painting on canvas became much more popular, so businesses began to sell ready-stretched and prepped canvases as a time-saving solution for artists who previously had to do it themselves.

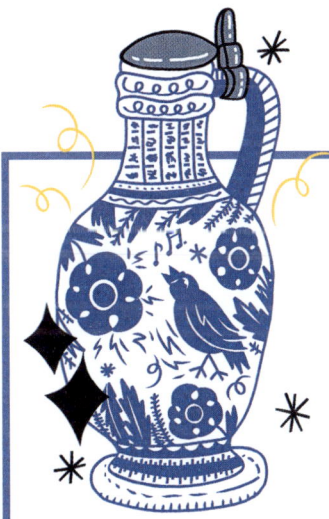

WHAT WAS BEING MADE?

Small-scale Dutch landscapes, Bible stories, portraits, domestic scenes and still lifes were all popular, while the market for prints took off thanks to new tech, and a new style of porcelain – known as Delftware – developed, inspired by goods imported from China.

WHERE COULD PEOPLE KEEP ALL THEIR COOL STUFF?

Like a first draft of a modern museum, *Wunderkammern* – cabinets of curiosities – were rooms that collectors filled with items from their travels and trades; Rembrandt's included artworks from around the world, dried fish, spears, ancient coins, Venetian glass and a large lion skin.

HOW WERE PAINTINGS KEEPING PEOPLE HUMBLE?

Vanitas paintings featured luxurious subject matter but with something amiss: perhaps one lemon in a banquet is peeled or a single bloom in a bouquet is wilting, designed to remind viewers that wealth is vanity and we all die in the end (cheery).

WHAT WAS A TRONIE?

Tronies (Dutch for 'faces') were works that depicted an exaggerated facial expression or characteristic – for example in Adriaen Brouwer's *The Bitter Draught* and Joos van Craesbeeck's *The Smoker,* where both blokes look like they'd be great value on a night out.

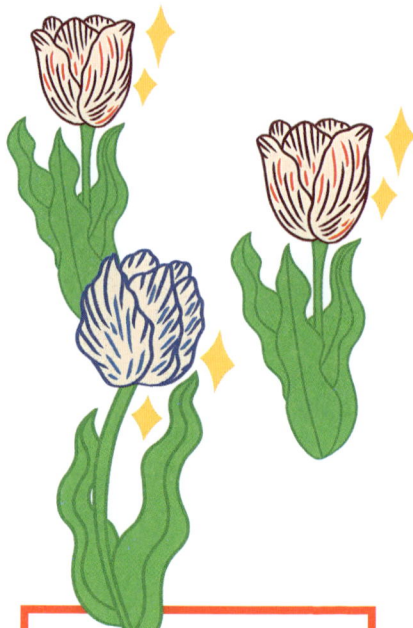

WHAT WAS WITH THE OBSESSION WITH TULIPS?

'Tulip Mania' hit the Netherlands in the early seventeenth century when the flowers, originally from central Asia, were first grown in Leiden's Botanical Gardens; such was their exotic charm that in 1623, ten tulip bulbs were bought for more than the cost of an Amsterdam townhouse.

3 KEY ARTISTS

Frans Hals (c.1582–1666)

Dutch painter who had money issues; the 'Elder' and most famous of the two Frans Hals (an inconveniently popular name – he was once confused with yet another Frans Hals, earning him a wrongful reputation for abusing his wife, who was actually already dead).

Clara Peeters (fl.1607–1621)

Flemish painter and foodie; hid self-portraits in her paintings by appearing reflected in the glass and silverware.

Jan Steen (c.1626–1679)

Dutch painter whose chaotic domestic scenes inspired the phrase *een huishouden van Jan Steen* ('a Jan Steen household') meaning an untidy but jolly home.

3 KEY ARTWORKS

Rembrandt, *Militia Company of District II under the Command of Captain Frans Banninck Cocq* (1642)

A.K.A. *The Night Watch,* it isn't actually happening at night: the painting just had a thick layer of varnish and grime when it was given its nickname in the eighteenth century.

Judith Leyster, *A Boy and a Girl with a Cat and an Eel* (c.1635)

Representing the adage 'he who plays with cats gets scratched' (fuck around and find out), this image of naughty siblings is typical of Dutch Golden Age paintings, which often used children as conveyors of moral messages.

Johannes Vermeer, *Girl with a Pearl Earring* (c.1665)

Perhaps the most famous tronie of all time, the 'pearl' being worn was most likely a painted glass bauble, because a real pearl of that size would have been ludicrously expensive.

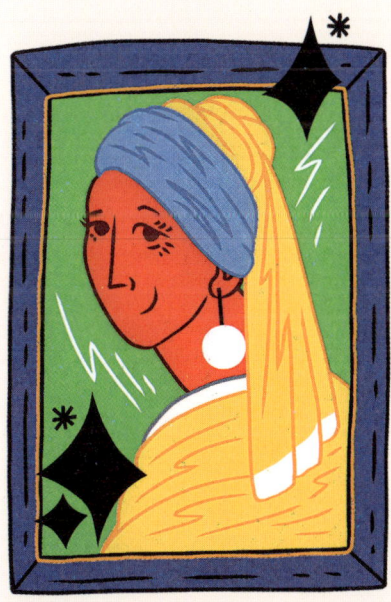

WHAT WAS BAROQUE?

The Baroque was a style characterised by realism (showing things as they look to us in real life), grandeur and high emotional tension called *affetti*.

Baroque

1600s–1700s

ITALY

WHERE DOES ITS NAME COME FROM?

The word comes from the Portuguese term *barrocco*, meaning an irregularly shaped pearl (not a fizzy orange drink), and although this sounds like it could be a compliment, it was really meant to emphasise the movement's misshapenness compared to the art of the Renaissance.

WHERE DID IT BEGIN?

As if starting the Renaissance (see page 12) and Mannerism (see page 22) wasn't enough for the Italians, they kickstarted the Baroque too, which then spread to the rest of Europe.

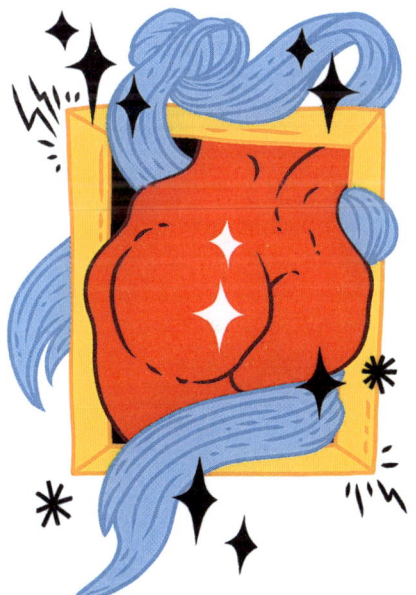

WHAT IS *CHIAROSCURO*?

Meaning 'light-dark' in Italian, *chiaroscuro* was a technique popular with Baroque painters wanting to create heavy, moody contrast between areas of shadow and highlight.

IS THAT SOME BODY POSITIVITY I SEE?

At the time, plumpness was a symbol of wealth and health, and artists including Peter Paul Rubens painted many such upper-class women, leading to the compliment 'Rubenesque' – however, Rubens also believed that the ideal woman was inherently horse-like, which is less complimentary, unless you really like horses.

I'M SPOTTING SOME PEOPLE WHO AREN'T BIBLICAL FIGURES OR TOFFS; I'M SURE THEY'RE BEING PORTRAYED REALLY RESPECTFULLY, RIGHT?

For the first time, really, Baroque artists began to include common people in their work but these were often unkind caricatures, designed to give the wealthy owners of the paintings a good laugh.

HOW MUCH DID BAROQUE ARTISTS WANT TO CAPTURE EMOTIONAL DEPTH?

Gian Lorenzo Bernini once sculpted a self-portrait showing him as a damned soul, and so committed was he to properly representing this that he apparently repeatedly burned his hand on a candle while looking in the mirror to capture that authentic 'Ow ow ow, I'm burning in Hell!' look.

WHY HAS CARAVAGGIO GOT SUCH A BAD-BOY REP?

Throughout art history there have been a lot of nasty fellas, and

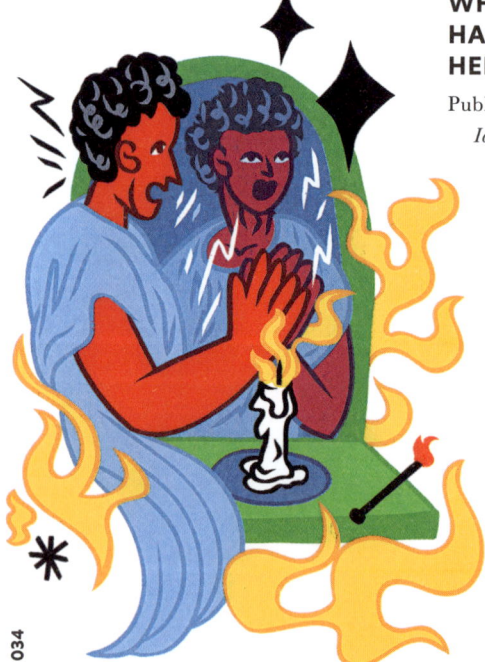

Caravaggio is one of the best-known because he literally murdered someone (stabbing Ranuccio Tomassoni in the femoral artery – so probably aiming for his family jewels – during a duel).

WHO WAS JOHNNY BOLLOCKS?

The painter and art historian Giovanni Baglione had beef with Caravaggio, who then wrote an unkind poem about Bagione in which he called him 'Gian Coglione' – John Testicle – for which Baglione had him put in prison for libel.

WHAT DOES IT MEAN WHEN AN OLD WOMAN HAS AN OWL ON HER HEAD?

Published in 1593, Cesare Ripa's *Iconologia* was a highly influential text on symbols and allegories; artists leaned into these meanings in their paintings, so an image of an old woman with an owl on her head was a classic symbol of superstition.

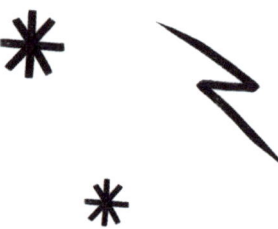

3 KEY ARTISTS

Caravaggio (1571–1610)
Italian painter, credited as the creator of tenebrism (*chiaroscuro* with even more extreme shadows); his first name was Michelangelo but that was already taken.

Nicolas Poussin (1594–1665)
French painter who spent most of his time in Rome despite a tasty job offer from the French King to be his First Painter; seen as the daddy of French Art.

Claude Lorrain (c.1600–1683)
French painter and competitive frenemy of Poussin; worked initially as a pastry chef in Rome – although the urban legend that he invented puff pastry sadly isn't true.

3 KEY ARTWORKS

Artemisia Gentileschi, *Judith Beheading Holofernes* (c.1612–1613)
Interpreted as an expression of feminine power and rage, this work is a particularly bloody rendering of the biblical story and was created shortly after a lengthy public trial between Gentileschi and the artist Agostino Tassi, who was convicted of raping her.

Gian Lorenzo Bernini, *The Rape of Proserpina* (1621–1622)
Featuring perhaps the most famous thigh in art history, *The Rape of Proserpina* is so realistically carved that you can see the imprint of the god Pluto's fingers on her leg (ugh).

Diego Velázquez, *Las Meninas* (1656)
In this group portrait we see the Infanta Margarita Teresa (who would become Holy Roman Empress, Queen of Hungary, Queen of Germany, Queen of Bohemia, and the Archduchess of Austria, all before dying at 21 – what have you achieved?), but is the framed image of her parents in the background a portrait or a mirror reflection?

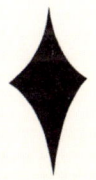
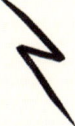

WHAT WAS ACADEMICISM?

It was a style of painting and sculpture promoted by the official art academies of Europe, whose purpose was to train artists and display their artwork in regular exhibitions.

Academicism

1600s–1800s

INTERNATIONAL

WHICH ACADEMIES?

The first official art academies were opened in Italy in the sixteenth century (yes, we get it Italy, you're massively important), but perhaps the most powerful influences on European art came from the academies in Paris and London.

WHAT WAS THEIR INFLUENCE ON AUDIENCES?

The academies and their juries for exhibitions acted as taste-makers, deciding which artists would be given academic training and passing judgement on which artworks were Hot or Not.

WHAT WAS THEIR INFLUENCE ON ARTISTS?

In many ways, the academies replaced the old guild system (see page 13): artists were taught there instead of in the workshops of masters, and if they succeeded at the salons they had the chance to win prizes, travel abroad and sell their artworks.

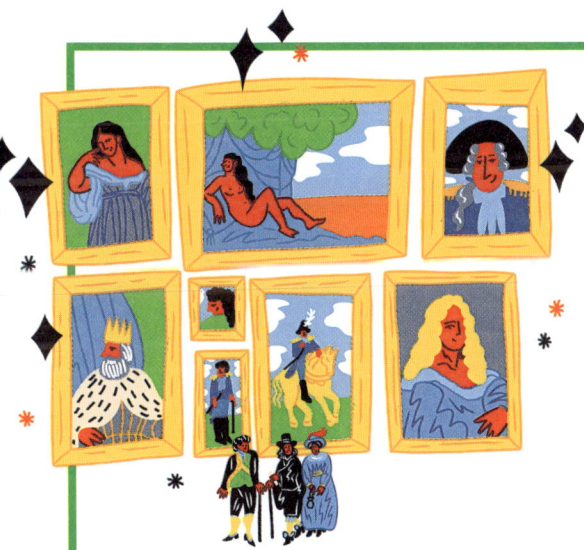

WHAT WERE SALONS?

Salons were the annual exhibitions of the academies, with artworks selected by a jury of academicians filling the galleries from floor to ceiling (called a 'salon hang'); the best paintings were given prime spots at eye level.

WHAT SORT OF THING WERE THEY INTO?

The academies favoured works with moral messages and narrative paintings of Bible stories or tales from Asia and the Middle East; style-wise, they preferred the Neoclassical (see page 46) and Romantic (see page 50).

WHICH SUBJECT WAS THE BEST?

The subjects of art were graded, with history painting (showing serious moments from a story) being the most highly valued, followed by portraiture, genre painting (people doing everyday things), landscapes, and still lifes at the bottom of the pile (sorry still lifes).

WHO WINS WHEN RUBENS FIGHTS POUSSIN?

Rather than the artists literally squaring up to each other, 'rubenistes' and 'poussinistes' were rivals in the academies – poussinistes seeing line as the most important element of art, and rubenistes believing it was colour.

WHY DID IT GO OUT OF STYLE?

The problem was that the academies' tastes didn't really develop much over the course of 200 years (if it ain't broke, and the upper classes still like it…) and artists and audiences eventually got tired of its idealism, turning instead to art that better represented our not-always-lovely world.

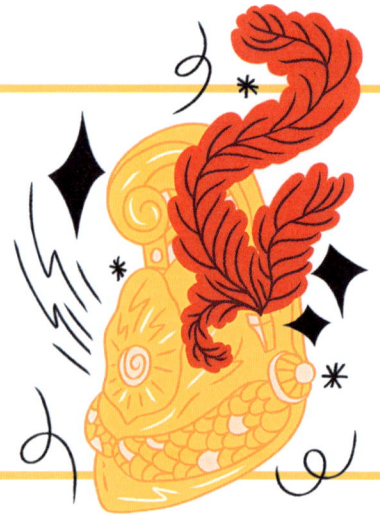

WHAT WAS *L'ART POMPIER*?

In the nineteenth century, when Academicism was dying out and seen as deeply unfashionable, history paintings were sometimes mocked as *L'art pompier* ('fireman art'), because of the similarity between ancient military helmets in the paintings and those worn by French firemen.

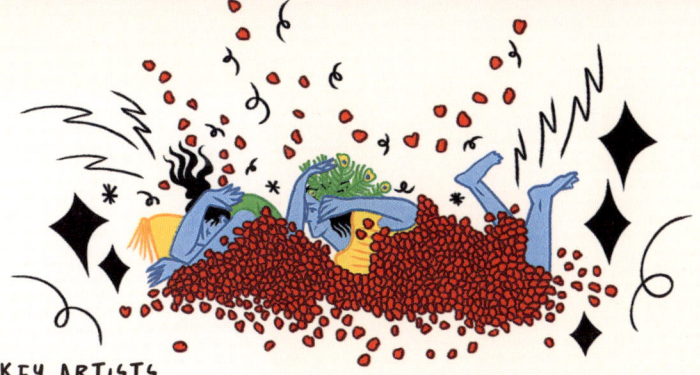

3 KEY ARTISTS

Joshua Reynolds (1723–1792)

English painter, founder of London's Royal Academy of Arts, unkindly called Sir Sloshua by the Pre-Raphaelites (see page 64).

Edwin Landseer (1802–1873)

English painter and sculptor who painted a lot of animals and could apparently paint with both hands at the same time (show off).

Jean-Léon Gérôme (1824–1904)

French painter, sculptor and early photography fan, his painting *Pollice Verso* ignited a debate about whether a thumbs-down was really used in ancient Rome to indicate that a defeated gladiator should be killed.

3 KEY ARTWORKS

Benjamin West, *Death of General Wolfe* (1770)

This work shows a key moment in American military history, and was seen as quite radical in portraying people in contemporary, instead of classical, costumes.

William-Adolphe Bouguereau, *The Birth of Venus* (1879)

Known for his 'licked style' (when the surface of a painting looks so smooth it could have been licked clean), this work by Bouguereau is massive at almost 3 m (10 ft) tall (and would have taken a lot of licking).

Lawrence Alma-Tadema, *The Roses of Heliogabalus* (1888)

Alma-Tadema had roses sent to him in England from France every week for four months in order to accurately paint this scene of the Roman emperor Elagabalus accidentally smothering some of his dinner guests to death under falling petals.

WHAT WAS ROCOCO?

Also known as Late Baroque, it was a heavily ornamental (decorative) style of art, architecture and design, known for its scenes of the aristocratic classes luxuriating in meadows, flirting and generally having a lovely, rich time.

Rococo
1730s–1770s

FRANCE

HOW DID IT EVOLVE FROM THE BAROQUE?

In comparison to earlier Baroque artworks (see pages 32), Rococo art is characterised as more 'feminine', using softer colours, featuring less earnest subject matter and being more swirly.

WHERE DID THE NAME COME FROM?

Rococo takes its name from the French word *rocaille*, which referred originally to a mix of shells and pebbles used to decorate Renaissance grottos and later to elaborate designs during the reign of Louis XIV.

WHAT MADE IT LOOK SO DECADENT?

Rococo paintings are incredibly ornate, and focus on the sort of lives the wealthy patrons who commissioned the artworks would have been living, so they are filled with beautiful colours, luxurious fabrics and glamorous settings.

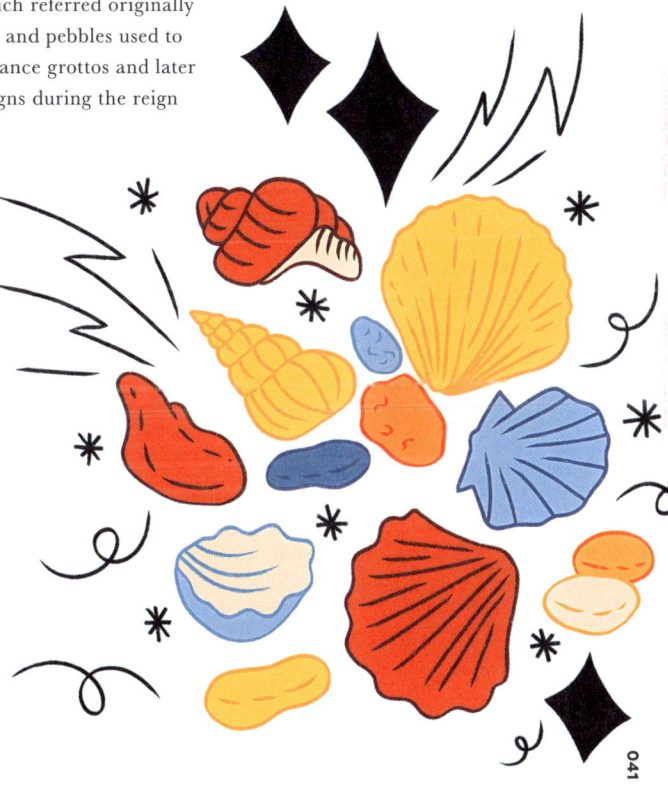

THESE ALL LOOK VERY CLASSY; SURELY NOTHING PERVY IS GOING ON?

Even the Rococo artworks with bare bottoms on show seem tame now (because we've put them on public display in galleries and museums for years), but many of these artworks would have originally been kept in the private homes of the aristocracy, who were well up for a bit of naughty fun.

WHAT ARE *FÊTE GALANTE* PAINTINGS?

In 1717, when Antoine Watteau's works didn't neatly fit into the existing categories at the academy, they created a new category – *fête galante* – just for him; paintings showing aristocratic outdoor activities like lounging about, having a bit of a dance and then lounging about again.

DID THEY STOP AT PAINTINGS?

No; the applied arts – practical objects that are artistically tarted-up, including furniture and household items (as opposed to fine arts, which serve the sole purpose of being art) – also got the Rococo treatment.

WHAT DID THAT LOOK LIKE?

Rococo furniture was heavily decorated with motifs (images) from nature as well as with curly, asymmetrical designs directly inspired by decor from East Asia (called 'Chinoiserie' in Europe), which had been imported into the continent for around 200 years.

WHAT ENDED THE ROCOCO ERA?

French revolutionaries despised the luxurious, frivolous lifestyles of the aristocracy (the French Revolution itself didn't start until 1789 but bad vibes were brewing long before that); unfortunately Rococo was the total embodiment of this, so the style and its artists fell out of favour – sometimes violently.

WHAT'S SNUFF GOT TO DO WITH IT?

Snuff – powdered tobacco taken up the snout – was a popular vice among the aristocracy, and Rococo artists like Rosalba Carriera had the opportunity to begin their careers by painting miniatures on the ivory lids of snuff boxes.

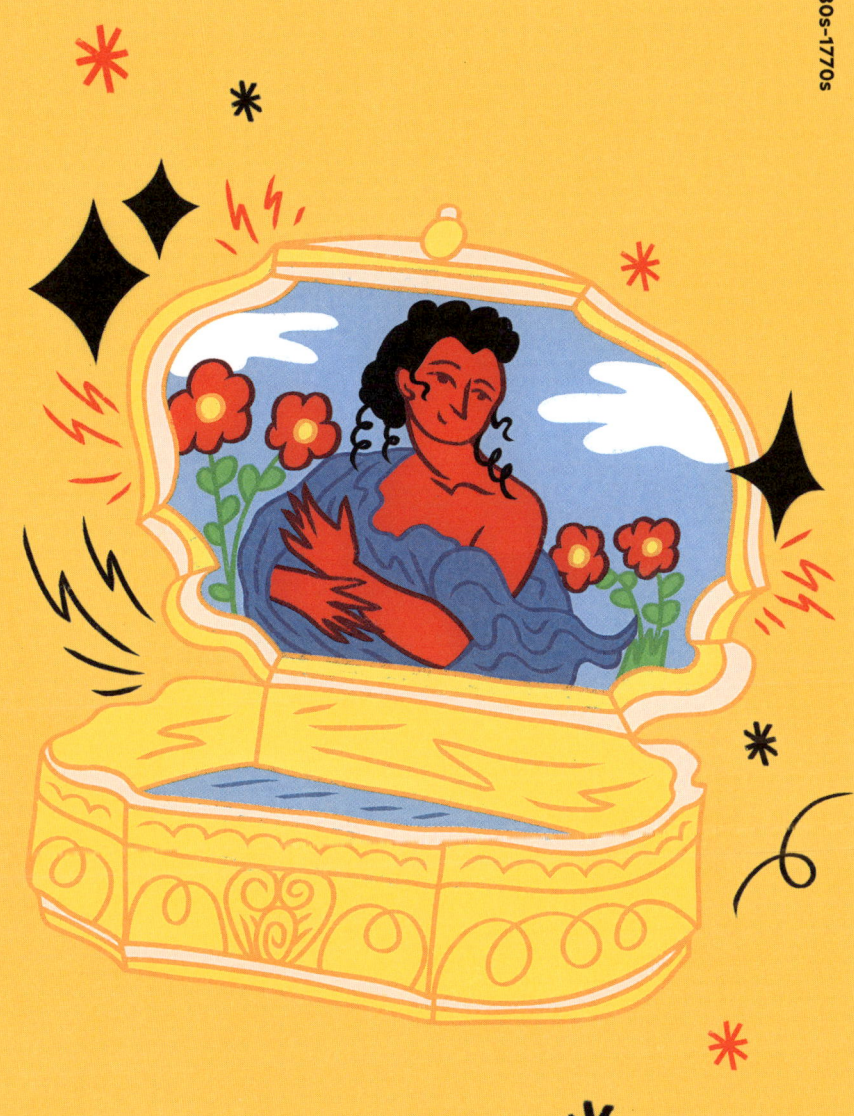

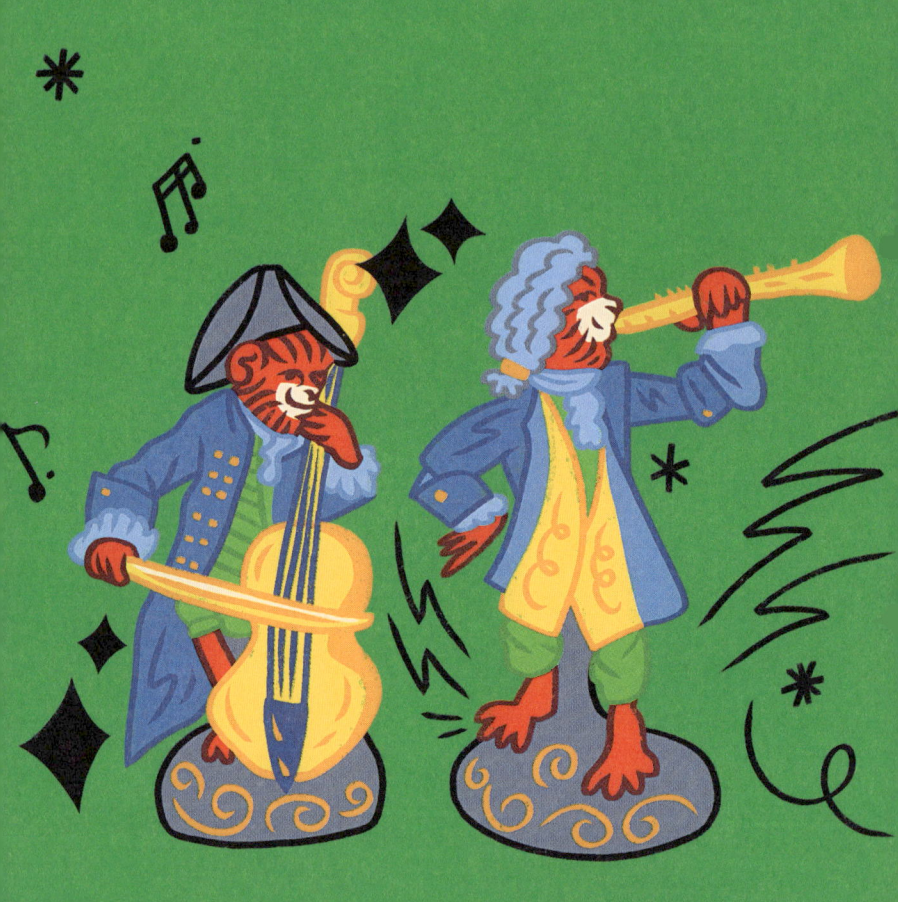

3 KEY ARTISTS

Jean-Antoine Watteau (1684-1721)

French painter considered the father of Rococo, painter of Italian *Commedia dell'arte* – a popular comedy theatre type with set characters including clowns, rich old men, arrogant captains and young lovers.

François Boucher (1703-1770)

French painter and etcher, favourite artist of Louis XV's chief mistress Madame de Pompadour and designer of several key prints for her porcelain factory, which had been gifted to her by the King (don't settle for less, ladies).

Johann Joachim Kändler (1706-1775)

German sculptor and arcanist (someone who knows the secrets of porcelain making – mysterious); designer of a hugely popular orchestra of porcelain monkeys in full Rococo outfits and powdered wigs.

3 KEY ARTWORKS

Jean-Honoré Fragonard, *The Happy Accidents of the Swing* (1767-1768)

Commissioned by a member of the French court who wanted a painting of his mistress being pushed on a swing (originally by a bishop) while he gets to have a good gawp up her skirt from below, this Rococo masterpiece isn't as innocent as one might first assume.

Thomas Gainsborough, *The Blue Boy (Portrait of a Young Gentleman)* (c.1770)

It was said that Gainsborough painted this as an act of rebellion against London's Royal Academy, where it was being taught that paintings should be mostly made up of warm colours (yellows and reds), with cool colours like blue reserved for small details.

Élisabeth Vigée Le Brun, *Marie Antoinette in a Chemise Dress* (1783)

Vigée Le Brun painted Marie Antoinette more than thirty times, but this was likely the most controversial portrayal: it shows Marie in a white muslin dress and straw hat more likely to be seen on a farmer's wife than the Queen.

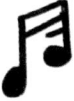
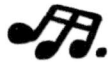

WHAT WAS NEOCLASSICISM?

Neoclassicists looked back at the art of ancient Greece and Rome for inspiration, aiming to create moralistic work that was harmonious, simple and idealistic.

Neoclassicism
1760s–1850s

INTERNATIONAL

I THOUGHT IT WAS THE RENAISSANCE THAT WAS ALL ABOUT HARKING BACK TO THE PAST?

Neoclassicism (which until the mid-nineteenth century was known as the 'true style') wasn't necessarily about recreating the art of the past, but rather taking those past aesthetic attitudes and using them, even on modern subjects.

WHAT WAS IT AGAINST?

Neoclassicists reacted against the highly decorative and theatrical Baroque and Rococo movements, wanting to see art return to a calm and simple beauty, using less harsh *chiaroscuro* and dramatic movement, and more symmetry.

WHAT WAS THE GRAND TOUR?

A key part of an upper-class gentleman's education, the Grand Tour was a trip that could last several years, in which young men would visit significant historical sites to view artefacts and monuments, soak up the culture and probably get a venereal disease.

WHAT SORT OF THINGS DID THEY PAINT?

Popular topics included historical events, portraits of political figures and scenes from recent history too, made grander by the stylings of the past.

WHY THE PAST?

The preference for the past was partly a political choice; at a time of great turmoil (revolutions were brewing and the Enlightenment was calling fundamental beliefs into question – see page 48), artists sought to imbue their work with the stoic, patriotic and noble ideals of a bygone age.

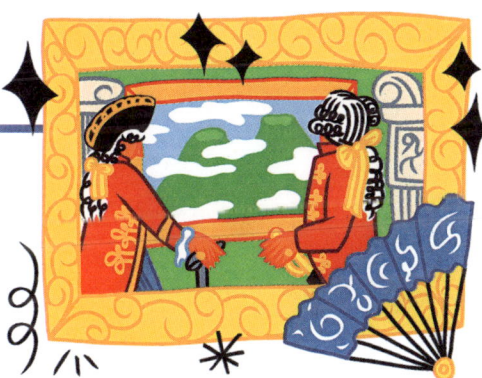

HOW WAS SCIENCE CHANGING THINGS?

This was the Age of Reason (A.K.A. the Enlightenment) – a period of major scientific discoveries and philosophical debate – and Neoclassicism followed the Enlightenment philosophy that the best course of action was to be rational rather than emotional (looking at you, Baroque and Rococo).

WHO WAS THE BEST-DRESSED ART HISTORIAN?

Author of the seminal book *History of Ancient Art*, Johann Joachim Winckelmann was a huge proponent

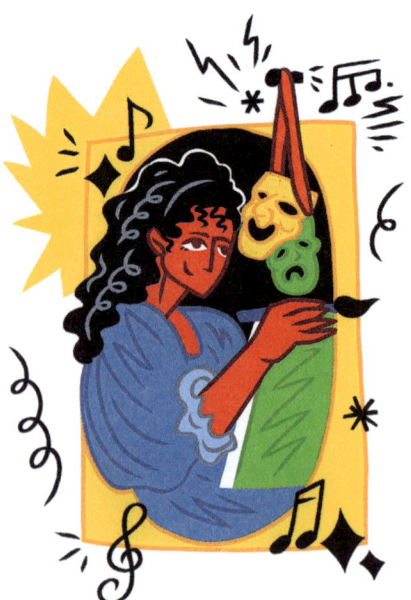

of Neoclassical art after seeing a storeroom of ancient statues in Dresden, and an equally big fan of wearing skin-tight leather trousers.

HOW DID A VOLCANIC ERUPTION, 1,700 YEARS EARLIER, AFFECT THINGS?

In the early eighteenth century, the ancient Roman cities of Pompeii and Herculaneum, buried under ash when Mount Vesuvius erupted in AD 79, were rediscovered and news of newly excavated artworks and architecture ignited interest in the ancient past.

WHAT DID THEY RECKON PEOPLE SHOULD WEAR?

In 1794, Jacques-Louis David was commissioned to design a range of outfits for the citizens and officials of the new French Republic, but the flamboyant, classical-inspired numbers (all colour-coded and toga-esque) sadly never got the go-ahead because David's friend Robespierre was busy being overthrown and executed (bad timing).

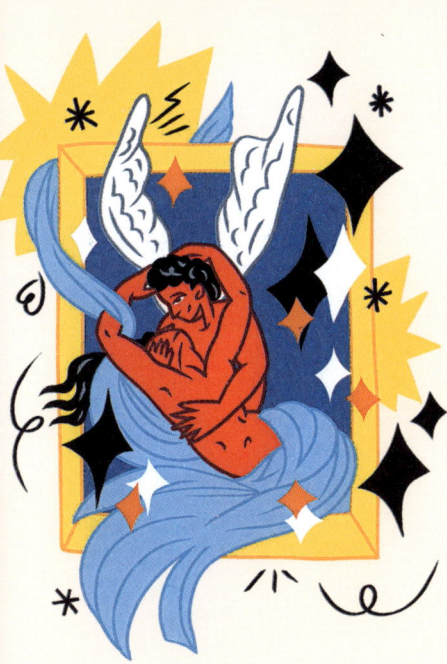

3 KEY ARTISTS

Angelica Kauffmann (1741–1807)
Swiss painter, one of two female founding members of London's Royal Academy; chose a career in art over one in music after a priest warned her about the sorts of people who work at the opera.

Jacques-Louis David (1748–1825)
Notoriously anti-social French painter who managed to avoid being guillotined because of a well-timed stomach ache and was put in prison instead (twice).

Anne-Louis Girodet de Roussy-Trioson (1767–1824)
French painter who studied under David; known for the not-so-discreet erotic undertones in his paintings.

3 KEY ARTWORKS

Antonio Canova, *Psyche Revived by Cupid's Kiss* (1787–1793)
Canova's marble sculpture was designed with a convenient handle by the goddess's foot, to allow the sculpture to be rotated on its base so it could be viewed from all angles.

Marie-Guillemine Benoist, *Portrait of Madeleine* (1800)
This piece was named *Portrait of a Black Woman* until 2019, when the subject was identified as a Guadeloupean servant to the Benoist family during the brief window in which slavery was abolished in France in 1794, before being reintroduced in 1802.

Jean-Auguste-Dominique Ingres, *Napoleon I on His Imperial Throne* (1806)
Ingres' portrait of Napoleon's coronation as French emperor takes its pose directly from drawings the artist had seen of an ancient statue of Zeus by Greek artist Phidias, from the fifth century BC.

WHAT WAS ROMANTICISM?

Romantic art – **not** just paintings of love stories – was a movement in both literature and fine art, which put an individual's feelings and unique perspective at the centre of artistic expression.

Romanticism
1760s–1850s

WESTERN EUROPE

WHERE DOES IT GET ITS NAME?

'Romanticism' was first used to describe Romantic literature, which was written in Romance languages (modern languages, including French and Italian) rather than in Latin.

WHAT WERE ROMANTICISTS PAINTING?

Romanticism was a broad church, with artists painting various subjects including wild landscapes, scenes of political uprisings, portraits of those who were othered in society and fantastical designs inspired by Romantic literature.

WHAT WAS *STURM UND DRANG*?

Meaning 'storm and stress', it was the first Romantic movement, emerging in Germany in the 1760s and questioning the Enlightenment obsession (see page 48) with rationality, suggesting instead that our experiences come from an internal emotional world rather than the external, law-bound one.

HOW DID IT DIFFER FROM NEOCLASSICISM?

Romanticism put more emphasis on individual points of view and emotions; scenes were more likely to depict modern, medieval or folk stories than tales from ancient history, and there was less focus on achieving visual harmony in compositions.

WHAT IS THE SUBLIME?

A key element in Romantic works, it is an artistic effect that causes viewers to feel a sense of awe, astonishment or reverence when looking at artwork.

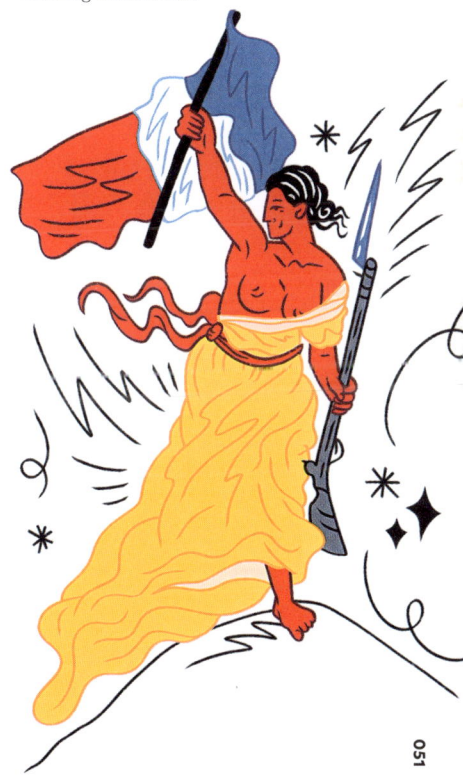

HOW DID J. M. W. TURNER GET UP CLOSE AND PERSONAL WITH STORMS?

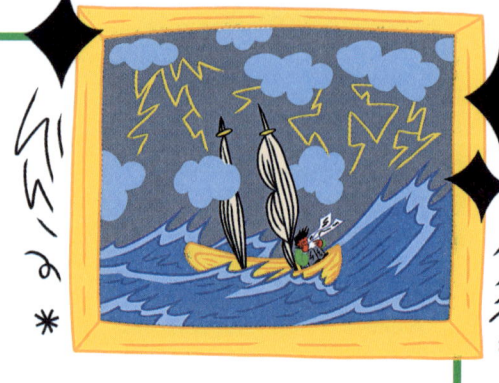

Turner claimed that he had sailors strap him to the mast of a steamship for four hours during a night-time snowstorm in order to observe the scene for a painting, but it's not clear whether this really happened, as it probably would have finished Turner off (being in his mid-sixties and in less-than-brilliant health).

WHAT WAS GOING ON IN THE WORLD AT THE TIME?

All sorts was changing: the Industrial Revolution came storming in during the 1780s, significant literature was being written about the rights of humankind, and uprisings and conflicts were breaking out around the world, so it's no surprise that creatives wondered if rationality was actually making things worse, not better.

WHAT COLOUR DID THE ROMANTICS THINK YOUR LIVING ROOM SHOULD BE?

Many Romantic artists were inspired by Johann Wolfgang von Goethe, who wrote about the way colours make us feel in his 1810 book *Theory of Colours*, in which he recommended green as an eye-pleasing colour for the rooms you're in most regularly.

I'M FEELING A BIT... WHAT'S THE WORD?

Weltschmerz – a German term for world-weariness literally meaning 'world pain' – was a key element in many Romantic artworks, which show a melancholy, solitary figure in a landscape, looking out sadly at the beauty of the world.

3 KEY ARTISTS

William Blake (1757–1827)
English artist and poet, although he preferred the title 'craftsman'; had intense, supernatural visions.

John Constable (1776–1837)
English painter and creator of idyllic scenes of the English countryside featuring modern artificial features like canals; heir to a corn mill.

Théodore Géricault (1791–1824)
French print-maker and painter who enjoyed painting horses and battles, and especially horses taking part in battles; died young from an infection following a horse-riding accident (but he did **love** horses).

3 KEY ARTWORKS

Eugène Delacroix, *Liberty Leading the People* (1830)
Showing the July 1830 Revolution, Liberty (with bosoms out in an ancient goddess-y type of way) leads revolutionaries through Paris; in the background you can spot a tiny tricolour flying on the roof of Notre-Dame cathedral.

Francisco Goya, *The Third of May 1808* (1814)
Created just six years after the event in which Spanish revolutionaries were executed by Napoleonic troops, Goya's brutal image of martyrdom was worlds away from previous depictions of war as noble and clean.

Caspar David Friedrich, *Wanderer above the Sea of Fog* (c.1818)
This landscape is an amalgamation of sketches Friedrich made of the Elbe Sandstone Mountains in Germany and Czechia, melding them to create an otherworldly range for his pensive figure to have a big think in.

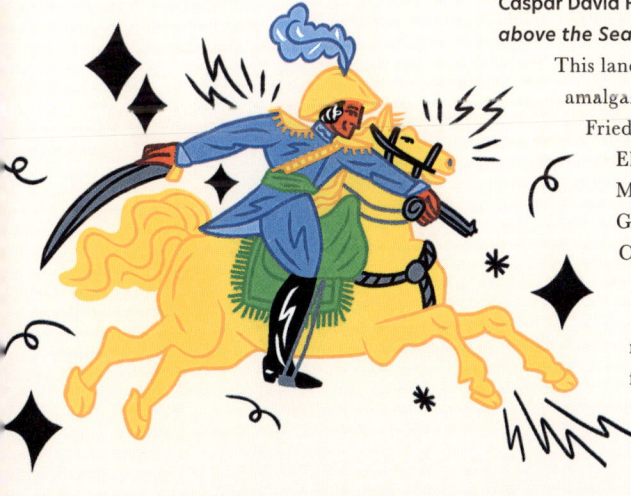

WHAT WAS THE HUDSON RIVER SCHOOL?

It was a multigenerational set of American artists whose work highlighted the country's natural beauty, based in New York State but capturing landscapes across the country in a Romantic style.

Hudson River School

1820s–1870s

US

WAS IT AN ACTUAL SCHOOL?

It wasn't a school, but a fraternity of painters who went on trips and exhibited together, although Thomas Cole did give art lessons to Frederic Church, so that relationship was a bit school-y.

WHAT WERE THEY TRYING TO DO?

When Cole created his first masterpieces, America as an independent, colonised country was less than sixty years old and largely unexplored – he and his fellow artists wanted to capture and immortalise its natural beauty before it was scuppered by the pollution seen in Europe.

WHAT WERE THEY INSPIRED BY?

As well as the vast, beautiful landscapes around them, the Hudson River artists were inspired both by the pioneering spirit of the US frontier, and the works being praised in Europe's academies.

WHY WAS IT CALLED THE HUDSON RIVER SCHOOL?

First used as a light dig at the group's landscapes when their style was losing popularity in the 1870s, the name simply came from the fact that many of their early works focused on areas of natural beauty around the Hudson River Valley area.

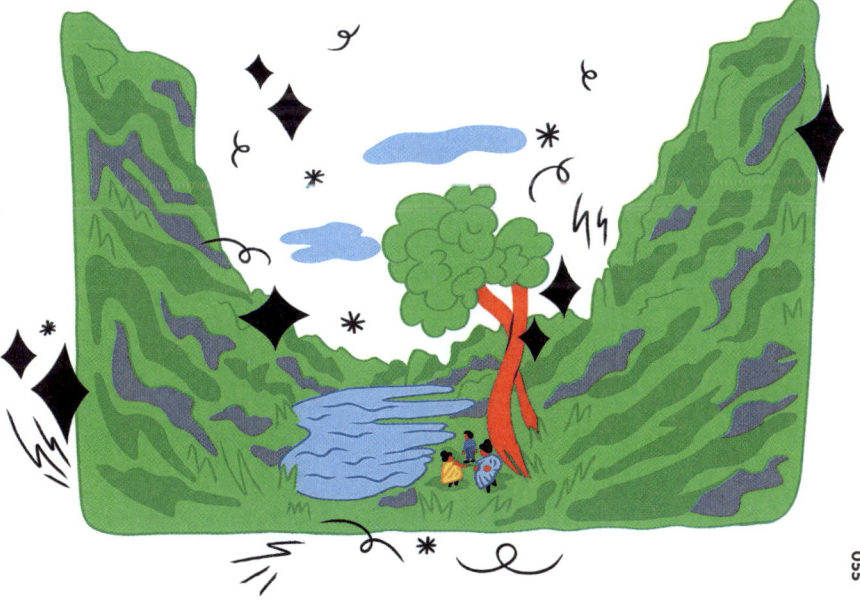

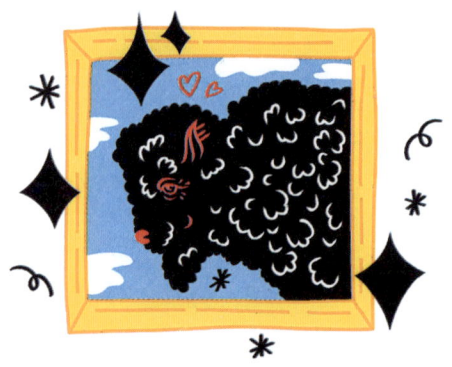

HOW DID IT RELATE TO ROMANTICISM?

HRS artists were really into the work of European Romantic artists (see page 50), sharing their enthusiasm for dramatic beauty and the desire to capture the Sublime before industrialisation ruined everything.

WHAT IS TRANSCENDENTALISM?

It was a nineteenth-century social, philosophical and literary movement, which held that the divine exists in all things and can be felt by us inherently; it can be felt in HRS art in the way it captures awe-inspiring beauty.

WHAT WERE THOMAS COLE'S PREDICTIONS FOR THE FUTURE?

Devout Protestant Cole was sceptical about the benefits of industrialisation and *The Course of Empire* (1833–36) is his seriously gloomy series of paintings showing an untouched landscape becoming a flourishing city state before its inevitable destruction, including lots of gory details and people flinging themselves into the sea.

WHY WERE THEIR FIGURES SO SMALL?

Figures in HRS landscapes are always tiny in relation to the rest of the composition, often tucked away and easy to miss; this makes the landscapes seem even more epic and expansive, while also alluding to how humankind was beginning to tame and conquer the land.

IS IT AN EXHIBITION IF IT'S ONLY GOT ONE THING IN IT?

Frederic Church became known for his exhibitions of single paintings (which, to be fair, were massive), complete with theatrical lighting and opera glasses to help the paying customers get a better look.

3 KEY ARTISTS

John Frederick Kensett (1816–1872)

American painter and Luminist (a popular Hudson River School spin-off, focused on the light within landscapes); bought himself an island to work on (the dream).

Robert S. Duncanson (c.1821–1872)

American painter; a free Black man whose art was popular with anti-slavery abolitionists; perhaps the first internationally-renowned African-American artist.

Albert Bierstadt (1830–1902)

German-American painter, big on buffalo and younger sibling of the Bierstadt Brothers, who were pioneers of stereoscope and colour photography.

3 KEY ARTWORKS

Thomas Cole, *View from Mount Holyoke, Northampton, Massachusetts, after a Thunderstorm (The Oxbow)* (1836)

The Oxbow was painted when friends advised Cole to take a break from working on *The Course of Empire,* which they thought was making him depressed.

Asher Brown Durand, *Progress (The Advance of Civilization)* (1853)

A work with a deeply colonialist world-view, *Progress* shows three Native Americans standing in the wild landscape to the left of the painting, with a developing industrial town to the right, complete with canals, a church spire, and steam train.

Frederic Edwin Church, *Rainy Season in the Tropics* (1866)

This work features an Alexander's band – a double rainbow in which the colours in one rainbow are reversed in the other – both rainbows comprising just three colours, as did most rainbows in art at that point.

**WHAT WAS
REALISM?**

It was an initially a
movement in which artists
focused on portraying
life in an authentic,
warts-and-all way.

Realism

1840s–1900s

INTERNATIONAL

WHAT'S THE DIFFERENCE BETWEEN 'REALIST' AND 'REALISTIC'?

Anything that tries to show things accurately is 'realistic', but Realist refers to art of a specific period, when artists turned away from sentimental depictions of grand subjects and chose instead to portray the potentially uglier side of life.

WHY WAS IT CALLED REALISM?

After his work was rejected for the World Exposition of 1855, Gustave Courbet set up his own pop-up gallery next door to the Exposition called the Pavilion of Realism and displayed forty of his artworks, inspiring the 'Realism' label.

WHAT OPTIONS DID YOU HAVE IF YOUR WORK WAS REJECTED BY THE SALONS?

Not getting into official shows was a big blow for artists so in 1863, the *Salon des Refusés* was created as an opportunity for those whose work had been rejected – its first exhibition included important work by Courbet and Édouard Manet.

HOW DID IT DIFFER FROM OTHER REALISMS?

Realism wasn't the only Realist art movement but it was the first, with later movements including Social Realism (see page 200) and Socialist Realism (see page 204), which were stylistically Realist, but with their own specific focus.

WHAT SORT OF THINGS WERE THEY PAINTING?

Realists painted scenes from modern life, showing everyday people and those deemed as at the edge of society; the artists were reacting against what they saw as Romanticism's sentimental excess (see page 50).

WHAT IS POSITIVISM?

It's a philosophy which maintains only that which can be rationally proven can be taken as true (putting religious faith in an uncomfy position), leading people – including the Realist artists – to examine and look critically at society.

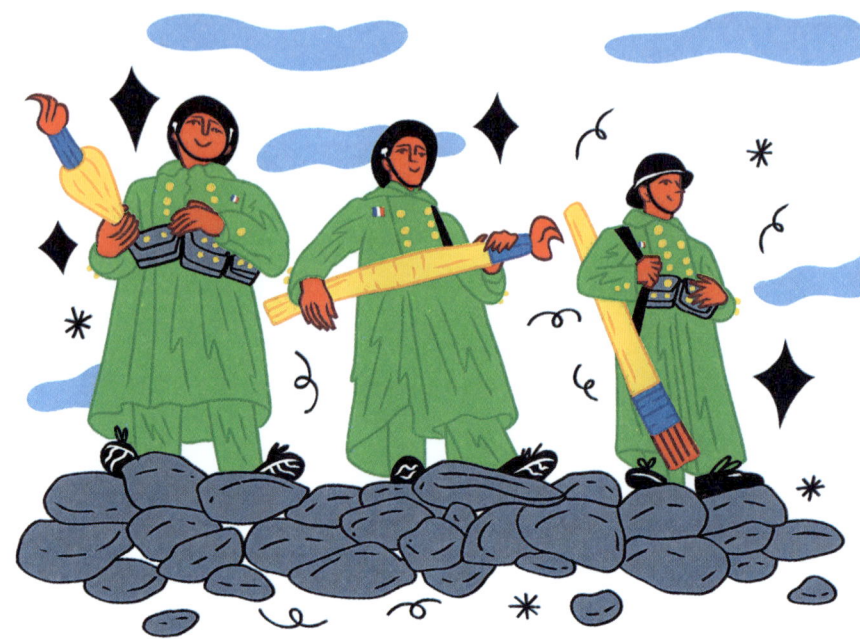

WHAT MAKES SOMETHING AVANT-GARDE?

Taken from the French term for the foremost row of soldiers advancing in battle, in the nineteenth century 'avant-garde' came to mean those at the cutting edge of art and culture.

WHY DID COURBET NEVER PAINT AN ANGEL?

Realism was all about painting what was in front of you and, well, Courbet hadn't ever seen an angel, so when he was asked to paint one for a commission from a church, he famously asked them to show him one first.

WHAT HAPPENED WHEN THEY TOOK PHOTOGRAPHY TO COURT?

Photography, invented in 1822, called into question whether or not artworks had to be made directly by an artist's hand to be considered 'proper' art, so in 1862 the French supreme Court of Cassation gave their ruling that photography was, indeed, art (not a machine product) and therefore protected under copyright law.

3 KEY ARTISTS

Théodore Rousseau (1812–1867)

French painter and founding member of the Realist Barbizon School; rejected so often from the Paris Salon that he earned the nickname *Le Grand Refusé*.

Rosa Bonheur (1822–1899)

French painter who achieved great fame for her paintings of animals; obtained permission from the French police to be allowed to wear trousers.

Ilya Repin (1844–1930)

Ukrainian-born Russian painter and member of the Russian Realist Wanderers (*Peredvizhniki*) group; got in trouble for a depiction of Ivan the Terrible showing the tsar after he had maybe just beaten his son to death (whoops!)

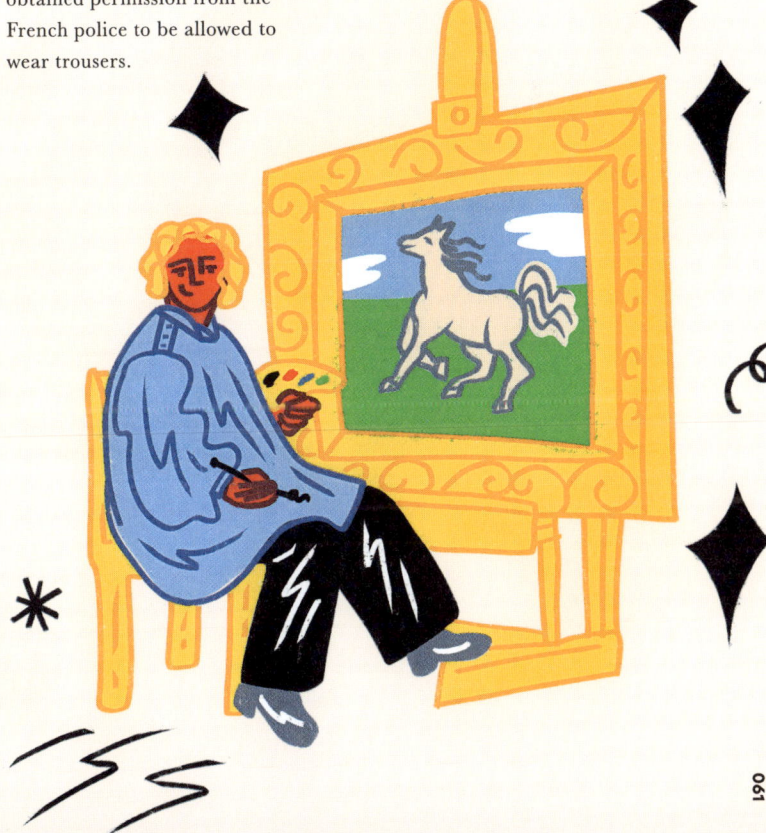

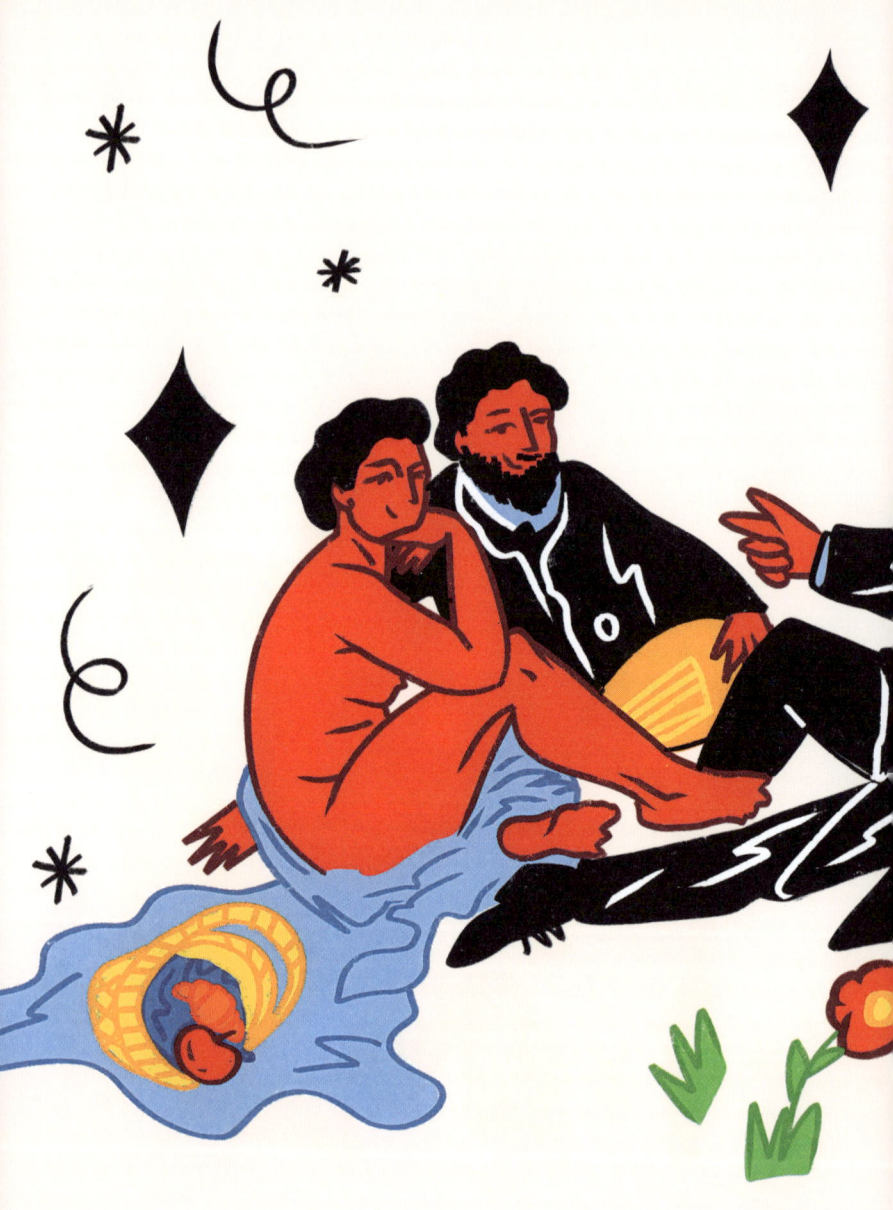

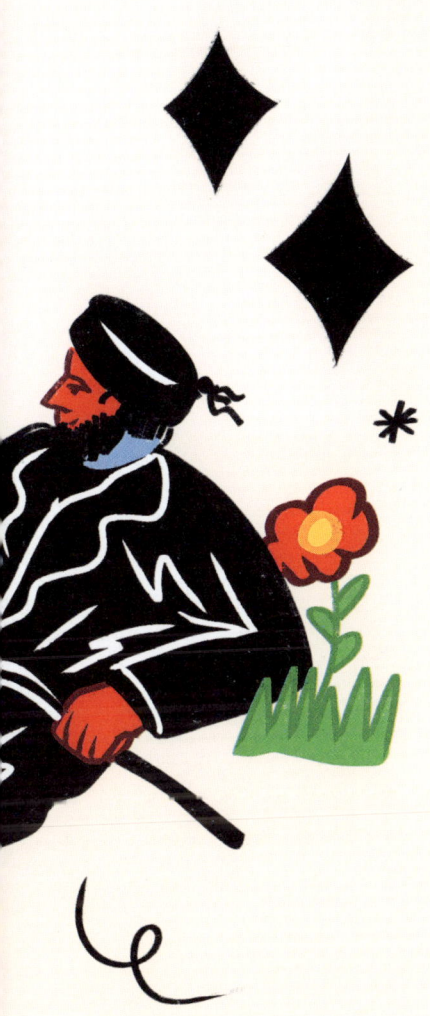

3 KEY ARTWORKS

Jean-François Millet,
***The Gleaners* (1857)**
When first exhibited in 1857,
The Gleaners was met with disgust
by gallery-goers who saw the
subject matter of three peasant
women as unsuitable, especially
on such a large canvas, which
would usually have been reserved
for depicting noble subjects.

**Édouard Manet, *The Luncheon
on the Grass* (1862–1863)**
Having ruffled feathers for many
reasons (What's going on? The
brushwork is a bit loose, isn't it?
Why has she got her kit off but the
blokes are in full suits?), Manet's
painting was rejected by the 1863
Salon and instead exhibited at the
first *Salon des Refusés*.

**Gustave Courbet, *The Origin
of the World* (1866)**
Believed to have been
commissioned by an Ottoman
diplomat for his collection of
horny paintings, this remains one
of art history's most shocking
artworks, displaying (seriously)
up-close-and-personal nudity
and not even in a classy,
ancient-historical way.

**WHAT WAS THE
PRE-RAPHAELITE
BROTHERHOOD?**

The Brotherhood was a
tight-knit group of young
artists who worked with
each other to create artworks
inspired by Romantic poetry,
medieval stories and
fourteenth-century
Italian art.

Pre-Raphaelite Brotherhood

1840s–1850s

BRITAIN

WHY DID THEY CALL THEMSELVES THAT?

The group longed for a return to the beautiful, realistic art of the fourteenth and fifteenth centuries, before High Renaissance stars – like Raphael – began putting too much emphasis on classical and idealised figures for their liking.

'BROTHERHOOD' – NO WOMEN, THEN?

Women played a key role in the development of the Pre-Raphaelite style, and although many of the PRB's female models were artists in their own right (including painter Elizabeth Siddal and embroiderer Jane Morris), they are often remembered only for their roles as muses.

WHEN WERE THEY MAKING THEIR WORK?

In 1848, some of the key players in what would become the Brotherhood gathered at John Everett Millais' parents' house (aw) in London for their first meeting, but just six years later all artists involved had stopped signing their works with the 'PRB' mark.

WHAT DIDN'T THEY LIKE ABOUT THE ART SCENE?

The Pre-Raphaelites weren't fans of sentimental Victorian paintings that beautified their subjects and lacked political edge, and they also disagreed with the way art was taught and displayed, which was based on gaining the approval of a small number of academicians.

WHAT ELSE INSPIRED THE BROTHERHOOD, APART FROM NOT-RAPHAEL?

They loved literature and depicting scenes from stories – a list compiled by Dante Gabriel Rossetti and William Holman Hunt named some of their heroes as Dante, Homer, Shakespeare, Chaucer, Barrett Browning, Tennyson, Keats, Shelley, Byron and Poe.

WHY IS EVERYONE GINGER?

Uncommon in England, red hair was associated with lustiness and deviousness (Millais got in big trouble with Charles Dickens for portraying Jesus as ginger in his 1850 painting *Christ in the House of His Parents*), and the Brotherhood loved to portray their female figures as wild, sexually available and otherworldly.

WEREN'T THEY ALL SIBLINGS OR MARRIED TO EACH OTHER?

Thomas Woolner had proposed to William Holman Hunt's first wife Fanny; James Collinson married Christina Rossetti, sister of Dante Gabriel Rossetti, whose muse was Jane Morris (who was married to William Morris); and PRB cheerleader John Ruskin had his marriage to PRB model Effie Gray annulled on the grounds of non-consummation (apparently because he hated her pubic hair), leaving her free to marry John Everett Millais – so yeah, sort of.

WHAT WAS THE PRB'S RELATIONSHIP TO THE ARTS AND CRAFTS MOVEMENT?

Both movements fancied the idea of medieval craftsmanship, when people made beautiful things by hand, and key Pre-Raphaelite players – including Rossetti, Edward Burne-Jones, Morris and Ruskin – were instrumental in the development of the Arts and Crafts Movement (see page 82).

WHAT WAS MUMMY BROWN?

Produced between the sixteenth and twentieth centuries, Mummy Brown was a brown pigment made from actual mummified remains, and when Burne-Jones found out what it was made from, he held a funeral for his last tube.

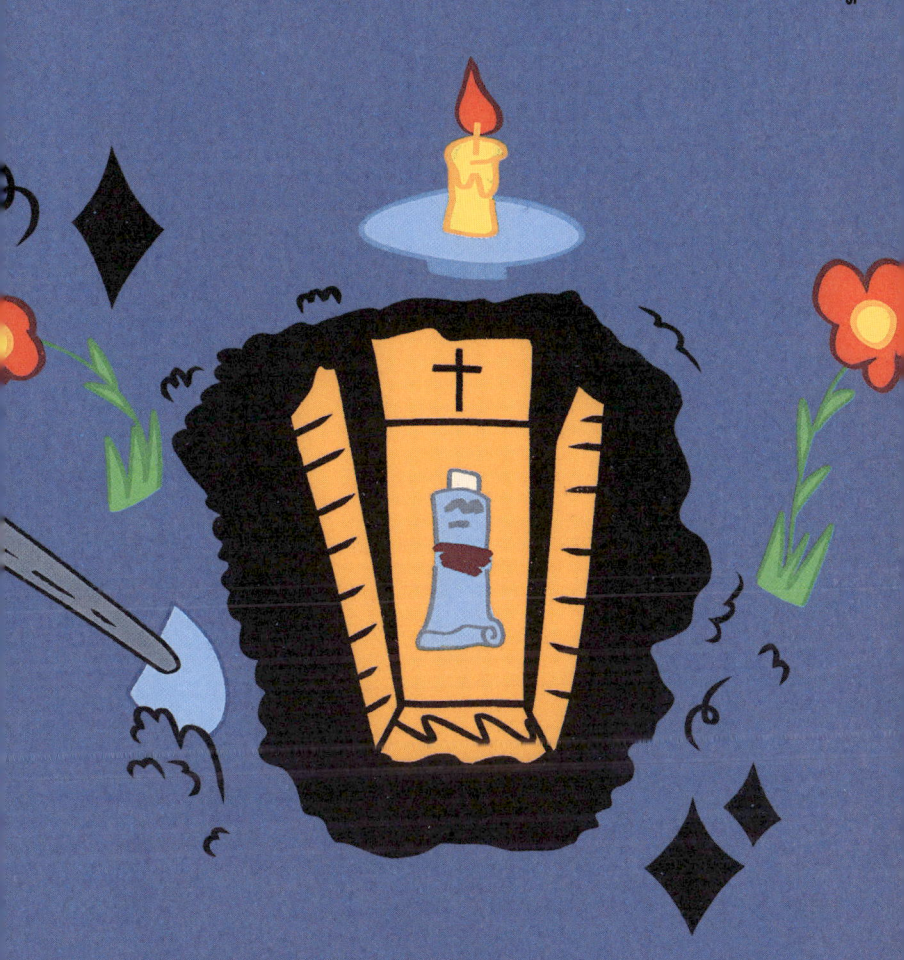

3 KEY ARTISTS

Thomas Woolner (1825–1892)
English poet and sculptor who briefly emigrated to Australia in 1852 to work in the goldfields (so confident he'd make his fortune that he left his sculpting tools at home); the only founding Pre-Raphaelite sculptor.

Elizabeth Siddal (1829–1862)
English artist and poet, the only woman to exhibit work at the 1857 Pre-Raphaelite exhibition; often poorly.

Simeon Solomon (1840–1905)
English painter who created work highlighting his Judaism and focusing on figures from the Old Testament; sentenced to hard labour for homosexuality.

3 KEY ARTWORKS

Dante Gabriel Rossetti, *The Annunciation (Ecce Ancilla Domini!)* (1849–1850)
With his sister Christina posing as Mary, this depiction of the Annunciation was controversial,

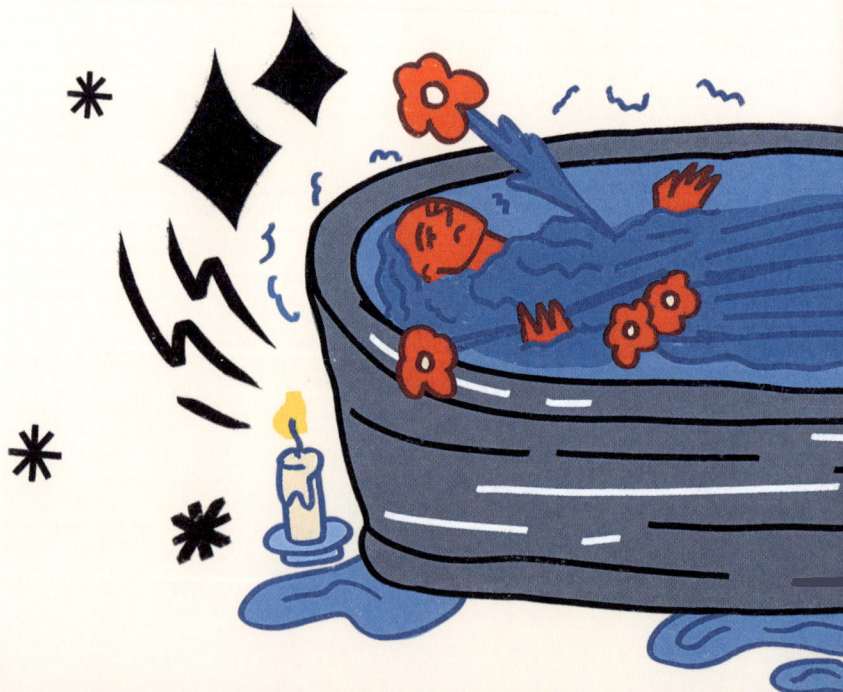

showing the Virgin sat in bed in her nightgown and a wingless Angel Gabriel naked beneath a cheeky little number with a big slit down the side.

John Everett Millais, *Ophelia* (1851–1852)

Showing the moment in Shakespeare's *Hamlet* when Ophelia drowns herself in a river, a then 19-year-old Elizabeth Siddal posed for the painting by lying, fully clothed, in a tin bath filled with water 'warmed' by oil lamps, which went out while Millais was engrossed in painting, causing Siddal to catch a terrible cold.

William Holman Hunt, *The Awakening Conscience* (1853)

Portraying a mistress who suddenly wakes up to her wicked ways, the frame Hunt designed for the work features bells (a symbol of warning), marigolds (associated with grief and despair) and a star at the top (representing her moment of spiritual realisation).

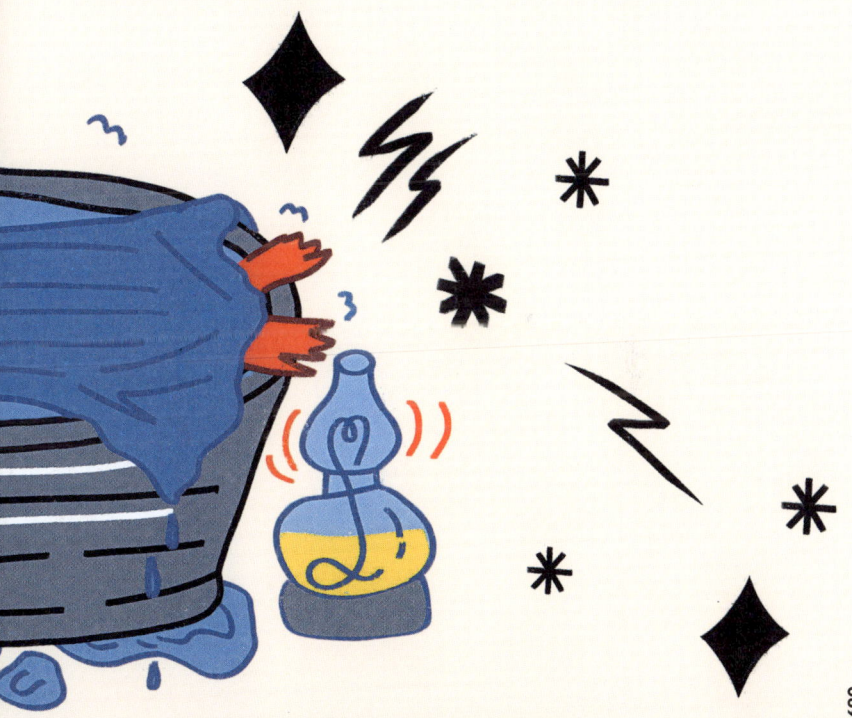

They were a loose group of artists creating artwork that reflected the developing modern world around them, with a focus on capturing light and movement through loose brushstrokes and a colourful palette.

Impressionism
1860s–1880s

FRANCE

WHERE DID THE NAME COME FROM?

The critic Louis Leroy called the group 'Impressionists' in a tongue-in-cheek review in 1874, referencing Claude Monet's painting *Impression, Sunrise* (1872) and saying that a preliminary drawing for wallpaper was more finished than Monet's seascape (harsh).

WHAT DID THEY DO WHEN THE SALONS WOULDN'T HAVE THEM?

Impressionist artists got fed up with being constantly rejected (or hung in poor positions) at the Salon of the *Académie des Beaux-Arts*, so created their own society and set up independent exhibitions, the first of which was held in 1874 in the studio of photographer Félix Nadar.

WHEN WERE THEY MAKING THEIR IMPRESSIONS?

A total of eight Impressionist exhibitions took place between 1874 and 1886, but some people argue that Impressionism didn't truly die until Monet did, in 1926.

WHAT INSPIRED THEM?

The Impressionists wanted to represent what it was like (mostly for the middle and upper classes) to live in cosmopolitan society, capturing the new forms of entertainment available on the recently-built Parisian boulevards, and creating compositions heavily influenced by the Japanese *ukiyo-e* woodcut prints that had become popular in Europe in the 1850s.

WHY SO BLURRY?

The Impressionists questioned the traditional way of painting favoured by the academies, which aimed to paint their scenes in exact detail, instead arguing that the way we actually see the world isn't always in perfect focus.

WHAT IS IMPASTO?

It's a technique, often used by the Impressionists, of applying paint so thickly to a canvas that it creates a three-dimensional texture, standing out and showing exactly where – and how – the artist has created their marks.

WHAT WAS MONET'S FAVOURITE COLOUR?

The first true violet pigment was created in 1856; Monet loved it so much that he called it the true colour of the atmosphere, and the Impressionists used it so enthusiastically that they were said to be suffering from 'Violetomania'.

AND HIS LEAST FAVOURITE COLOUR?

Monet was such a passionate fan of bright colours that it is said that at his funeral, his friend, the French politician Georges Clemenceau, cried out, removed the black cloth draped over the coffin, and replaced it with a colourful one instead.

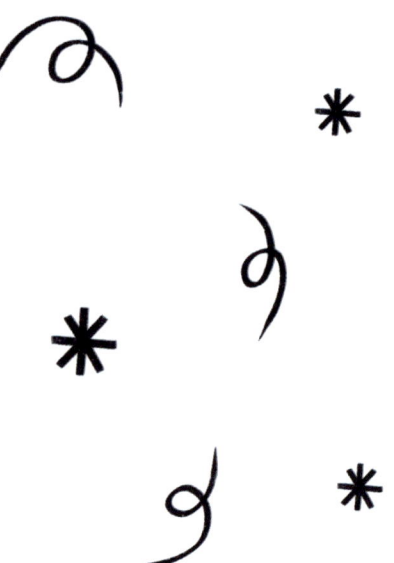

HOW WERE THEY HELPED BY DEVELOPMENTS IN THE PAINT INDUSTRY?

The invention of zinc tubes in 1841 meant that artists could conveniently carry their paints outdoors to paint *en plein air* ('in the open air'), which was popular with Impressionists because it allowed artists to observe and capture the effects of sunlight live.

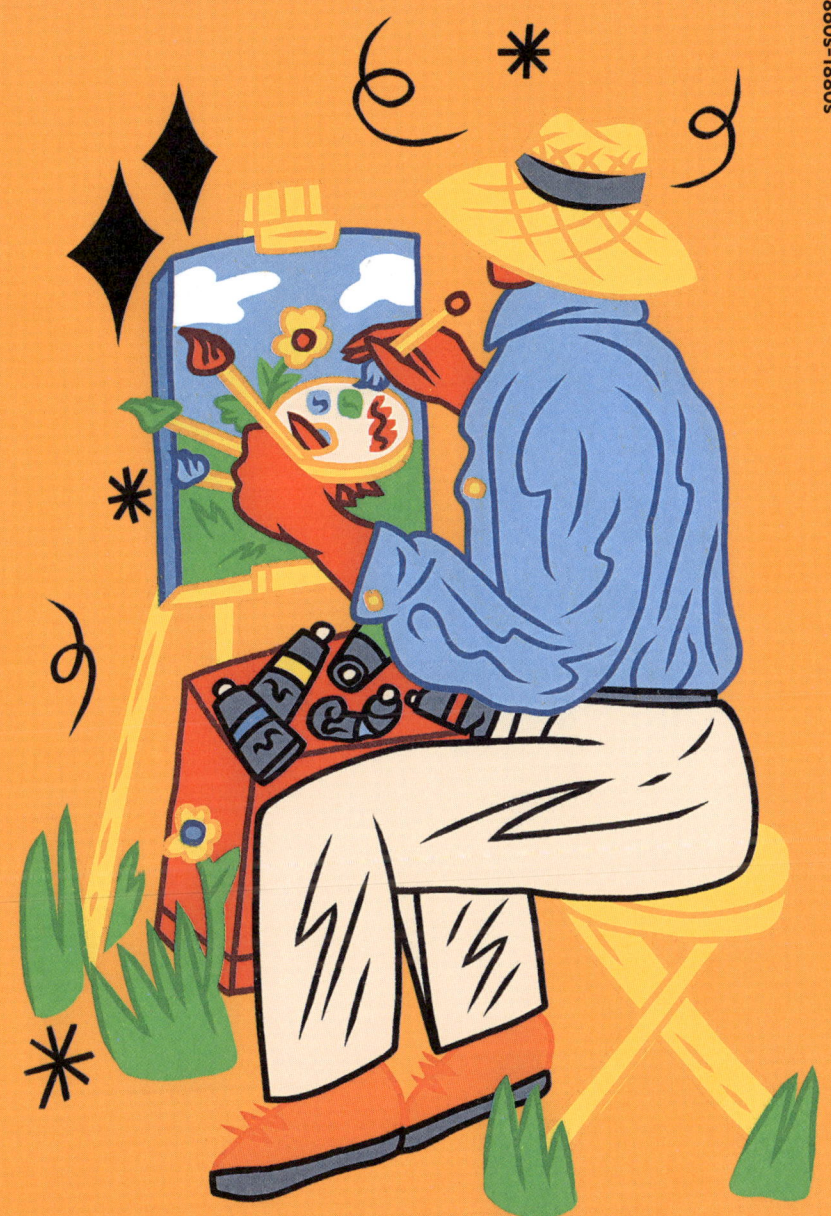

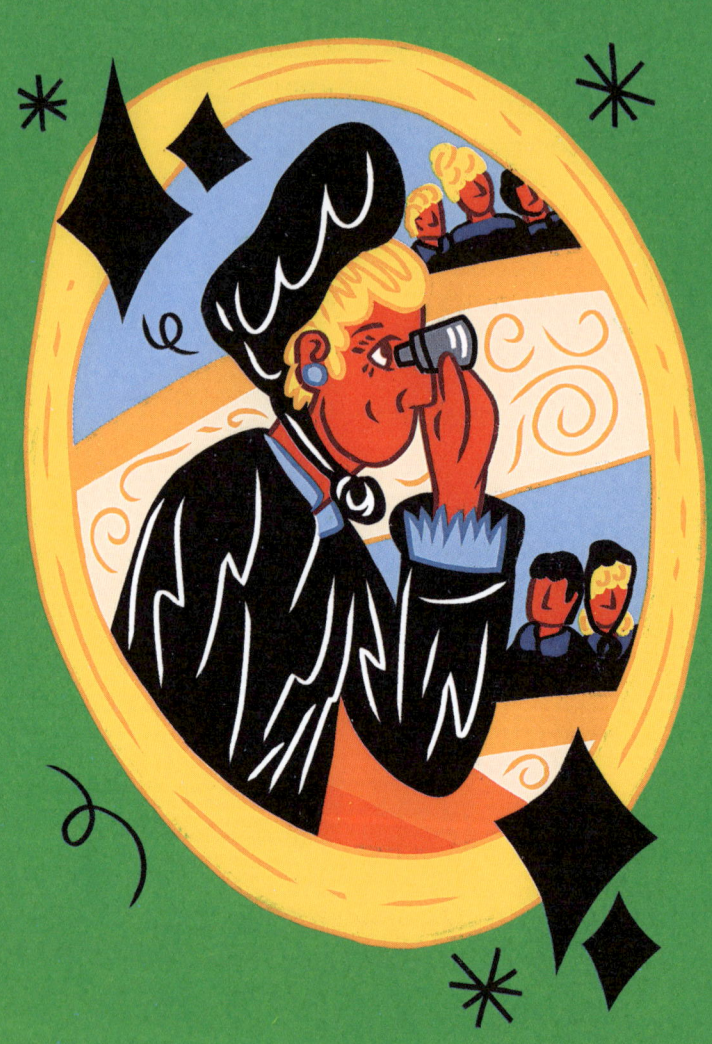

3 KEY ARTISTS

Camille Pissarro (1830–1903)

Danish-French painter, the only artist to display work at all eight Impressionist exhibitions; loads of his major works were lost during the Franco-Prussian war when soldiers apparently used his paintings as doormats while he was away in London.

Edgar Degas (1834–1917)

French artist famous for his ballerinas, he reckoned the government should set up a special armed force to tackle all the artists that were painting *en plein air*.

Berthe Morisot (1841–1895)

French painter and the only female founding member of the Impressionists' society, Morisot featured in more Impressionist exhibitions than Monet.

3 KEY ARTWORKS

Claude Monet, *La Gare Saint-Lazare* (1877)

One of a series of twelve views of the newly-expanded Gare Saint-Lazare railway station in Paris, Monet created the sketches for these paintings while sitting at the side of the track and on the concourse.

Mary Cassatt, *In The Loge* (1878)

Seen as a sly comment on how women are subjected to the male gaze, the painting shows a woman watching a performance through opera glasses, seemingly unaware that a man is using **his** opera glasses to stare directly at her.

Pierre-Auguste Renoir, *Luncheon of the Boating Party* (1881)

Renoir included portraits of lots of his mates in this jolly get-together and the work was generally well-received, apart from one comment in a French newspaper that said it would have been a better painting if only Renoir had learned to draw (ouch).

WHAT WAS AESTHETICISM?

Guided by the idea of 'art for art's sake', Aestheticism valued art's beauty above its ability to convey meaning.

Aesthetic & Decadent Movements

1860s–1900s

BRITAIN

WHAT WAS IT INSPIRED BY?

Aestheticism was inspired by Romanticism (see page 50) as well as by artwork imported from Japan and China, and rejected the Victorian belief – held by the likes of the Arts and Crafts group (see page 82) – that art has a moral duty to fulfil.

HOW DID PEOPLE REACT TO AESTHETICISM?

Most people rolled their eyes at the Aesthetes, viewing them as pretentious hipsters – and they were regularly mocked in the satirical magazine *Punch*, shown wearing shocking green and yellow (colours that consequently took on connotations of disease and sexual perversion).

WHAT WERE OSCAR WILDE'S HOT TAKES ON ART?

Seen as the closest thing to an Aesthete manifesto, Oscar Wilde's *The Decay of Lying* (1891) put forward four key artistic points: art doesn't express anything other than itself; bad art is the result of looking too earnestly at real life and nature; lying is the true aim of art; and 'Life imitates Art far more than Art imitates Life'.

WHAT BECAME THE UNLIKELY BEAUTY STANDARD?

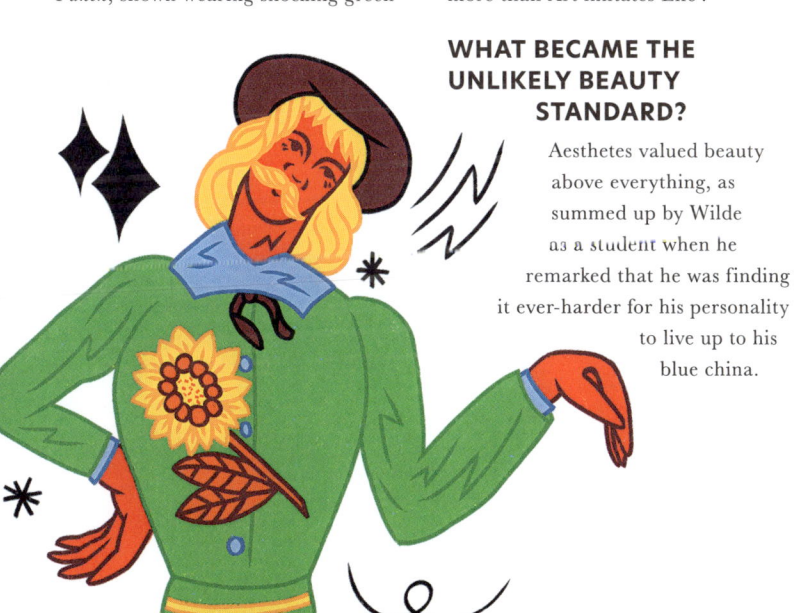

Aesthetes valued beauty above everything, as summed up by Wilde as a student when he remarked that he was finding it ever-harder for his personality to live up to his blue china.

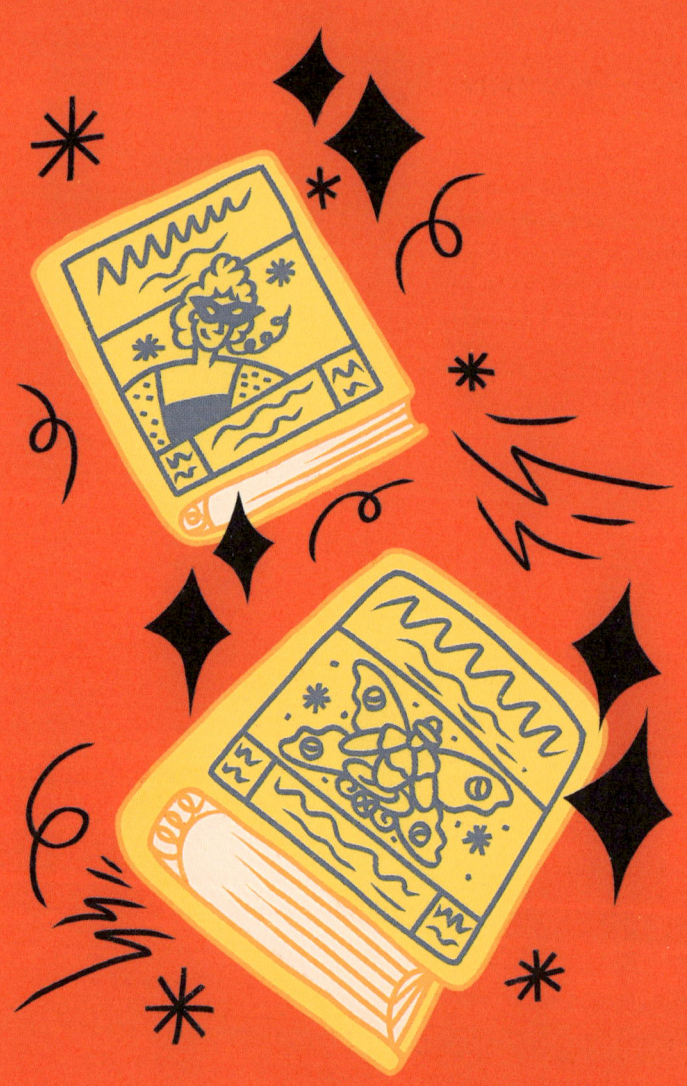

HOW LONG DID IT TAKE WHISTLER TO CREATE *NOCTURNE IN BLACK AND GOLD*?

During a court case for libel, when the artist James McNeill Whistler was asked how he could possibly charge so much for a work that took just a couple of days to make, he defended himself by saying that the price reflected the knowledge he had built up over a lifetime.

WHAT WAS DECADENTISM?

Decadentism was the result of Aestheticism's developing interest in hedonism and pleasure, so its artwork and writings are often immersed in dark and erotic fantasy.

JUST HOW HORNY WAS SOME OF IT?

Decadent illustrators had a reputation for using intensely sexual imagery, and in Aubrey Beardsley's case this was compounded by the fact that he also had tuberculosis, which in Victorian times was seen as a sexy illness, in a pale, sickly way.

WHAT IS THE *FIN DE SIÈCLE*?

The term refers to the end of the nineteenth century, a period full of radical approaches to art and rebellions against social norms; the period is also called the 'Yellow Nineties' after *The Yellow Book* and the Aesthetes' yellow dandy culture.

WHAT WAS *THE YELLOW BOOK*?

Published quarterly between 1894 and 1897, *The Yellow Book* was a radical periodical containing illustrations and writing associated with the Aesthetic and Decadent movements, named after the saucy Parisian books that booksellers would wrap in yellow paper.

3 KEY ARTISTS

Franz von Bayros (1866-1924)
Croatian-born Austrian Decadent
artist who moved to Germany
after his nasty divorce from the
stepdaughter of composer Johann
Strauss II; got himself arrested and
exiled for his infamous portfolio
Tales from the Dressing Table,
which is almost laughably porny.

Charles Conder (1868-1909)
English-born Australian Aesthete,
lover of ladies and libations, and
a key member of the Australian
Impressionist Heidelberg School.

Aubrey Beardsley (1872-1898)
English Decadent illustrator and
co-founder of *The Yellow Book*, he
asked his publisher to destroy his
lewd drawings after he converted
to Catholicism a month before his
early death, but his request was
ignored (bad for Beardsley, great
for pervs).

3 KEY ARTWORKS

James McNeill Whistler, *Symphony in White, No. 1* (1861-1862)
Embodying the 'art for art's sake'
approach, this painting perplexed
audiences trying to work out what
it was about, because it wasn't
about anything – it was simply
a girl in white in front of a
white curtain.

Félicien Rops, *Pornocrates* (1878)
Rops' best-known work features a
blindfolded *femme fatale* (see page
96) being guided by a pig with a
golden tail (a symbol of luxury)
on top of a classical frieze
showing four allegories of the arts,
suggestive of the Decadent ideal
that sensual pleasure is more
important than philosophical art.

James Hadley, *Teapot* (1882)
This Royal Worcester teapot
mocks the pretentiousness of
the Aesthetes and hints at their
sexually transgressive reputation
by depicting a man on one side
and a woman on the other, who
look almost identical.

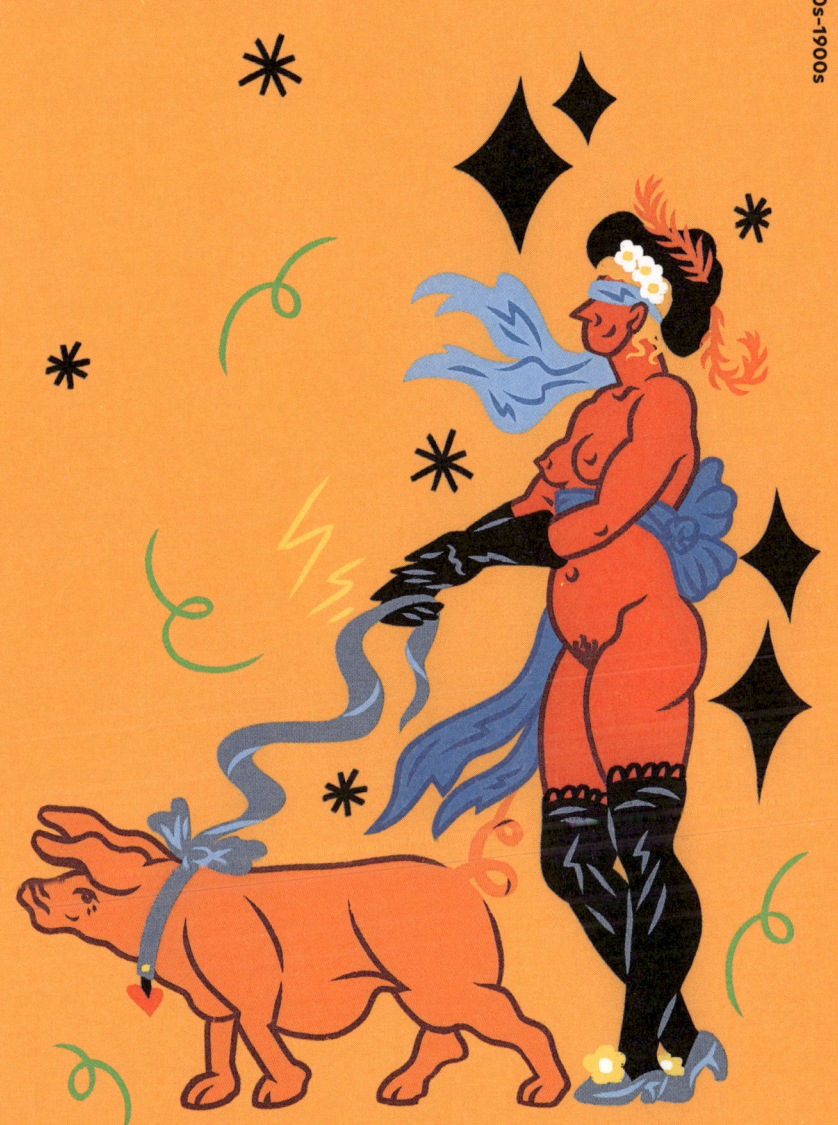

WHAT WAS ARTS AND CRAFTS?

It was a movement – inspired by the socialist ideology of William Morris – that was all about beautiful and useful objects made by hand by craftspeople, as they had been in medieval times.

Arts and Crafts

1880s–1920s

BRITAIN

WHAT WERE THEY UPSET ABOUT?

Arts and Crafts artists and thinkers believed that following the Industrial Revolution, the objects in our homes had become poor-quality, and that truly beautiful things could only be made by skilled artisans who were suitably paid for their labour (chance would be a fine thing, am I right?)

WHO WERE THEY INSPIRED BY?

The art critic John Ruskin (see page 66 for him being upset by pubes) was a key Arts and Crafts theorist, believing that poorly made, mass-produced goods were impacting society's morals, and that even a bad workman would create something inherently beautiful, as long as they made it by hand.

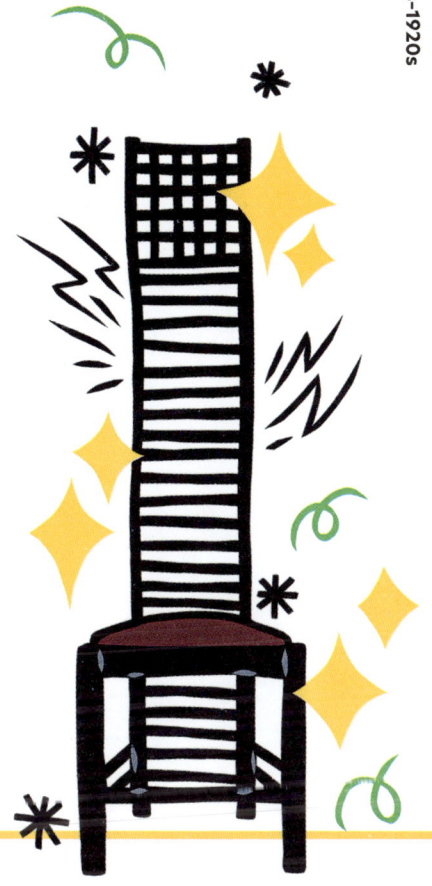

WHY WERE MACKINTOSH'S CHAIRS SO TALL?

Scottish designer Charles Rennie Mackintosh designed his iconic high-backed chairs with, well, very high backs, because it created an illusion of an additional wall behind people sitting around a table, increasing the sense of intimacy (phwoar).

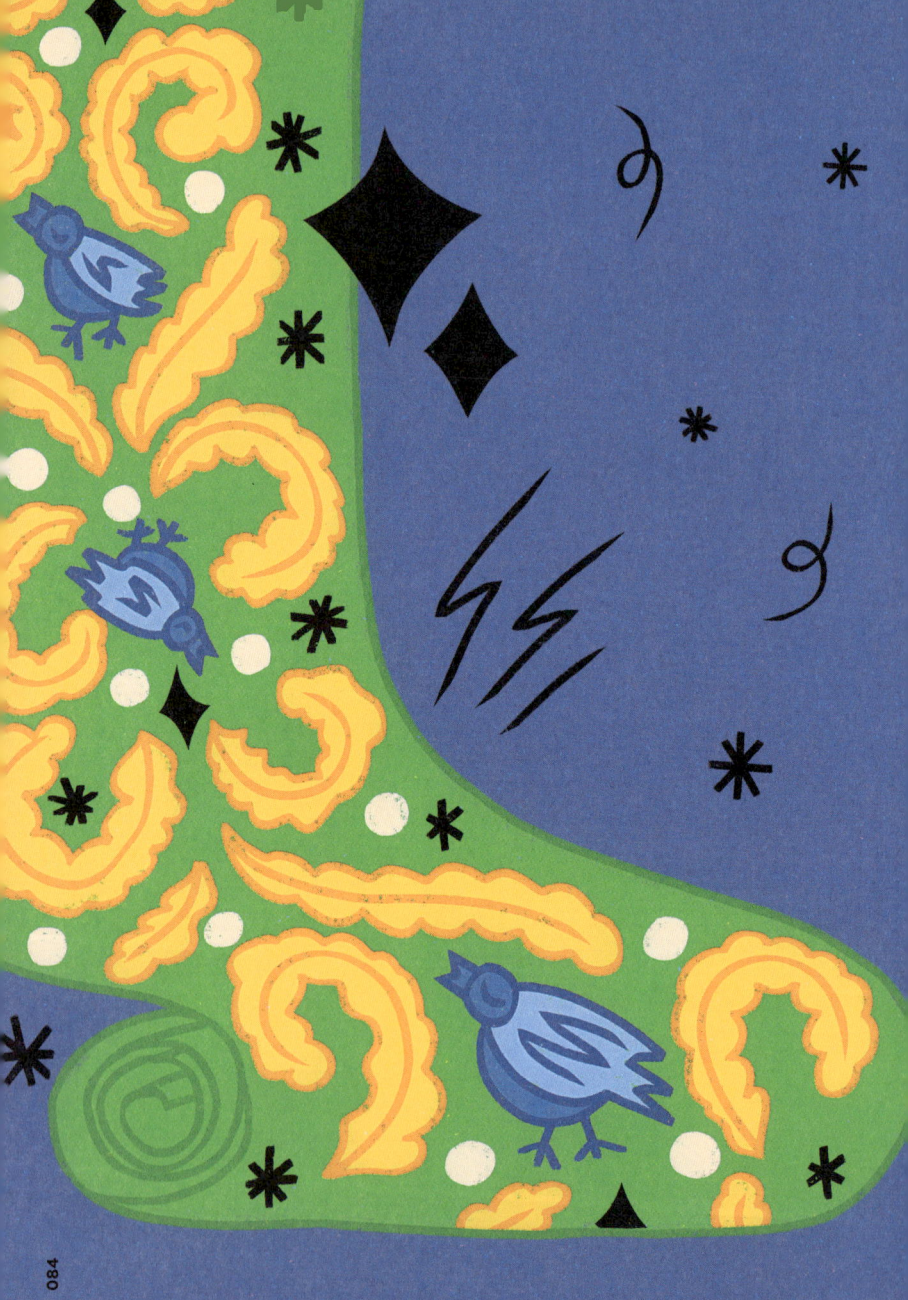

SO WAS ALL MACHINERY FROWNED UPON?

Machinery itself wasn't necessarily bad – artists at Morris & Co. had access to state-of-the-art Jacquard looms to create their tapestries – as long as it was helping individual craftspeople to do their thing, save time and create truly quality products.

WHAT WAS MORRIS' WALLPAPER PROBLEM?

Morris' firm designed and made wallpaper, seen as an easy way for people to make their homes more beautiful; but in the 1860s, a string of child deaths was tied to high levels of arsenic in wallpaper dyes.

AH, SO I GUESS THE COMPANY STOPPED MAKING WALLPAPER IMMEDIATELY?

Well, coincidentally Morris was a director of his family mine in Devon, which happened to be one of the world's largest producers of arsenic; he did, however, **eventually** bow to pressure and created a line of special, arsenic-free wallpaper.

WHAT DID THE ARTS AND CRAFTS MOVEMENT INSPIRE?

It was hugely influential, both visually – impacting everything from architecture to carpets – and in its attitude towards unifying fine and applied arts, which was big for movements like *Art Nouveau* (see page 102) and Bauhaus (see page 188).

HOW DID IT DIFFER FROM *ART NOUVEAU*?

Although both movements focused on natural motifs and beautiful ornate designs, *Art Nouveau* didn't have the same political chops as Arts and Crafts, and the Arts and Crafts lot definitely didn't approve of how the *Art Nouveau* lot used machinery to mass-produce some of their designs.

WHAT WAS GOING ON ELSEWHERE?

It wasn't just in Britain that people were looking longingly back at their folk-art traditions – in Poland, the *Młoda Polska* (Young Poland) movement drew inspiration from the folk crafts of the Gorals highlanders.

3 KEY ARTISTS

William Morris (1834-1896)

English designer, writer, activist and massive socialist; co-founder of Morris & Co. and also 'co-founder' of May Morris.

May Morris (1862-1938)

English designer who became director of the embroidery department at Morris & Co. at 23 (can you be a socialist nepo-baby?); she founded the Women's Guild of Arts in 1907 when the Art Workers' Guild wouldn't accept female members.

Charles Rennie Mackintosh (1868-1928)

Scottish designer, born 'McIntosh' but changed it and no one's really sure why; once arrested on suspicion of being a German spy.

3 KEY ARTWORKS

Kate Bunce, *The Keepsake* (c.1898-1901)

Held in a fantastic frame created by her older sister Myra, this work was inspired by a Gabriel Dante Rossetti poem that tells of the return of keepsakes to a princess whose boyfriend had been killed while on pilgrimage (although she doesn't really look that fussed).

Phoebe Anna Traquair, *The Awakening* (1904)

Also inspired by a Rossetti poem, this bright oil-on-panel painting shows the awakening of the human spirit, with an angel pointing at a pile of people snoozing in a field.

Veronica Whall, *Stained Glass Windows in King Arthur's Great Halls, Cornwall* (c.1933)

Whall created seventy-two windows telling the story of King Arthur for the HQ of the Order of the Fellowship of the Knights of the Round Table (whose members saw less sword-fighting than in Arthurian times and which was led not by a mythical king, but a man who ran a custard-powder firm).

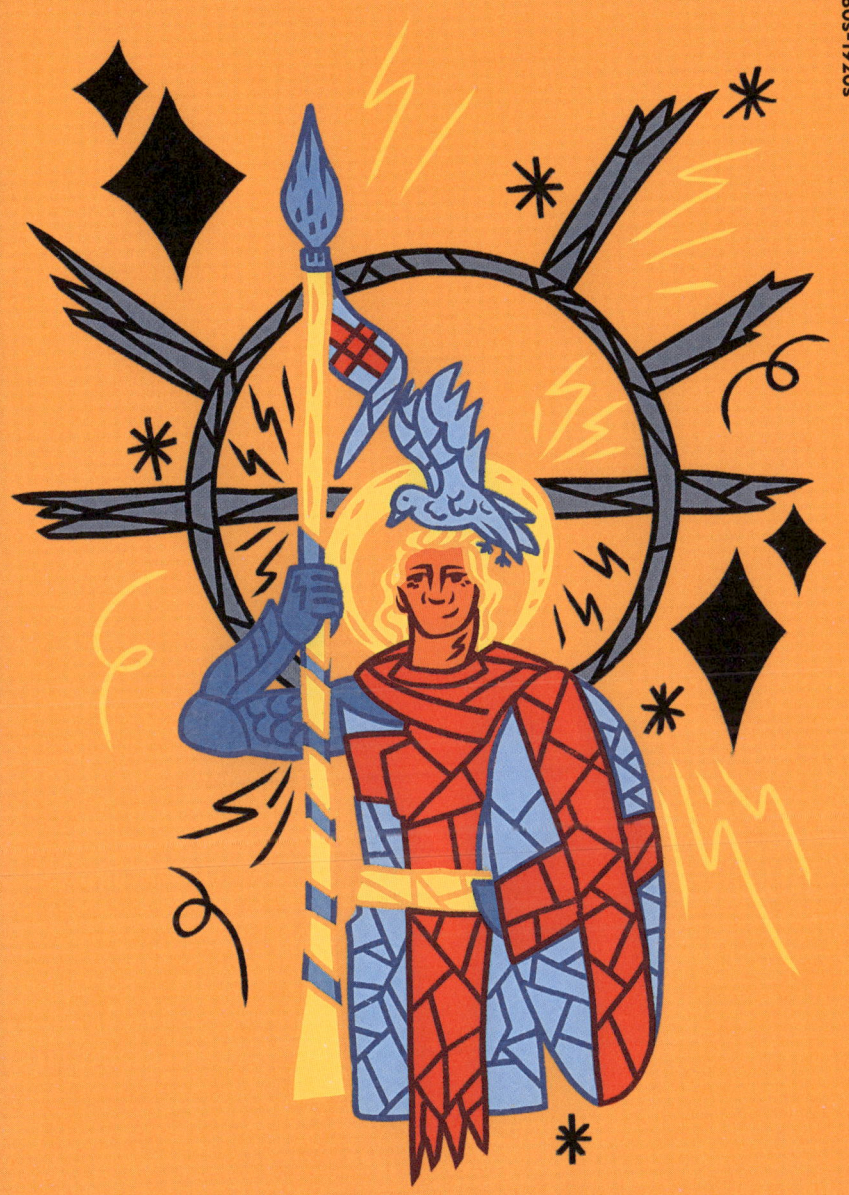

WHAT WAS POST-IMPRESSIONISM?

The Post-Impressionists were a set of artists (who wouldn't have thought of themselves as any type of group, let alone one called the Post-Impressionists) who sought to take art further on than where the Impressionists (see page 70) had left it.

Post-Impressionism
1880s–1900s

FRANCE

IN WHAT WAY WERE THEY 'POST'?

While the Impressionists were big on light, the Post-Impressionists were more interested in colour and capturing emotion in their work, rather than making impressions of fleeting moments.

HOW DID THEY GET THEIR NAME?

It wasn't until the end of the period (when all the major Post-Impressionists were already dead) that Roger Fry (see page 131) gave them their name with his 1910 exhibition, Manet and the Post-Impressionists, at London's Grafton Galleries.

WHAT INSPIRED THEM?

The Post-Impressionists loved colour (particularly the bright, new pigments being manufactured at the time) as well as the art coming out of Japan (Van Gogh made his own versions of designs from Utagawa Hiroshige's *One Hundred Famous Views of Edo*).

DID THE POST-IMPRESSIONISTS KNOW EACH OTHER?

While they didn't all know each other personally, Paul Gauguin and Vincent van Gogh certainly did, living together in France in the famous Yellow House, until a nasty quarrel between them apparently prompted Van Gogh to sever his ear in distress.

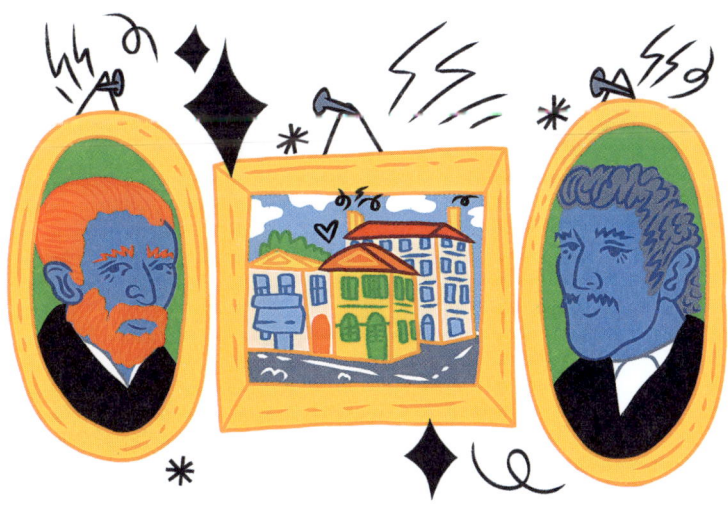

IF VAN GOGH ONLY SOLD ONE WORK IN HIS LIFETIME, HOW IS HE SO FAMOUS?

After Vincent and his brother Theo died, Theo's widow, Jo, published a collection of the 900+ letters the brothers exchanged while Theo was bankrolling his big brother's artistic career; this gave people an insight into the man behind the paintings, cementing his legacy.

WHY DOES SOME OF IT MAKE MY EYES HURT?

Pointillism was a technique developed by Post-Impressionists Paul Signac and Georges Seurat, in which small dots of contrasting colours were placed together to create a composition brimming with colour and light when viewed from a distance (but which can be a bit headache-y when viewed up close).

WHAT DID THEY PICK UP FROM THE CHEMIST?

Colour theory: Michel Chevreul was a French chemist whose works on colour theory, particularly on 'simultaneous contrast' – how two opposite colours on a colour wheel impact each other when placed close together – was also deeply impactful for both the Impressionists and Post-Impressionists.

WHAT IS CLOISONNISM?

It's a Post-Impressionist technique where areas of flat colour are separated by dark borders, taking its name from the practice in stained glass and ceramics making, where wires ('cloisons') are used to define glass- or enamel-filled boundaries.

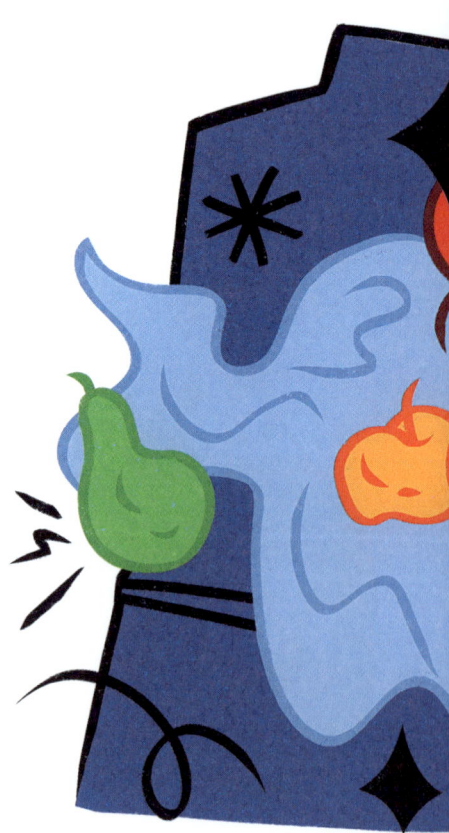

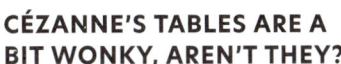

CÉZANNE'S TABLES ARE A
BIT WONKY, AREN'T THEY?

Paul Cézanne regularly rearranged the objects in his
still lifes while painting, and moved his easel to paint
from different viewpoints – so while the perspective
sometimes feels a little off, Cézanne captures a more
honest representation of how we actually see things,
with two eyes that are always moving about.

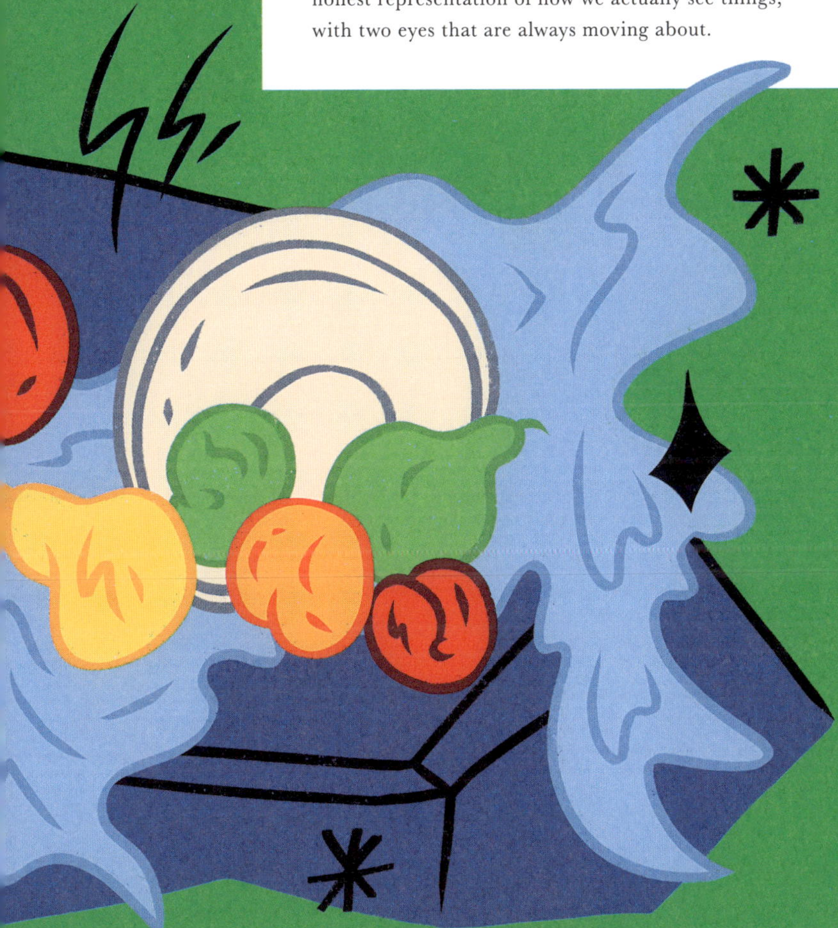

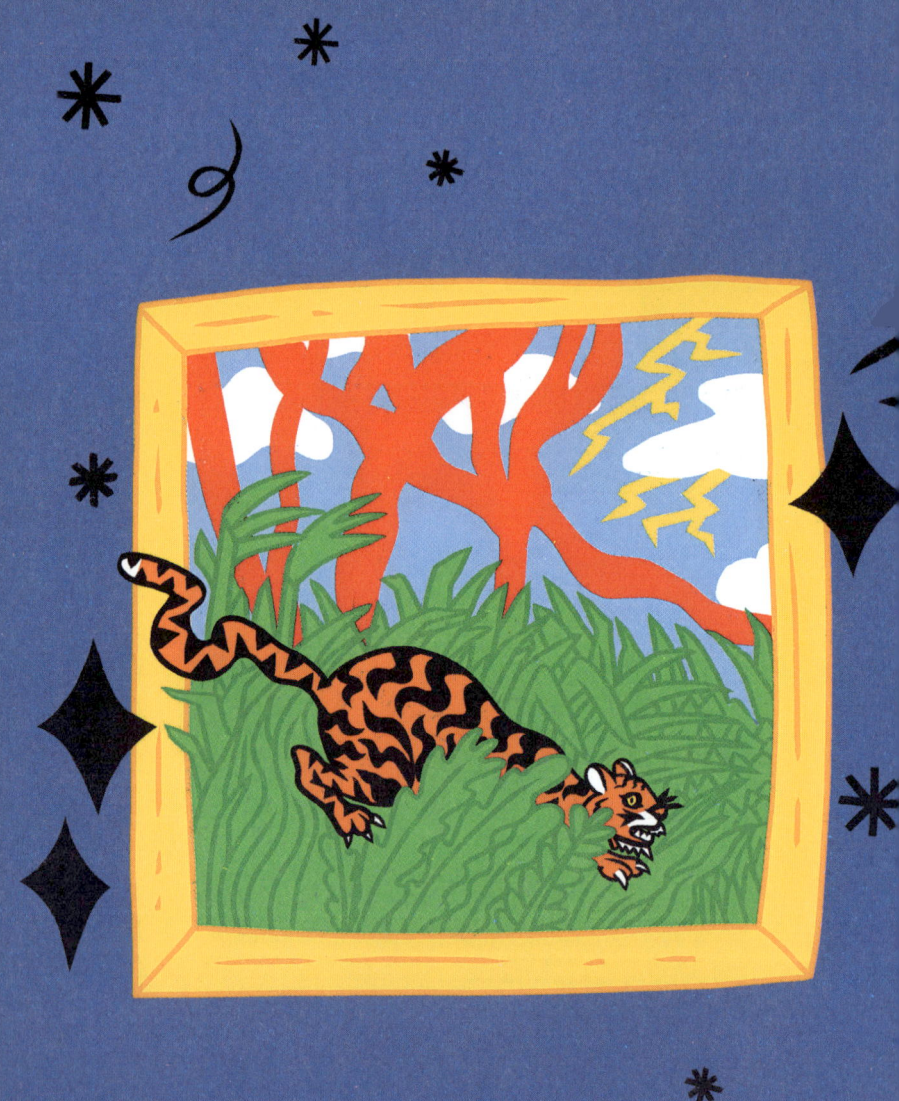

3 KEY ARTISTS

Paul Cézanne (1839–1906)

French painter, encouraged by his father to become a lawyer (whose father hasn't encouraged them to become a lawyer?); tricky to categorise as he also exhibited at the first Impressionist exhibition.

Paul Gauguin (1848–1903)

French artist of Spanish-Peruvian noble stock, he left Paris (and his wife and children) for Tahiti because he believed France had become morally bankrupt; painted a largely made-up version of Tahiti and married a 13-year-old.

Vincent van Gogh (1853–1890)

Dutch painter, originally going to be a preacher but ended up doing a stint as a substitute teacher in Ramsgate first; deeply troubled.

3 KEY ARTWORKS

Henri Rousseau, *Tiger in a Tropical Storm (Surprised!)* (1891)

This was the work that got Rousseau – an entirely self-taught artist who worked until he was 49 as a tax collector (hence his nickname '*Le Douanier*') – noticed by the art establishment.

Henri de Toulouse-Lautrec, *Le Lit (The Bed)* (1892)

Like many of his works, *Le Lit* was made from observations Toulouse-Lautrec made in Paris brothels, the places in which, he said, he felt most at home (aw).

Georges Seurat, *A Sunday Afternoon on the Island of La Grande Jatte* (1884–1886)

Reminiscent of the still and sideways-on figures in the friezes of ancient Egypt and Greece, this pointillist Parisian scene features a small monkey in the foreground which may be a hint that its owner is a sex worker.

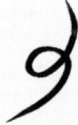

WHAT WAS SYMBOLISM?

Also a literary style, Symbolist art addressed fundamental truths about life and death via metaphorical imagery, often drawn from mythology or fantasy.

Symbolism
1880s–1910s

WESTERN EUROPE

WHAT WAS MAKING THEM GET ALL SYMBOLIC?

At a time when industrialisation and scientific developments had people thinking about what mattered spiritually, the Symbolists created art all about the soul, with symbolic meanings hidden in their compositions.

WHAT WERE THE FLOWERS OF EVIL?

A pioneering work of Symbolist literature, Charles Baudelaire's *Les Fleurs du mal* dealt with some of the Symbolists' favourite things – original sin, erotica, and death – and earned the poet a hefty fine for public indecency.

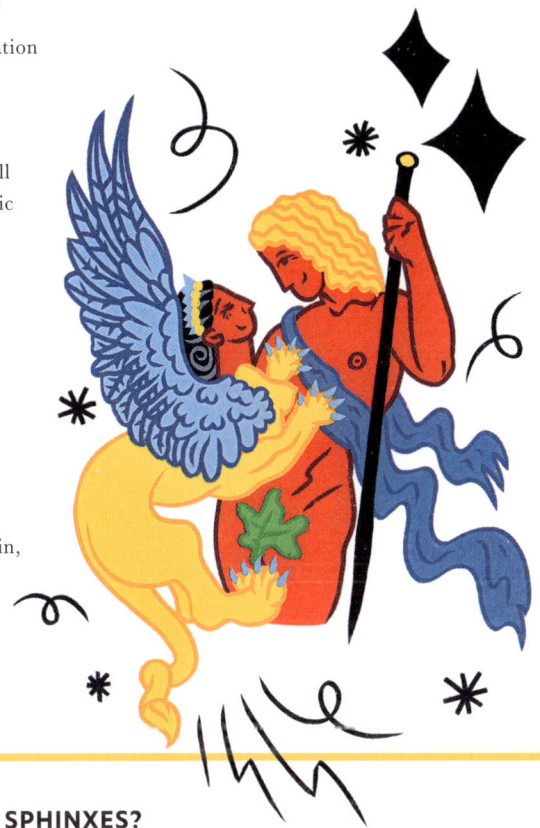

WHY SO MANY SPHINXES?

In the story of Oedipus (you know the one, very close with his mum), the Sphinx challenges people to solve a riddle, and this character is featured in several Symbolist artworks as the embodiment of themes like femininity, animal-ness and ancient and Eastern wisdom.

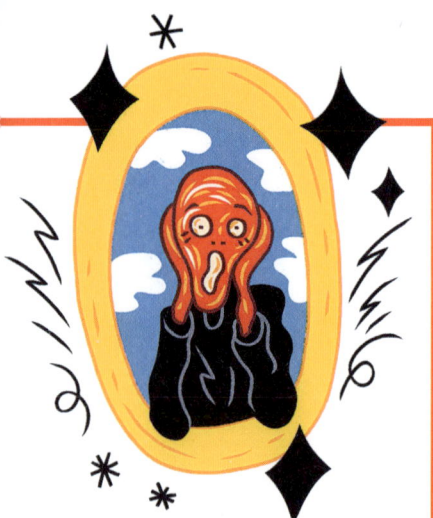

HOW LOUD IS THE GUY SCREAMING IN *THE SCREAM*?

Trick question: the figure in Edvard Munch's 1893 painting (considered a Symbolist masterpiece for the way it explores human anxiety) is actually **hearing** a scream, and the piece was originally titled *Der Schrei der Natur (The Scream of Nature).*

WHAT WAS *LE FIGARO*?

France's oldest national newspaper, it played a key role in art history by printing the (literary) Symbolists' manifesto, and in 1909 it would do the same for the Futurists (see page 144).

WHY ARE SO MANY CENTRAL FIGURES WOMEN?

Women have long been a favourite subject of male artists (often in a pervy way), seen by them to contain deep, mystical knowledge and used as symbols for sex, birth, beauty and also madness (women were still being diagnosed with 'hysteria' in the late nineteenth century).

WHAT IS A *FEMME FATALE*?

An archetype dating back to ancient times, the *femme fatale* is a mysterious, sexually awakened and dangerous woman: she is a key trope in Symbolist art.

WHAT DID JESUS LOOK LIKE?

In James Ensor's artwork *Christ's Entry into Brussels in 1889*, depicting a huge parade welcoming Jesus into the Belgian capital, Christ coincidentally looks **exactly** like James Ensor (humble, eh?)

WHAT WAS THE *SALON DE LA ROSE + CROIX*?

It was a set of six artistic salons featuring work by Symbolist artists, hosted by writer Joséphin Péladan, who made himself out to be a kind of high priest under the name of Sâr Mérodack, wearing big robes and claiming to be able to do religious magic.

3 KEY ARTISTS

George Frederic Watts (1817-1904)

English artist who created the Watts Gallery, a museum dedicated to himself (and his wife, Mary Fraser Tytler, a bit); 'England's Michelangelo' (although Michelangelo didn't marry a 16-year-old when he was 46…)

Gustave Moreau (1826-1898)

French artist, already wealthy and generally wanted to be left alone so turned down various significant exhibition opportunities.

Evelyn De Morgan (1855-1919)

English painter, also associated with the Pre-Raphaelites (see page 64), her mother bribed Evelyn's drawing tutor to tell her that she wasn't very good in the hope that she would quit.

3 KEY ARTWORKS

Max Klinger, *Death at the Lake* (1880)

Skeletons were frequent motifs in Symbolist artworks; sometimes a solemn reminder of death, sometimes a bit more playful, like this one who is happily pissing into a lake (which is probably still about death because you definitely don't want death-piss in the water supply).

Odilon Redon, *The Cyclops* (1898-1914)

Depicting the Greek myth of Polyphemus the Cyclops who was in love with the nymph Galatea (who was in love with the river god Acis), Redon's Cyclops comes across as shy and heartbroken, and not as if he is about to crush Acis with a great big rock.

Mikalojus Konstantinas Čiurlionis, *Rex* (1909)

A musical composer as well as an artist, Čiurlionis explored concepts like spirituality and the nature of the universe, and in *Rex* – his biggest work – he shows two towers, representing benevolent and malevolent forces.

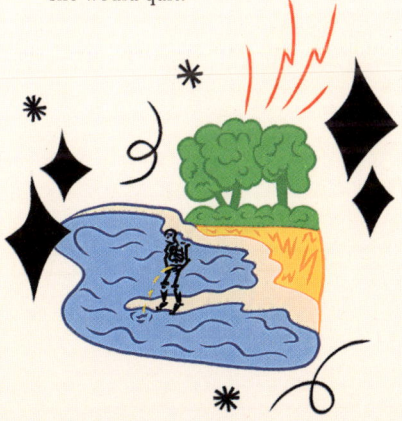

WHO WERE
LES NABIS?

Les Nabis was a blokes-only group, many of whom had met as students at Paris' *Académie Julian*, who were creating Symbolist- (see page 94) and Post-Impressionist- (see page 88) inspired artworks, with a particular focus on private domestic scenes from everyday life.

Les Nabis
1880s–1900s

FRANCE

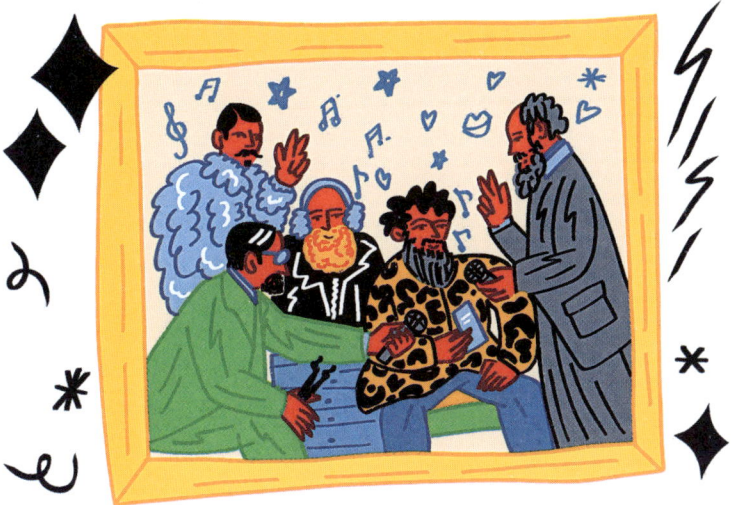

WHY 'NABIS'?

The group named themselves after the Hebrew word for prophet, positioning themselves – not massively humbly – as leaders of new modern art.

WHAT INSPIRED THEM?

They were inspired by the Post-Impressionists (see page 88) Paul Gauguin, Paul Cézanne and Georges Seurat for their approaches to colour, as well as by the newly-more-accessible medium of photography, becoming some of the first artists to embrace it and to use photos as references for paintings.

WHAT WERE THEY AIMING FOR?

The Nabis wanted to bring a sense of sacredness back into painting, rejecting strict rules about perspective that had dominated traditional art since the Renaissance and instead leaning into the power of colour as a way to express soul.

IN WHAT WAY WERE THEY LIKE THE SPICE GIRLS?

Each of the Nabi members also had a nickname, including 'Danish Nabi' (Mogens Ballin), 'Obelisk Nabi' (Jan Verkade), and 'Nabi who is even more Japanese than the Japanese Nabi' (Paul Ranson) – none of which are as catchy as Sporty, Scary, Ginger, Posh or Baby.

BIT CULTY?

The Nabis had a whole secret-society vibe going on, growing beards together and signing their letters '*E.T.P.M.V. et M.P.*' ('In your palm, my words and my thoughts'); a Nabi's studio was called an '*ergasterium*' (Latin for 'factory'), while Ranson's studio was 'the Temple'.

WHAT WAS *LE TALISMAN*?

In 1888 Sérusier created *Paysage au Bois d'Amour* in Brittany under the instruction of Nabi idol Paul Gauguin; the resulting vivid painting (originally meant only to be a sketch) became known as 'the Talisman', which the Nabis believed was charged with a special spiritual energy.

WHO DID THEY INSPIRE?

The Nabis' attitude to using intense and emotionally-charged colour was a big inspiration for the Fauvists (see page 124) around a decade later.

WHAT WAS INTIMISM?

Sounding sexier than it actually was, Intimism was a movement spearheaded by Édouard Vuillard and Pierre Bonnard following the disintegration of the Nabis, which continued the artists' interest in portraying domestic scenes.

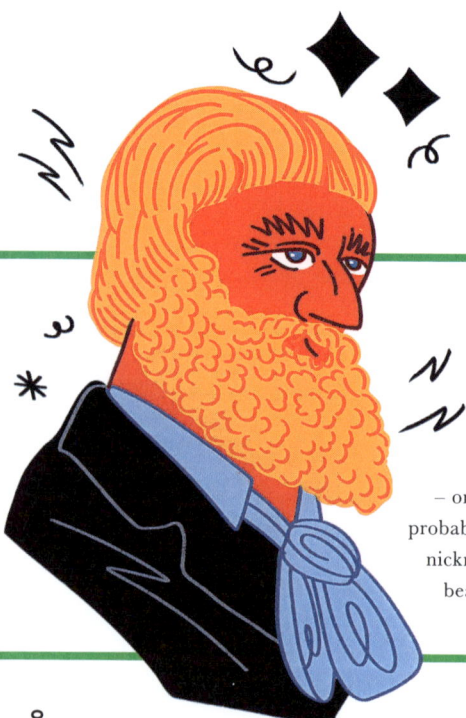

WAIT, WHAT WAS THAT ABOUT BEARDS?

Several Nabis had beards (it was part of the whole 'I'm a prophet' look), but Paul Sérusier – one of the leading members – probably had the best one as he was nicknamed 'Nabi with the brilliant beard' for his luscious facial hair.

3 KEY ARTISTS

Pierre Bonnard (1867-1947)
French artist nicknamed *le Nabi le très japonard* for his admiration of Japanese woodblock prints; couldn't keep away from his paintings even when they were on display in galleries, and regularly came back to make changes.

Jan Verkade (1868-1946)
Dutch painter who became a monk; son of the creator of Verkade confectionery.

Maurice Denis (1870-1943)
French painter and critic, deeply religious (but religiously one-upped by Verkade becoming a literal monk); 'Nabi of the beautiful icons' (nice!).

3 KEY ARTWORKS

Édouard Vuillard, *The Flowered Dress* (1891)
Vuillard specialised in interior scenes focused on women, and *The Flowered Dress* shows his grandmother, sister and mother – with whom he lived until he was 60 – at work as seamstresses.

Félix Vallotton, *The Waltz* (1893)
One of Vallotton's first Nabi paintings, *The Waltz* shows almost abstract swirling couples on an ice rink that used to be on the roundabout of the Champs-Élysées.

Henri-Gabriel Ibels, *Salon des Cent* (1894)
At a time when colour lithography – a process for making multi-colour prints – was relatively new, Ibels built his reputation creating adverts like this poster for the *Salon des Cent* exhibition in 1894.

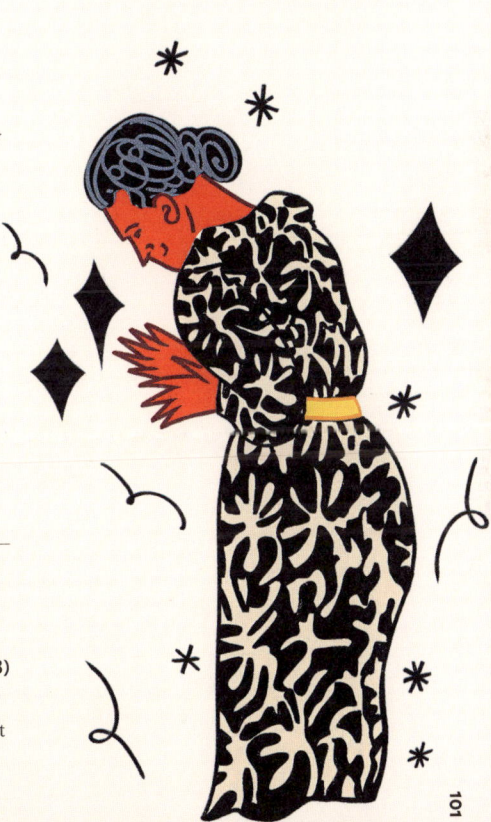

**WHAT WAS
ART NOUVEAU?**

It was a style of art, design
and architecture known for
its stylised ornamentation
(decorative bits) that often
referenced nature.

Art Nouveau

1890s–1910s

INTERNATIONAL

WHAT WAS IT INSPIRED BY?

As well as the philosophy of the Arts and Crafts artists (see page 82), which sought to fill both public and private places with beautiful things, *Art Nouveau* artists were inspired by the ornate applied art of Japan, ancient Celtic and Saxon designs, and Rococo (see page 4) flamboyance.

WHY THE NAME?

Art Nouveau went by many names across Europe, including *Jugendstil* in Germany and *Style Métro* after Hector Guimard's beautiful Parisian Metro station entrances, but it's believed the name was popularised when art dealer Siegfried Bing opened his *Maison de l'Art Nouveau* gallery in Paris in 1895.

WAS THAT NAME THE BEST OPTION?

Definitely not because they were calling it *Paling Stijl* – literally 'eel style' – in Belgium, which is brilliant.

HOW IS IT DIFFERENT TO ARTS AND CRAFTS?

Like Arts and Crafts, *Art Nouveau* artists wanted to unite fine and applied arts, but they were less fussed about their designs being made by hand (and less into the general socialist vibes of the A&C crowd), as long as what was being made was beautiful.

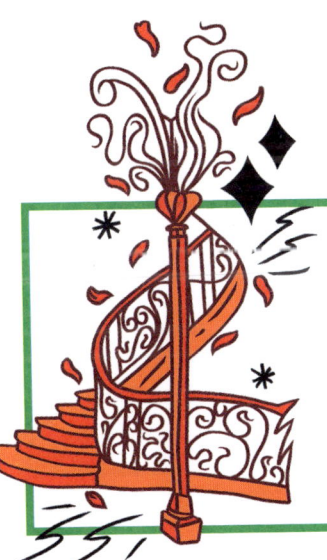

WHAT'S THE BEST BIT OF A PLANT?

The Belgian architect Victor Horta was a pioneer of *Art Nouveau* style, and believed that in the design of an ornate column you should discard the flowers and leaves and keep the stem (and now that you look at it, *Art Nouveau* is massively stemmy, isn't it?)

WHAT WAS *LA BELLE ÉPOQUE*?

French for 'the beautiful era', this was a rare period of peace for Western Europe between the end of the Franco-Prussian War in 1871 and the beginning of the First World War in 1914, during which people had the chance to get a bit indulgent and many new art styles blossomed as a result.

WHAT WAS THE DARMSTADT ARTISTS' COLONY?

Home to twenty-three *Jugendstil* artists, the colony was founded in Germany in 1899 by the 23-year-old Grand Duke of Hesse, not entirely for the love of art, but also because he hoped it would boost the local economy and make him a bit of cash.

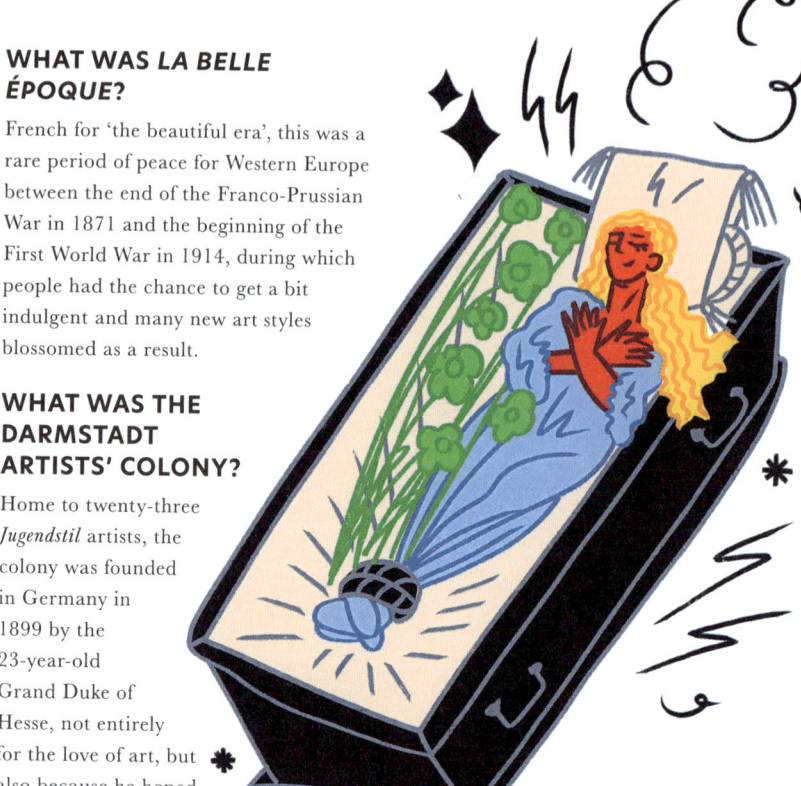

WHO WAS LOIE FULLER?

An icon of the *Art Nouveau* movement, Loie Fuller was a lesbian American dancer who regularly appeared at the *Folies Bergère* music hall in Paris, and was often portrayed by *Art Nouveau* artists performing her serpentine dance.

WHY DID IT END?

With the First World War disrupting its trajectory, and industrial advances leading the way to the Art Deco aesthetic, *Art Nouveau* fell out of fashion – so much so that, in Germany, it began to be called *Bandwurm* (tapeworm) style (like 'eel style' but so much worse…)

3 KEY ARTISTS

Eugène Grasset (1845–1917)
Swiss artist considered the father of *Art Nouveau* in Paris; did big things for the promotion of posters to the status of 'proper' art.

Alphonse Mucha (1860–1939)
Hugely patriotic Czech painter and illustrator; launched his career with images of the French actress and sculptor Sarah Bernhardt, who occasionally slept in a coffin.

Margaret Macdonald Mackintosh (1864–1933)
Scottish artist known for her roses; a member of The Four (also – and more coolly – known as the Spook School) along with husband Charles Rennie Mackintosh (see page 86), her sister and her brother-in-law.

3 KEY ARTWORKS

Louis Comfort Tiffany, *Education* (1890)
Tiffany's stained-glass designs brought Tiffany & Co. (owned by his father) to global prominence; *Education* showed a series of angels representing various subjects including art and music (lovely).

Mikhail Vrubel, *The Princess of the Dream* (1896)
Part of a major commission for an exhibition celebrating the coronation of the Russian emperor, the artwork was inspired by a play of the same name (in which Sarah Bernhardt starred in a later production).

Théophile Steinlen, *Tournée du Chat Noir* (1896)
In addition to this poster advertising the famous Black Cat club in Paris, Steinlen painted, sculpted and drew cats on the reg and would often feed the stray cats that roamed around Montmartre.

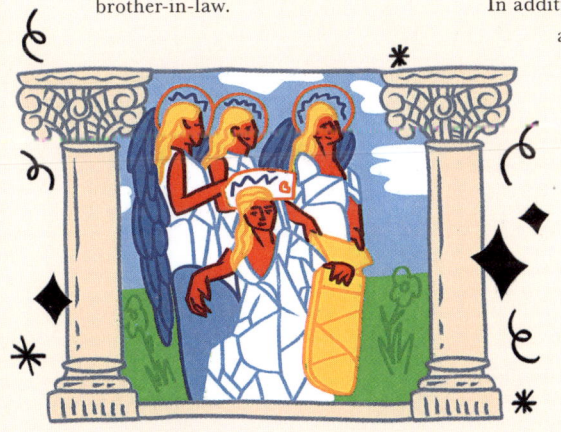

**WHAT WAS THE
VIENNA SECESSION?**

It was an *Art Nouveau*
movement founded by
artists and architects who
sought to redefine the
boundary between fine
and applied art and bring
avant-garde art to Austria.

Vienna
Secession
1890s–1900s

AUSTRIA

WHAT WAS GOING ON IN VIENNA AT THE TIME?

Following the shocking murder-suicide pact of the Austrian crown prince and his mistress in 1889, Vienna was going through a period of self-reflection, there was rising political tension from German Nationalists, and Austrian A-lister Sigmund Freud was publishing his groundbreaking treatise on the unconscious.

IF A SECESSION IS A WITHDRAWAL FROM A UNION, WHAT WERE THEY SECESSION-ING FROM?

The group wanted to free themselves from the rule of the conservative *Künstlerhaus* and the Academy of the Arts, institutions that controlled the exhibition of art in the city.

WHAT IS *GESAMTKUNSTWERK*?

Meaning total artwork, it was a guiding principle of the Secession and describes a universal approach to the arts, which includes all visual things – not just painting and sculpture, but furniture, typefaces, clothes and the objects in our homes, too.

WHO WERE THEY INSPIRED BY?

Vienna wasn't the only place having a Secession – Munich and Berlin were also having their own – and these avant-garde groups were all inspired by the spiritually expressive approach of the Symbolists (see page 94), the designs of *Art Nouveau* (see page 102), and the accessibility of Arts and Crafts (see page 82).

WHERE WOULD YOU FIND A SACRED SPRING?

Ver Sacrum (sacred spring) was the official Secessionist magazine, published twice a month from 1898 to 1903; its office was in the basement of the Secessionist Building, which had been built in 1898 by Joseph Maria Olbrich.

WHAT WAS THE PROBLEM WITH KLIMT'S NUDES?

The problem for Klimt's figures wasn't their nudity, per se (art history's full of it), but the way they embraced each other, contorted their bodies and had pubic hair: his art was often deemed pornographic and copies of *Ver Sacrum* containing his nudes were sometimes confiscated and taken off sale.

WHY DID KLIMT USE SO MUCH GOLD?

Klimt wanted to achieve a sense of sensual depth and give a nod to the heavenly in his work; also his father was a gold engraver with whom Klimt trained, which added to his expertise with the material.

WHY DID IT END?

The end came about due to a combination of changing tastes in Europe and some serious in-fighting – one group wanted to focus on getting Secessionist applied-art designs made on an industrial scale (called the Klimt Gruppe – guess whose idea that name was?), while others wanted to focus on fine art.

WHO WAS THE BEST-DRESSED?

Several of Gustav Klimt's most famous patterned dresses (such as in his 1903–1907 *Portrait of Adele Bloch-Bauer I*) were based on real garments designed by Klimt's life partner and muse, the fashion designer Emilie Flöge – who is also believed to be the model in Klimt's *The Kiss*.

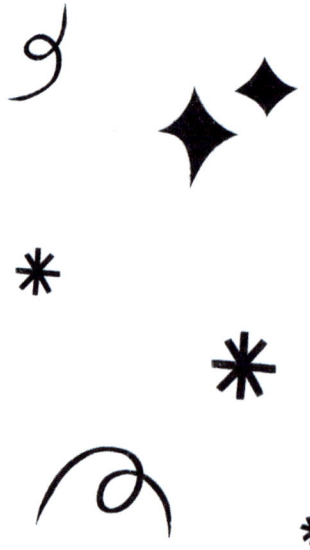

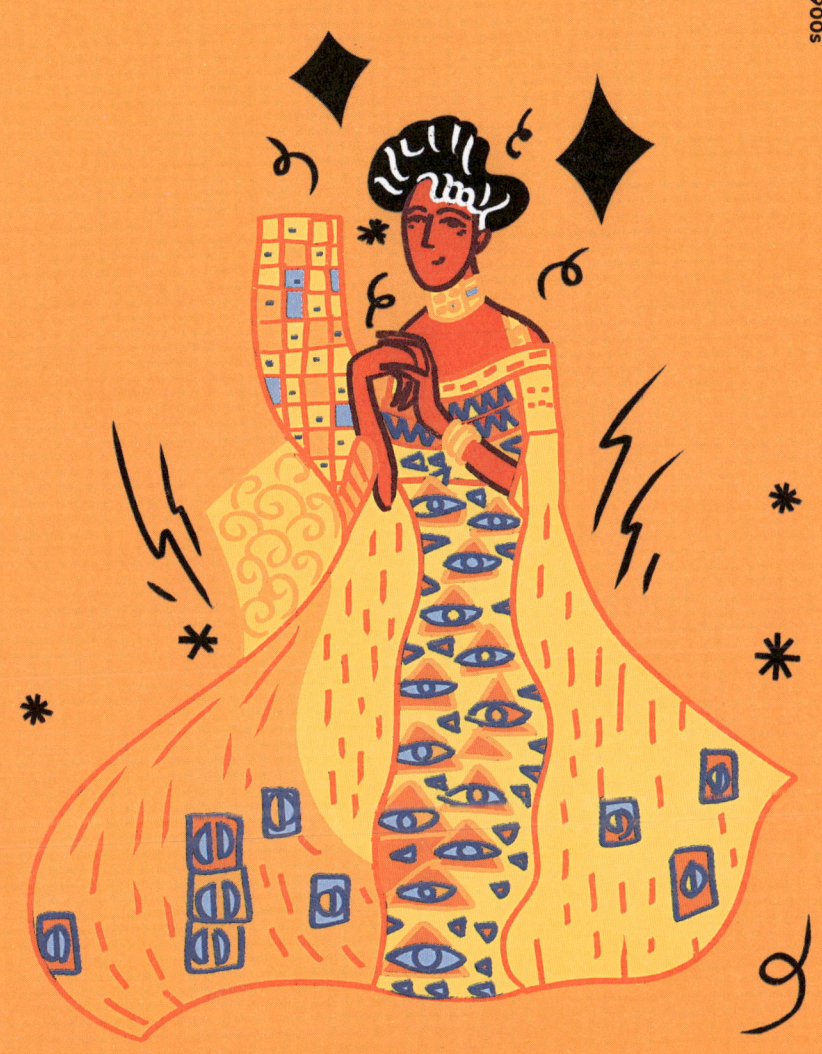

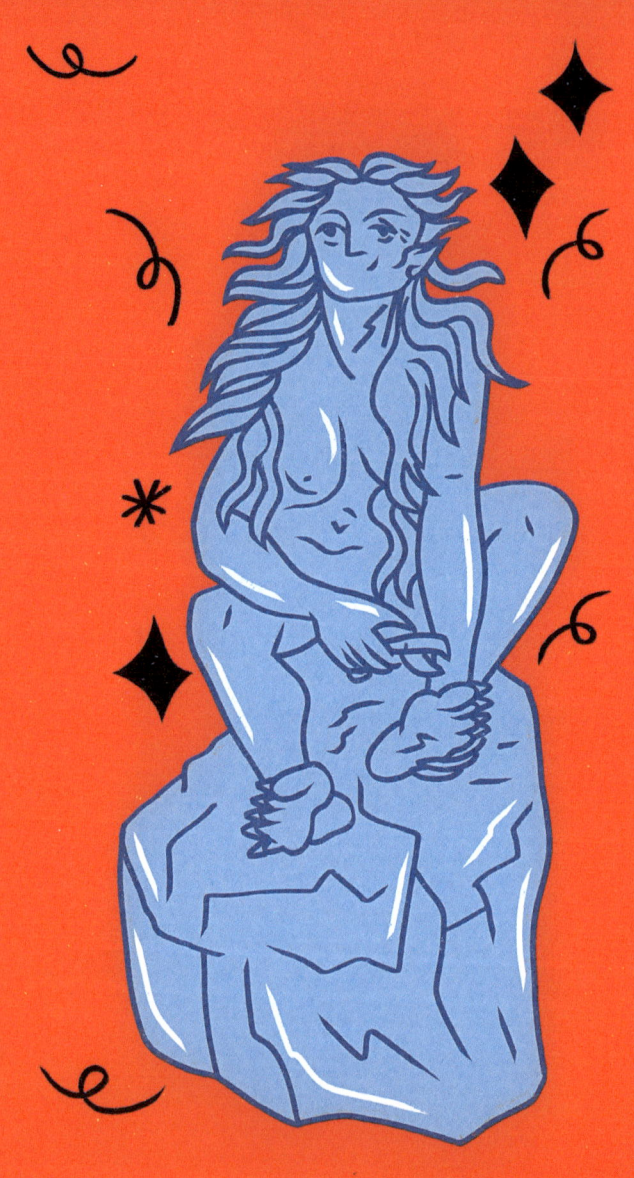

3 KEY ARTISTS

Alois Delug (1859–1930)

Austrian painter and founding member of the Secession; left after two years and became a professor at the Academy of Fine Arts in Vienna, where he may well have rejected the application of wannabe-art-student Adolf Hitler.

Teresa Feodorowna Ries (c.1866–1956)

Russian-born Austrian painter and sculptor and the first woman to exhibit with the Secession group; gained the attention of the Emperor with her sculpture of a nude witch cutting her toenails.

Josef Hoffmann (1870–1956)

Austrian-Moravian designer and architect, not as much into ornament as the others; trying to incorporate geometrical forms into *Art Nouveau* designs earned him the (patronising) nickname 'Little Square Hoffmann'.

3 KEY ARTWORKS

Maximilian Kurzweil, *Woman in a Yellow Dress* (1899)

A portrait of Kurzweil's wife, Marie-Josephine Marthe Guyot (Martha), this work was displayed

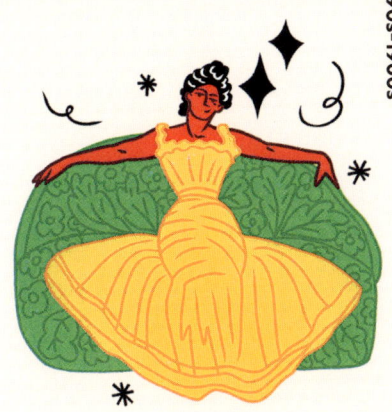

at the fourth Secessionist exhibition and received a lot of criticism for her relaxed pose (can women do **nothing**?!)

Maximilian Lenz, *A World* (1899)

Another founding member of the Secession, Lenz exhibited *A World* at the fourth Secessionist exhibition; it was so well received that it was shown with the Munich Secession as well (two-timer).

Gustav Klimt, *The Beethoven Frieze* (1901–1902)

Klimt's frieze was inspired by Beethoven's Ninth Symphony, including the six sister characters: sickness, madness, death, lust, unchastity and intemperance (every group of sisters has one of each, that's just the rules).

WHAT WAS THE ASHCAN SCHOOL?

It was a group of artists who aimed to show, through their art, the gritty realities of working-class life in the US.

Ashcan School

1900s–1920s

US

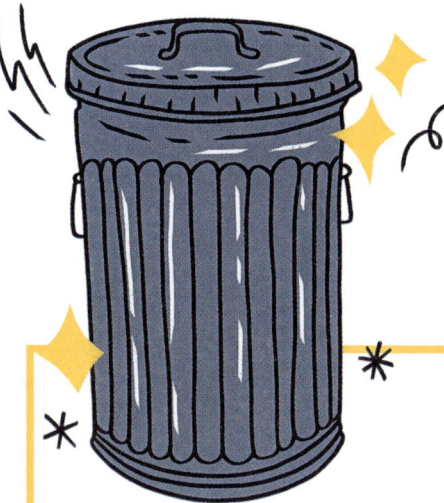

DID THEY KNOW EACH OTHER?

The Ashcans didn't necessarily think of themselves as a cohesive group working towards shared goals, but most of them did know each other, either having studied together at the Pennsylvania Academy of the Fine Arts or meeting while working as illustrators for newspapers in Philadelphia.

WAS IT A REAL SCHOOL?

It wasn't a literal school, and it wasn't even a school of thought – there were no set rules to the Ashcan style – 'school' was more tongue-in-cheek.

WHAT WERE THEY INSPIRED BY?

The Ashcan artists were determined to show what life was like for working Americans, portraying the people vital to city life, as well as shining a light on the issues of unemployment, poor factory conditions and society generally going to pot.

WHY WAS IT CALLED ASHCAN?

Ashcan artists took on the name as a cheeky reclamation of a 1916 cartoon in which it was complained that the group were producing too many ugly paintings of ashcans (rubbish bins), but they also called themselves the Apostles of Ugliness, which would have been a cooler name if they were a band.

WHO WERE THEY INSPIRED BY?

One inspiration was the Realist artist Thomas Eakins (who taught one of the Ashcan's teachers at the Pennsylvania Academy), an early supporter of letting women take part in life-drawing classes, but he was forced to resign after he removed a male life-model's loincloth in front of the ladies.

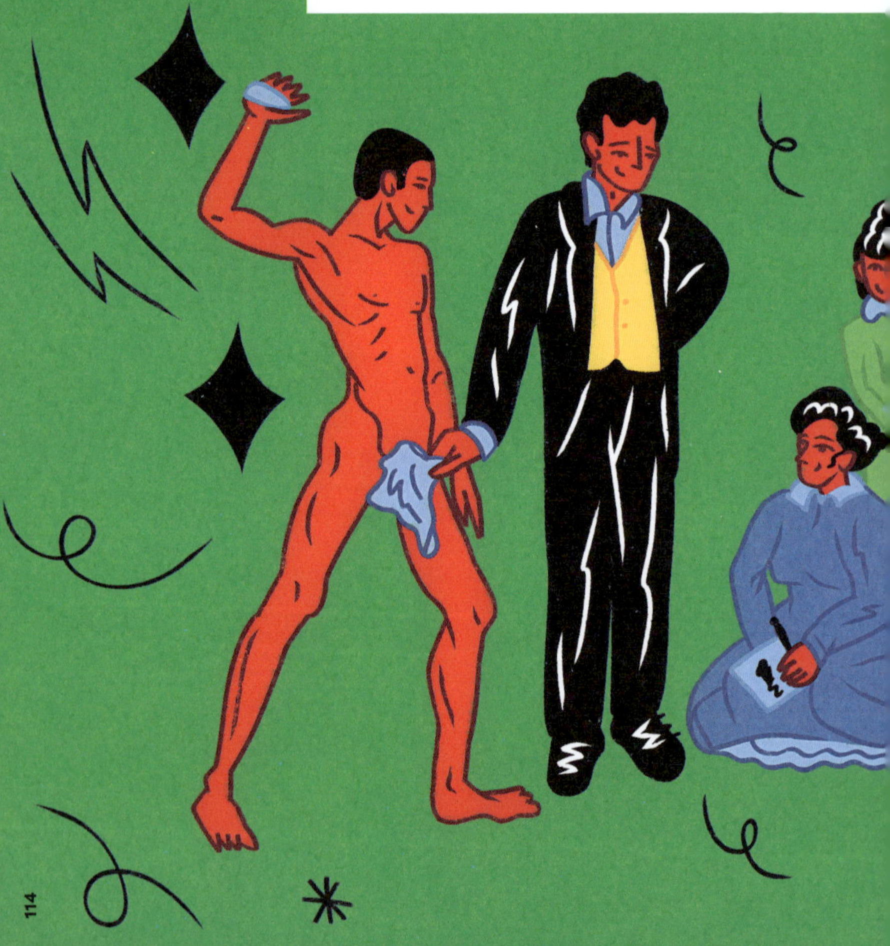

WHO WERE THE MUCKRAKERS?

Muckrakers – a name taken from a character in John Bunyan's 1678 *The Pilgrim's Progress* who ignored the offer of a 'celestial crown' to carry on raking muck – were photojournalists who exposed the terrible living conditions of people living in inner-city poverty, and whose work heavily influenced Ashcan art.

HOW MANY ARTISTS MAKE EIGHT?

Five key Ashcan artists are sometimes referred to as The Eight, named for the seminal 1908 exhibition they were included in (along with three other non-Ashcan artists – so the maths isn't actually off).

WHAT WAS THE ARMORY SHOW?

In 1913, two of The Eight, Arthur B. Davis and George Luks, helped to create the International Exhibition of Modern Art (later known as the Armory Show because it was held at the 69th Regiment Armory in New York), which showcased controversial, boundary-pushing modern art from Europe.

WHAT ENDED THE STYLE?

The end came partly because of the Armory Show (whoops!); Americans were at first shocked, but then enthralled by European Cubism (see page 138) and abstraction, which stole the Ashcan's thunder and the movement ultimately fizzled out.

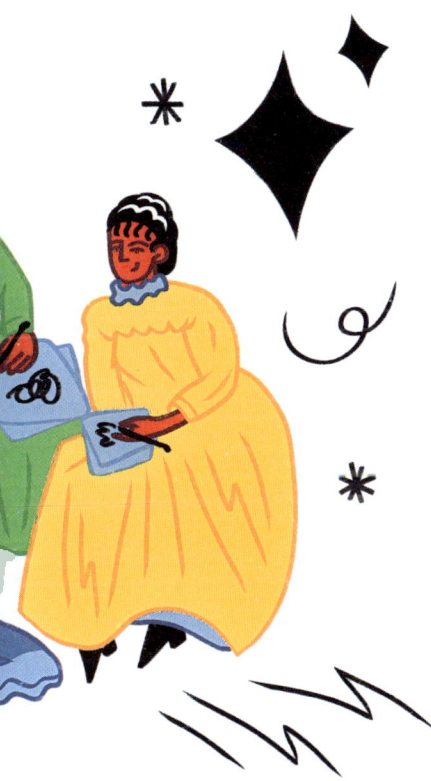

3 KEY ARTISTS

George Luks (1867-1933)
American painter and illustrator, heavily inspired by the Dutch Golden Age (see page 28), very masc and a bit fighty.

William James Glackens (1870-1938)
American painter and illustrator, Manet fan with a smooth domestic life compared to the other Eight.

Everett Shinn (1876-1953)
American painter and illustrator, annoyingly (for him) really good at capturing movement, given that the camera had just been invented; divorced three times in eleven years.

3 KEY ARTWORKS

Robert Henri, *Snow in New York* (1902)
Henri was encouraged to create this work for an upcoming solo show, but when little else at the exhibition sold, he turned his focus to portraiture instead (sad).

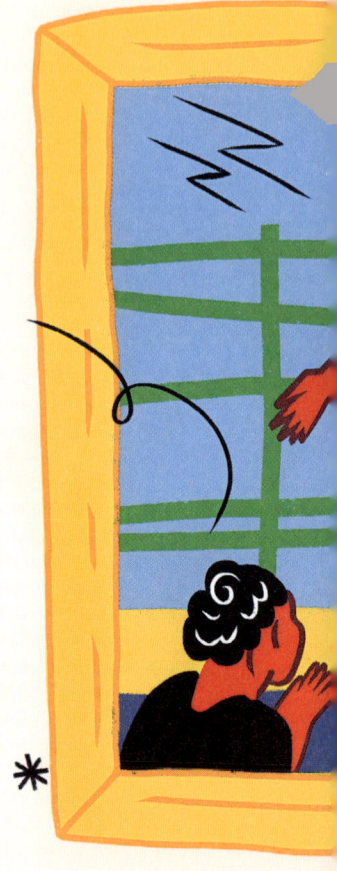

George Wesley Bellows, *Stag at Sharkey's* (1909)
Made at a time when public boxing was illegal in New York, so limited to private clubs, *Stag* shows two non- or temporary members ('stags') of the Athletic Club near Bellows' studio going at it.

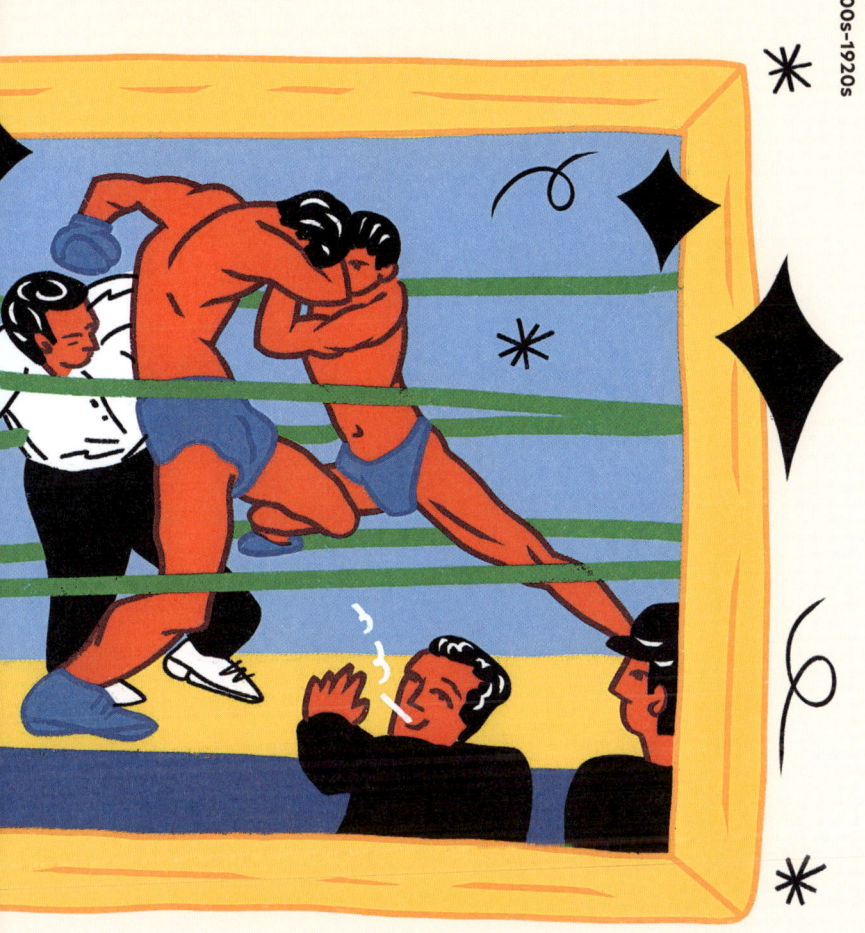

John French Sloan,
McSorley's Bar (1912)
McSorley's is the oldest surviving
Irish saloon in New York, and its

decor has been untouched since the
time of this painting (apart from a
pair of Houdini's handcuffs which
were later stolen from the bar).

WHAT WAS EXPRESSIONISM?

It's a broad category for art (as well as literature and theatre) that lays emphasis on the feeling that can be captured in a work rather than on the technical realism of its execution.

Expressionism

1900s–1930s

GERMANY

WHY 'EXPRESSIONISM'?

The term is believed to have been coined by Czech art historian Antonín Matějček, positioning the movement in opposition to 'Impressionism' (see page 70), as the artists prioritised **expressed** value over the accurate visual **impression** of their paintings.

HOW WAS IT ANTI-IMPRESSIONIST?

The Impressionists sought to depict the world around them (even though they were considered to be taking liberties with colour and brushstrokes), whereas the Expressionists were more interested in delving into our inner worlds, and did not shy away from life's darker topics while doing so.

WHAT INSPIRED THEM?

The Expressionists were inspired by the Symbolists (see page 94) for their emphasis on the feelings behind the image, and the Post Impressionists (see page 88) for their developments in the use of flat colour and images painted from their imaginations.

WAS EVERYONE A FAN?

Some German artists formed the *Neue Sachlichkeit* (New Objectivity) movement as a reaction against Expressionism, which they saw as smugly subjective, whereas they believed that the world needed art that dealt head-on with real political issues and the turmoil people were facing (and Germany was facing a **lot** of turmoil at the time).

WHEN MIGHT IT BE GOOD TO USE AN ARCHITECT RATHER THAN A PAINTER?

Thought of as the first Expressionist group, *Die Brücke* ('The Bridge') was a group of four architecture students in Dresden, who embraced their lack of fine-arts training and created a new visual style centred around feeling (and not accuracy, because all they had mostly drawn before were buildings).

WHAT ELSE WAS EXPRESSIONIST?

As a reaction against the increasingly-samey-but-heavily-invested-in mainstream German cinema, independent filmmakers adopted Expressionism, using warped backgrounds and keeping the camera in actors' faces for an uncomfortably long time to emphasise emotion.

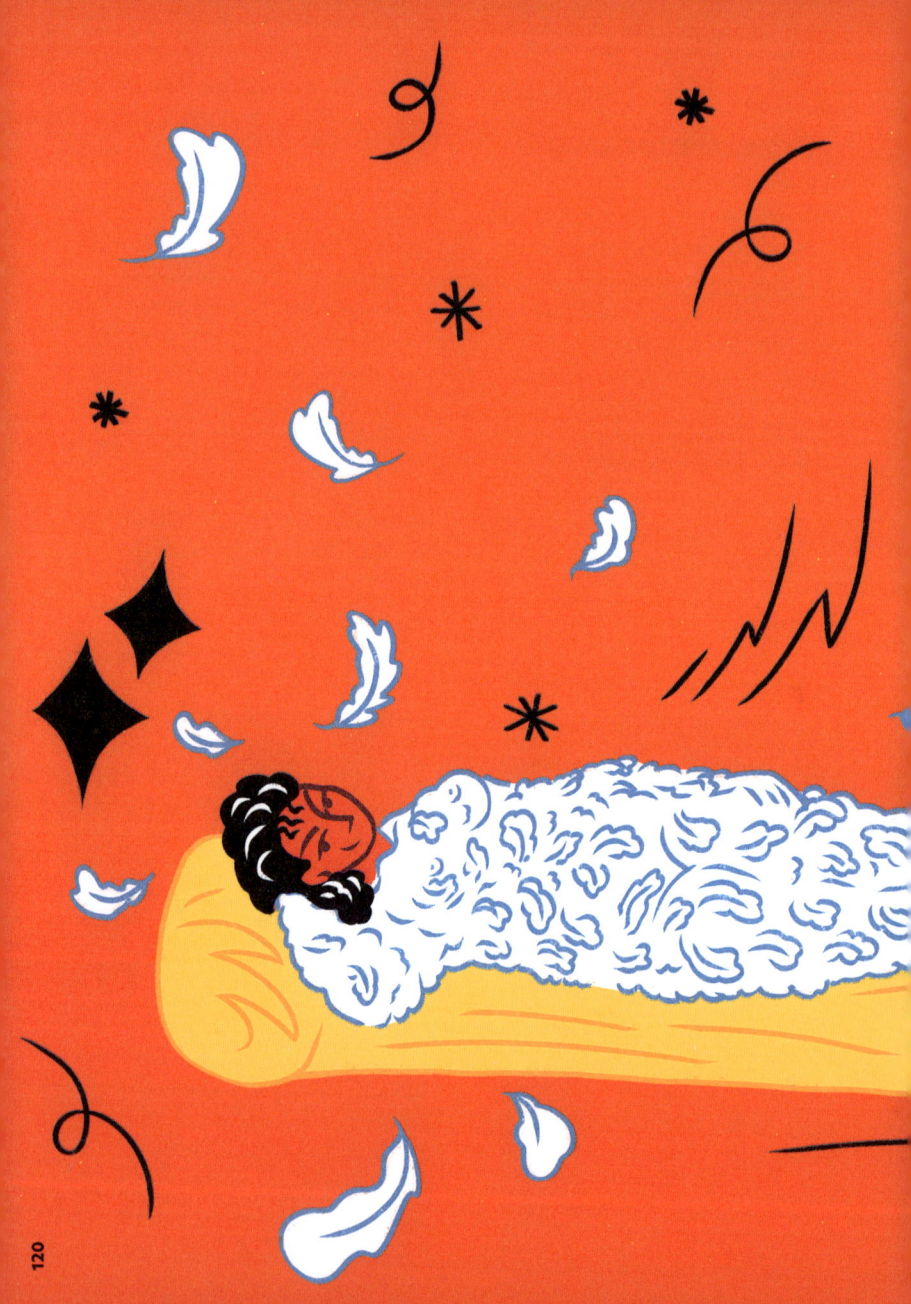

WHO WAS EXPRESSIONISM'S CREEPIEST MODEL?

When the Austrian Expressionist painter Oskar Kokoschka was dumped by fellow artist Alma Mahler, he commissioned a life-size, anatomically correct mannequin of her from the dollmaker Hermine Moos, which he then used as a model for over thirty paintings and took on dates to the opera (even though it was entirely covered in feathers).

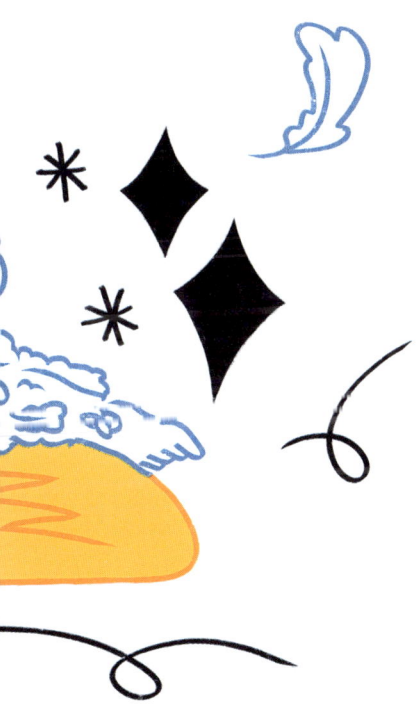

HOW DID THE SECOND WORLD WAR CHANGE THINGS?

As war approached, the sense of rebellion that favoured Expressionist artworks began to fade; the Nazis seized thousands of Expressionist works, displaying them in the (hugely popular) Degenerate Art Exhibition in July 1937 in Munich, alongside other modernist artworks.

HOW DID EMIL NOLDE AVOID HAVING MORE WORK SEIZED?

Nolde had the most artworks seized and was banned from painting (despite being a member of the Nazi party), so he swapped working with smelly oil paints to odourless watercolours, in order to fly under the radar if his house was raided.

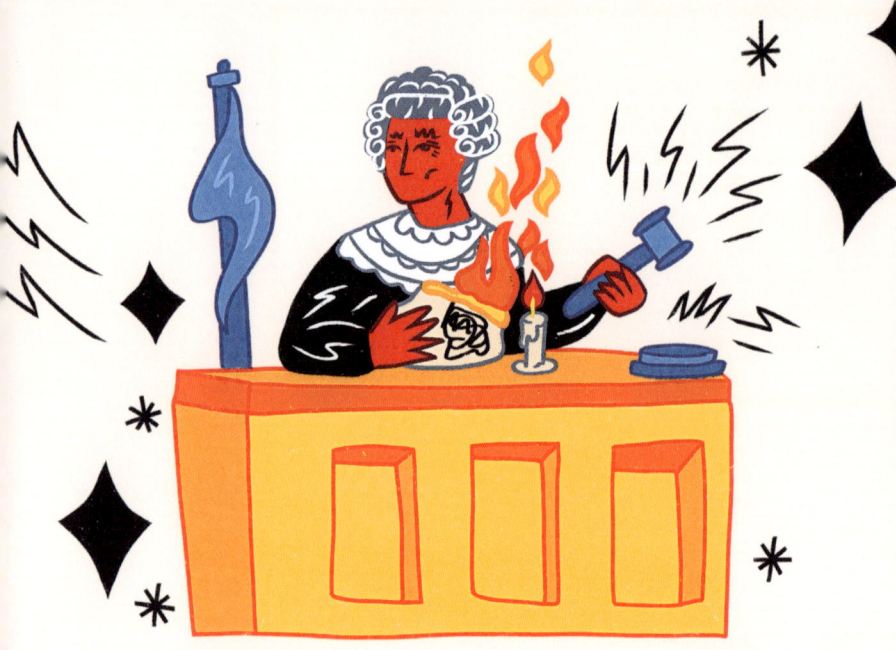

3 KEY ARTISTS

Marianne von Werefkin (1860-1938)
Russian painter nicknamed the Baroness for her aristocratic background; girlfriend of Expressionist Alexej von Jawlensky, but hid her paintings from him so as not to make him jealous.

Ernst Ludwig Kirchner (1880-1938)
German painter and printmaker, *Die Brücke* founder, had a studio in Dresden in an old butcher's shop where people would regularly strip and have it off with each other.

Egon Schiele (1890-1918)
Austrian painter, mentored by Gustav Klimt (see page 111), upset people with his erotic nude drawings (and his personal sexual behaviour), with one judge burning a drawing right there in the court.

3 KEY ARTWORKS

Käthe Kollwitz, *Woman with Dead Child* (1903)

A brutal portrait of grief, Kollwitz posed for this etching herself, with her then seven-year-old son, Peter.

Paula Modersohn-Becker, *Old Peasant Woman* (1907)

A prolific artist, best known for mother-and-child paintings and nude self-portraits (and the first woman to have a museum dedicated entirely to her work), Modersohn-Becker selected the model for this portrait from the local poorhouse.

Emil Nolde, *The Last Supper* (1909)

Nolde made this painting of Christ at his final dinner shortly after almost dying from drinking poisoned water, which turned his by-then-already-quite-religious paintings into super-dark-really-intense-religious paintings – his wife said she could only bear to look at them in quick glances.

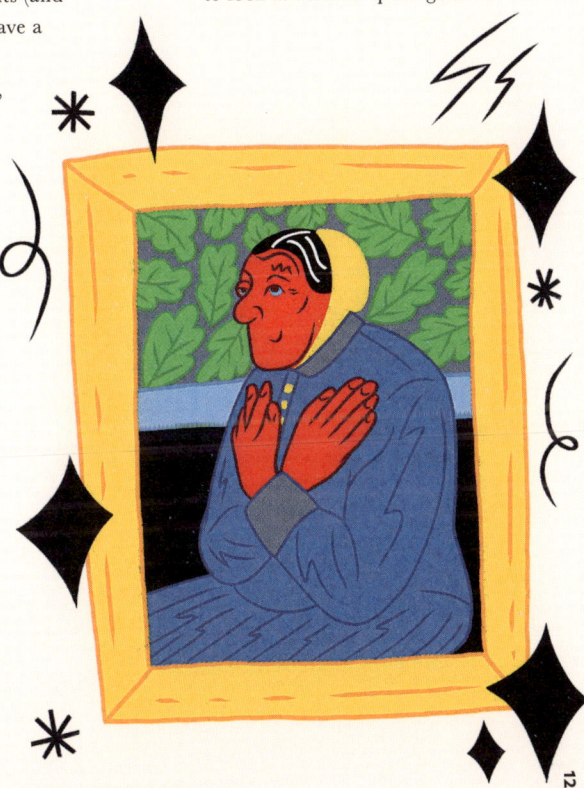

WHAT WAS FAUVISM?

The Fauves were a loose group of artists – working without strict rules or a manifesto – who used instinctive, bold brushwork and bright colours in order to communicate feeling in their work.

Fauvism
1900s

FRANCE

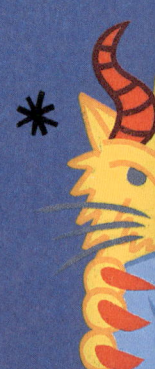

WHO GAVE IT ITS NAME?

When the Fauves first exhibited at the 1905 *Salon d'Automne*, art critic Louis Vauxcelles spotted a bronze by Donatello (see page 15) in the same room and wrote that Donatello was among '*les fauves*' (wild beasts), and the group reclaimed the insult.

WHAT INSPIRED THE FAUVES?

They were inspired by the attitudes to colour of the Symbolists (see page 94), Expressionists (see page 118) and Post-Impressionists (see page 88) – Maurice de Vlaminck once said that he loved Van Gogh more than his own father – and several Fauves also had a keen interest in African sculpture.

HOW WERE THE FAUVES DIFFERENT FROM THE SYMBOLISTS?

Both used intense colour as a way to provoke their viewers' senses, but for the Fauves, their colours did not have symbolic meanings, they were simply a way for the group to raise their compositions above reality.

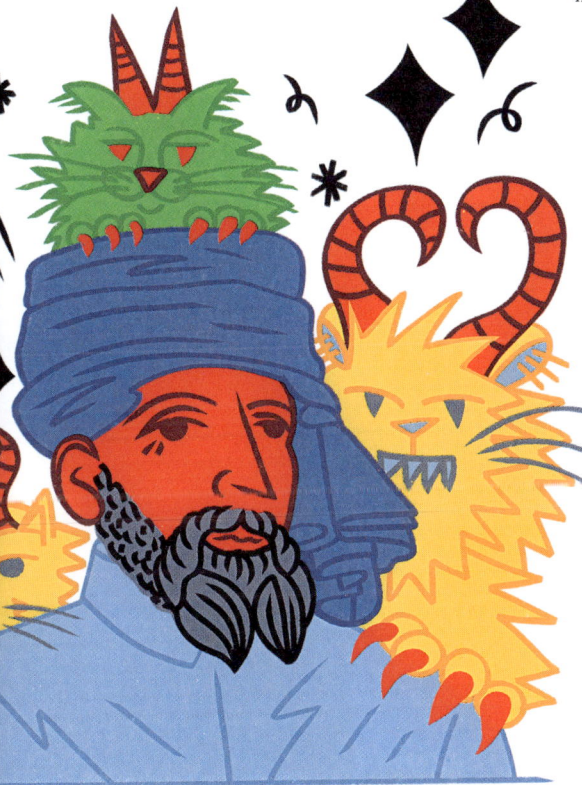

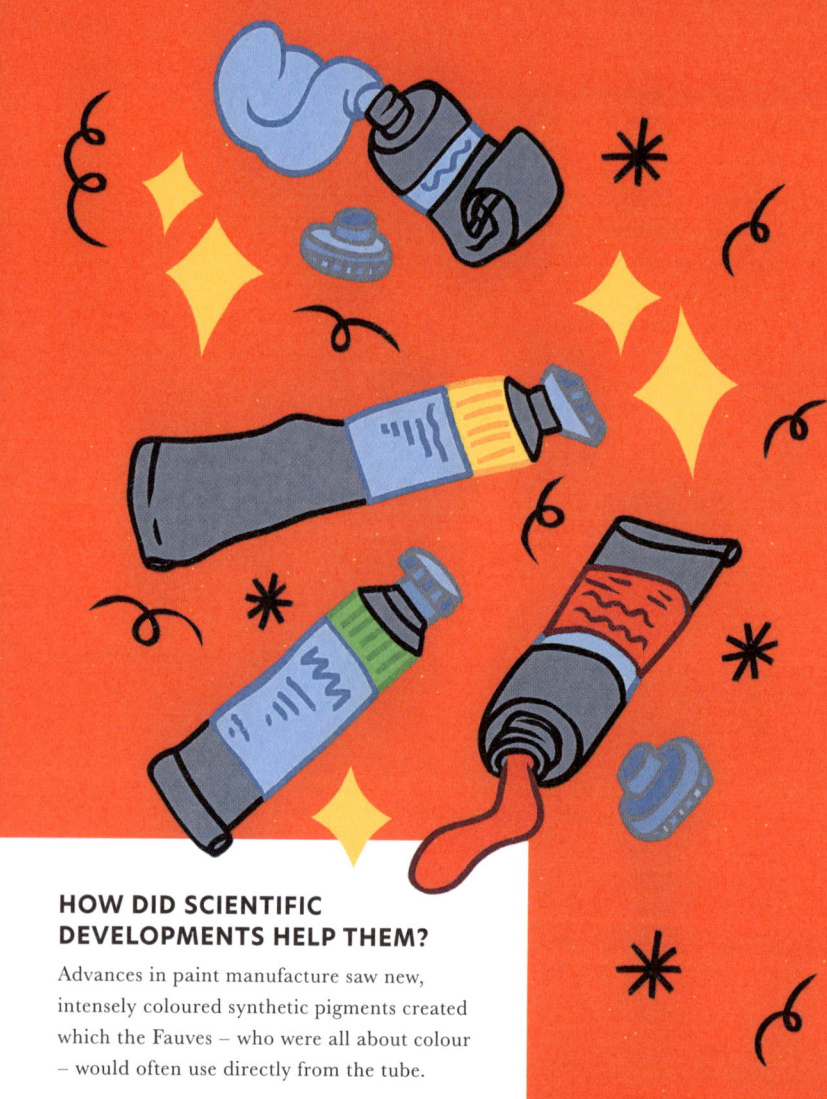

HOW DID SCIENTIFIC DEVELOPMENTS HELP THEM?

Advances in paint manufacture saw new, intensely coloured synthetic pigments created which the Fauves – who were all about colour – would often use directly from the tube.

HOW WERE THE FAUVES RECEIVED?

While audiences were shocked by the Fauves' wild approach, art collectors didn't hesitate to invest in the works, with one art dealer buying all the works in André Derain's studio, and the brother-and-sister duo Leo and Gertrude Stein becoming major collectors of Henri Matisse.

WOULD GUSTAVE MOREAU HAVE MADE A GOOD DRIVING INSTRUCTOR?

Symbolist painter Gustave Moreau taught several future-Fauves at the *École des Beaux-Arts* in Paris, and his impact on the young artists was summarised by Matisse, who said that rather than sending them down the right roads, Moreau guided them right off them.

WHAT WAS DIFFERENT ABOUT THE *SALON D'AUTOMNE*?

The *Salon d'Automne* – yes, another salon but this time juried by members of the public – was created in 1903 for artists to exhibit work they had made *en plein air* during the summer, because unlike other salons, which were held in the spring, this one was – you guessed it – held in the autumn.

WAS IT EASIER 100 YEARS AGO TO MAKE MONEY AS AN ARTIST?

Not always – like most artists today, de Vlaminck subsidised his developing art career by working several jobs, including professional cyclist, violinist, occasional wrestler and boxer, mechanic, billiards player and writer of porny novels (illustrated by his mate Derain).

WHAT FINISHED THE FAUVES?

Unlike some movements, Fauvism didn't end with a big bust-up – some artists, like Matisse, continued to make Fauvist art for years – but as a very loose group, the artists simply began to go their own ways, and the artistic community's attention soon turned to Cubism.

3 KEY ARTISTS

Henri Matisse (1869-1954)
French artist who quit his law career after appendicitis left him bed-bound with art supplies from his mum to help him kill time; considered so shocking that in 1913, students in Chicago sentenced a student dressed as Matisse to death in a mock trial.

Émilie Charmy (1878-1974)
French painter who displayed in some of the key avant-garde exhibitions of the day including the 1905 *Salon d'Automne* and the 1913 Armory Show; shocked viewers with her sexy nude ladies.

André Derain (1880-1954)
French painter and Fauvist co-founder, his series of thirty paintings of London were a high point for Fauvism, and a nice treat for London to have a brief moment of not looking completely miserable.

3 KEY ARTWORKS

Maurice de Vlaminck, *The Seine at Chatou* (1906)
Before Fauvism was even a glint in Matisse's eye, de Vlaminck and Derain shared a studio in Chatou, near Paris, where they created brightly-coloured works and called themselves the School of Chatou.

Raoul Dufy, *Jeanne with Flowers* (1907)
Dufy turned to Fauvism after seeing a painting by Matisse in 1905 (and later, he would be buried near his hero, which is nice), but we don't know who Jeanne is – likely she's one of his hundreds of (nine) siblings.

Kees van Dongen, *Modjesko, Soprano Singer* (1908)
This bright yellow singer is the African-American drag queen Modjesko (Edward Claude Thompson), also known as the Black Patti, whom van Dongen had first seen perform at Rotterdam's *Circus Variété*.

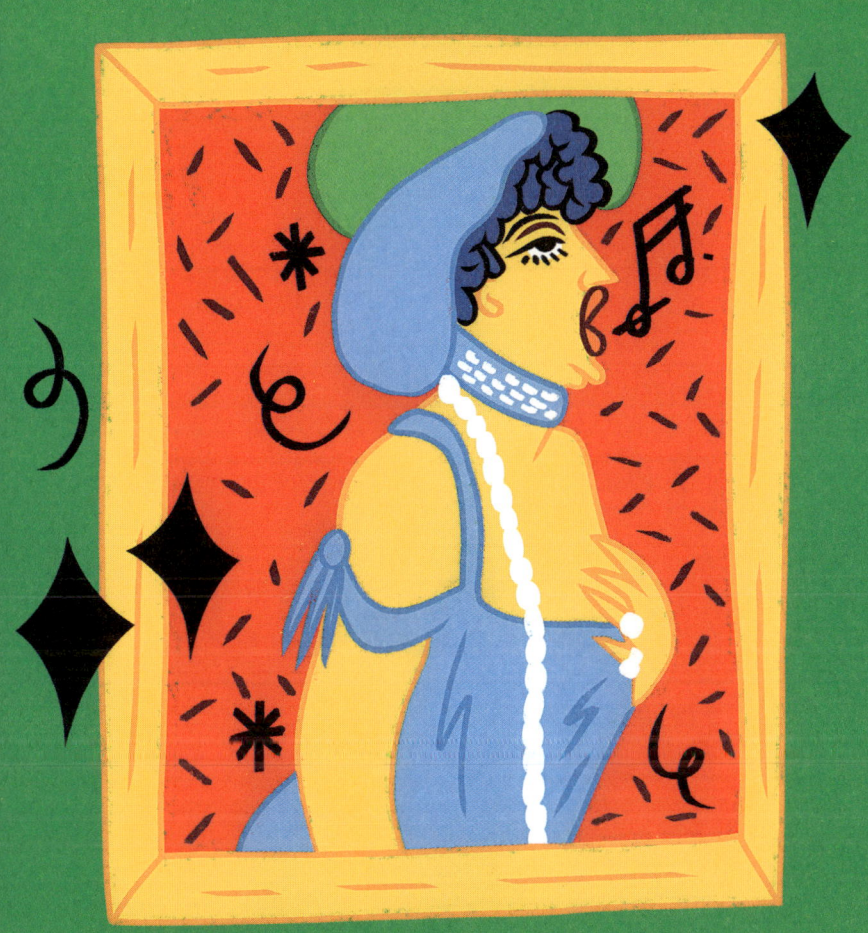

WHAT WAS THE BLOOMSBURY GROUP?

It was a circle of artists, writers and thinkers – many of whom had first met at the University of Cambridge – who turned their backs on strict Victorian sensibilities and became some of the first artists in Britain to create abstract work.

The Bloomsbury Group
1900s–1940s

BRITAIN

WHY 'BLOOMSBURY'?

The name (after the London area where the group met, in the homes of Vanessa Bell and her sister Virginia Woolf) was first given to the group by artist and art critic Roger Fry in his Second Post-Impressionist Exhibition in 1912.

WHAT WERE THEY UP TO ON THURSDAYS AND FRIDAYS?

In the early days of the group, in order to have the privacy to express themselves freely, the Stephen siblings – Vanessa (Bell), Virginia (Woolf), Adrian and Thoby – held a 'Thursday Evenings' literary discussion club and a 'Friday Club' for artists at their home in Gordon Square.

OTHER THAN THE ARTISTS, WHO ELSE WAS THERE?

As well as artists, the group was made up of writers including Lytton Strachey, art critics inlcuding Clive Bell, publishers Leonard Woolf and David Garnett, and the high-profile economist John Maynard Keynes.

WHAT WERE THE OMEGA WORKSHOPS?

It was a design company set up in 1913 by Roger Fry, producing avant-garde geometric designs for fabrics and household items designed by artists including Vanessa Bell and Duncan Grant (and Wyndham Lewis, who left and created the Rebel Art Centre – see page 162).

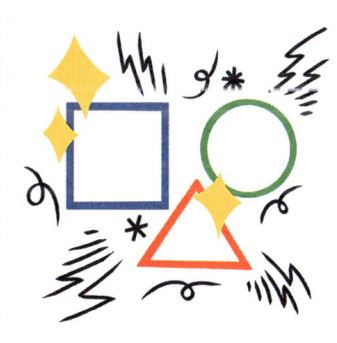

WHAT WERE THE INTERPERSONAL DYNAMICS LIKE?

The writer Dorothy Parker described the Bloomsbury Group as having lived in squares, painted in circles and loved in triangles – and to be fair, there was more than a little partner-sharing and swapping.

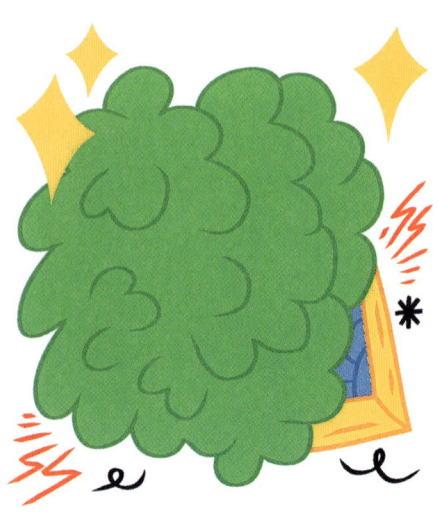

HOW DID PAUL CÉZANNE END UP IN A CHARLESTON BUSH?

During the First World War, Maynard Keynes attended the Paris auction of Edgar Degas' (see page 75) art collection, hoping to pick up some modern classics on the cheap; when he arrived back at Charleston with Cézanne's *Still Life with Apples* he had to leave the painting temporarily in a bush while he carried the rest of his luggage up the muddy path.

WHAT IS CHARLESTON?

Charleston Farmhouse, in East Sussex, became an artistic hub for the group when Duncan Grant, his lover David Garnett, his soon-to-be other lover Vanessa Bell and her husband Clive all moved there after Grant and Garnett registered as conscientious objectors during the First World War.

WHAT WAS THE MOST SHOCKING LIAISON?

In 1942 Angelica Bell – daughter of Bell and Grant – married her father's ex-lover Garnett, who had written a letter to the writer Lytton Strachey after Angelica's birth to say he would marry her one day…

WHAT 2000S WALL DECAL WOULD THE BLOOMSBURY GROUP CHOOSE?

A major inspiration for the group was the philosopher G. E. Moore, who saw the purpose of life as the pursuit of love, beauty and knowledge – so their decal of choice would probably be 'Live, Laugh, Love'.

3 KEY ARTISTS

Roger Fry (1866-1934)

English painter, critic, historian and namer of Post-Impressionism; added a layer of bricks to the Charleston fireplaces to retain more heat during freezing winters (maybe that's why everyone was sleeping with each other?)

Lady Ottoline Morrell (1873-1938)

English socialite who was both patron and friend of Bloomsbury; tall (and made herself even taller with hats and heels), and took hundreds of photos of the arty types of the day.

Dora Carrington (1893-1932)

English artist and friend of the group who visited Charleston in 1916 and wrote a letter expressing shock that none of them knew how to cook anything; fell in love with Lytton Strachey when she went to cut off his beard in the night.

3 KEY ARTWORKS

Vanessa Bell, *David Garnett* (1915)

One of the few portraits at the time of an undressed man by a female artist, this portrait was created while both Bell and Garnett were intimately involved with Duncan Grant.

Duncan Grant, *Bathers by the Pond* (1920-1921)

Showing male nudes luxuriating by the Charleston pond – a central point for social life at Charleston – this scene likely includes Grant's lovers David Garnett and John Maynard Keynes.

Stephen 'Tommy' Tomlin, *Lytton Strachey* (c.1928)

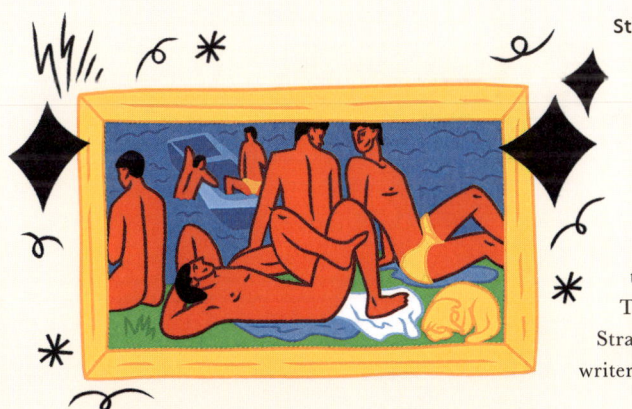

This bust – which the subject called 'repulsive' – was made around the time that Tomlin married Strachey's niece, the writer Julia Strachey.

**WHAT WAS
ART DECO?**

A popular style of art and
architecture, Art Deco
was known for its angular
designs and its association
with the exuberant
post-war period known
as the Roaring Twenties.

Art Deco
1910s–1930s

INTERNATIONAL

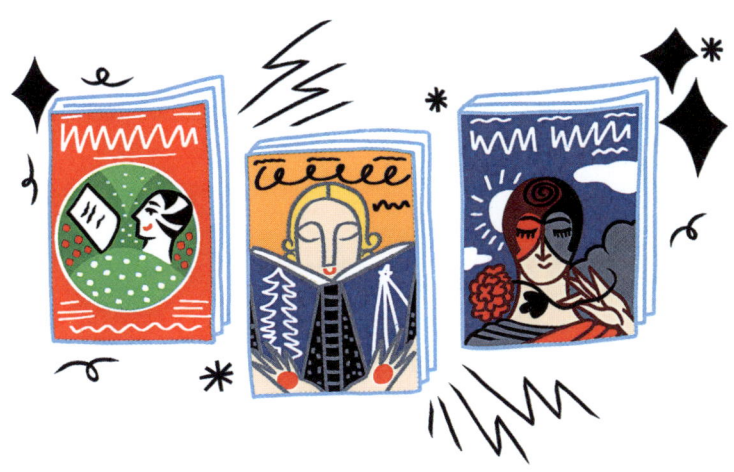

WHAT WAS IT INSPIRED BY?

Art Deco drew inspiration from all over the place: the avant-garde and the ancient past, industrial developments and folk stories, the aesthetics of both West and East (particularly the art of ancient Mesopotamia and Egypt), the new jazz culture coming out of North America as well as the traditional art of Central and South America.

WHY 'DECO'?

It wasn't until the 1960s that the term 'Art Deco' was popularised (it would previously have been thought of as *Style Moderne* or Jazz Style) – the name comes from the French *Exposition internationale des arts décoratifs et industriels modernes* held in 1925, where Art Deco designs were showcased for the first time on a major scale.

HOW DID IT GET SO POPULAR?

Art Deco designs were often seen on magazine covers – the Russian-French designer Erté designed over 200 covers for *Harper's Bazaar* – and this brought Art Deco into far more people's lives than artworks locked behind gallery doors could have.

WHAT MATERIALS WERE BEING USED?

Art Deco artists wanted to get across an air of luxury, so expensive and rare imported materials were often used, including mother-of-pearl, ivory, jewellery made from ancient beads taken directly from excavation sites and shagreen – a leather made from sharkskin.

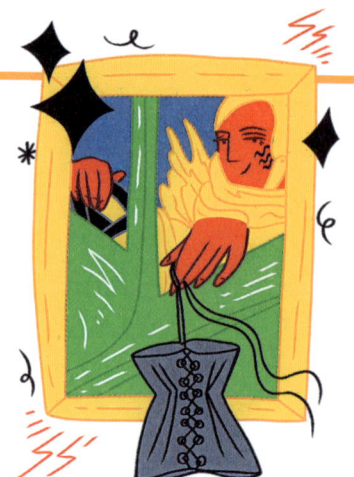

WHAT WAS THE IMPACT OF FASHION ON ART DECO DESIGNS?

Up until the 1920s, corsets had been central to women's fashion but when these went out of style, the newly corsetless woman (whose figure was now – like Art Deco designs – more angular than hour-glass) became a key symbol in Art Deco, representing a new era of (some) freedoms for (some) women.

IT'S ALL QUITE EGYPTIAN, ISN'T IT?

Archaeological digs around the world, new opportunities to travel further abroad, international mass media, and photographs all brought the influence of ancient societies to the West; and perhaps nothing sparked 'Egyptomania' so much as the discovery of the pharaoh Tutankhamun's tomb in 1922.

WHAT IS STREAMLINE MODERNE?

Also called *Style Paquebot* (ocean liner style) in France, Streamline Moderne was an international 1930s Art Deco style inspired by the sleek designs and curved lines of machines, locomotives, cars and ships (specifically the ocean liner SS *Normandie*, whose interior was designed by the Art Deco architect Pierre Patout).

OOH, THAT MUST HAVE BEEN A NICE CRUISE?

Not really – some passengers complained that the intensely patterned Art Deco interiors were making their seasickness worse.

HOW MANY CHILDREN DID TAMARA DE LEMPICKA HAVE?

The Polish painter – nicknamed 'the baroness with a brush' – lived a lavish lifestyle and was intent on gaining respect as an artistic pioneer, claiming her artworks were her only children, which must have been brutal for her actual daughter and biographer, Kizette de Lempicka-Foxhall.

3 KEY ARTISTS

Gerda Wegener (c.1886–1940)
Danish painter and illustrator, creator of (sometimes erotic) depictions of beautiful women; her main muse was her spouse Lili Elbe, one of the first transgender women to undergo gender reassignment surgery.

Winold Reiss (1886–1953)
German-born American artist best-known for his portraits of Native Americans of the Blackfeet Indian Reservation and major figures of the Harlem Renaissance (see page 184).

Paul Colin (1892–1985)
French artist who created over 1,400 posters; famous for his designs starring the cabaret celebrity and Roaring Twenties icon Josephine Baker.

3 KEY ARTWORKS

François Pompon, *Polar Bear* (c.1923)
Pompon's polar bear proved a huge hit at the 1925 Paris Exposition, securing its place as one of the most popular and widely reproduced Art Deco sculptures of all time, ranging in size from palm- to life-size.

Louis Lozowick, *New York* (1925)
Ukrainian-born Lozowick is best-known for his lithographs of US cities, inspired by his experiences with the Russian Constructivists (see page 174).

Tamara de Lempicka, *Autoportrait (Tamara in a Green Bugatti)* (1928)
Created for the cover of *Die Dame* magazine, Lempicka shows herself as the embodiment of the cool Art Deco woman, even though she never owned a Bugatti and was actually getting around in a little yellow Renault.

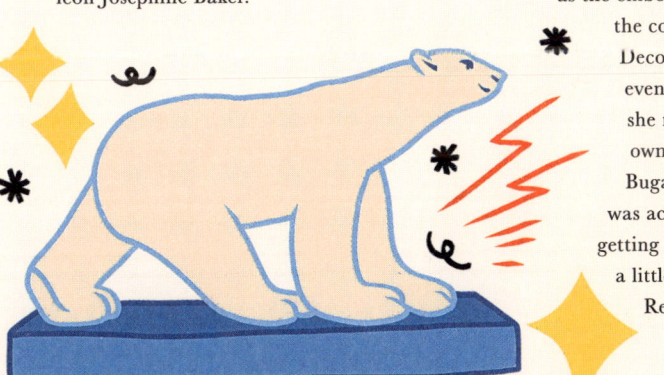

WHAT WAS CUBISM?

Developed by artists Pablo Picasso and Georges Braque, Cubism revolutionised how artists depicted the world, fragmenting their compositions and showing scenes from multiple perspectives at one time.

Cubism
1900s–1910s

FRANCE

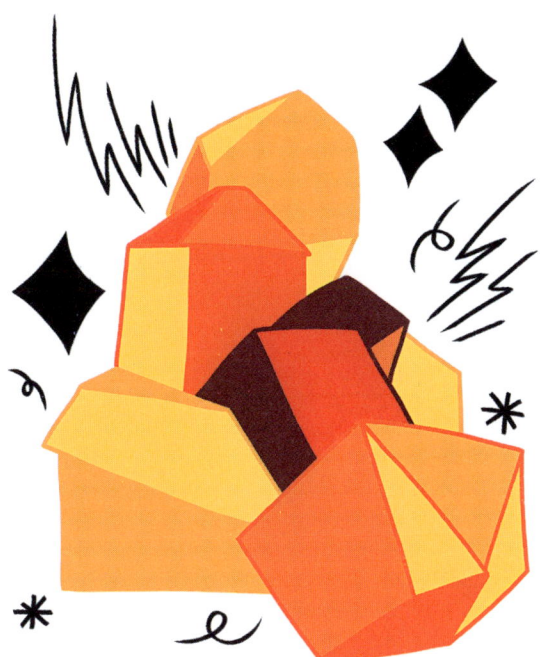

WHERE DID IT GET ITS NAME?

After seeing Braque's landscape *Houses at l'Estaque* in Paris in 1908, art critic Louis Vauxcelles (whose earlier insult gave the Fauves their name – see page 125) dismissed the works as '*bizarre cubiques*' (strange cubes) and the term 'Cubism' took hold.

WHY DOES EVERYTHING LOOK KIND OF ODD?

Cubism sought to portray the world not as it is seen from one perspective, but how it truly is: existing in many perspectives all at once (an object still has sides and a back, even if we're only looking at it from the front).

WHAT DID CUBISM HAVE IN COMMON WITH AMERICAN AVIATION?

So inspired were they by the Wright Brothers' development of the aeroplane, that Picasso and Braque affectionately nicknamed each other Orville and Wilbur, seeing themselves as similarly pioneering.

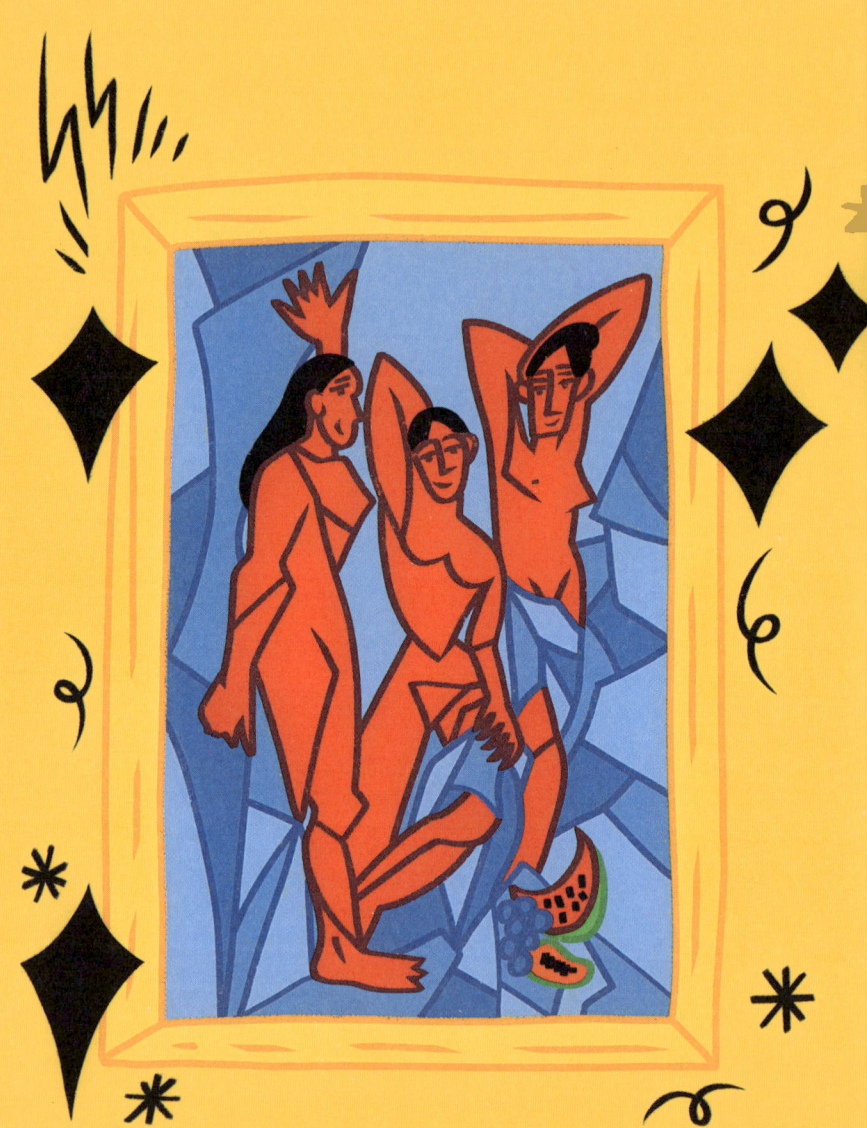

IF BRAQUE AND PICASSO INVENTED IT TOGETHER, WHY HAS PICASSO ENDED UP BETTER KNOWN?

A bit like George Michael and Wham!, Picasso ended up as the frontman of Cubism because he was more sociable, more prolific and more outspoken than Braque, who took his time with his work and was a much more private person.

HOW TIGHT WERE PICASSO AND BRAQUE?

Incredibly; during the creation of Cubism, the pair saw each other almost every evening in order to see what the other had made, with

(notorious womaniser) Picasso describing Braque as the woman that loved him the best, while Braque saw them as roped-together mountain climbers.

IS IT TRUE THAT BRAQUE AND PICASSO INVENTED COLLAGE?

People had definitely cut things up and stuck them down before, but Braque and Picasso gave this a name (taking 'collage' from the French verb *coller* – to glue or stick together) and introduced it as a fine-art medium.

WHAT IS THE DIFFERENCE BETWEEN ANALYTIC AND SYNTHETIC CUBISM?

Analytic Cubism came first and was really only interested in breaking down form, and Synthetic Cubism saw the introduction of more colour, symbolism, and collage.

WHAT BROKE UP THE CUBISTS?

The once-inseparable pair parted ways when Braque joined the French army in 1914; they never spoke again about their time creating Cubism together, with Braque explaining that only he and Picasso could ever understand what truly went on.

WHAT WAS THE FIRST CUBIST WORK?

Some consider it to be Picasso's *Les Demoiselles d'Avignon* (1907) – a scene in a Barcelona brothel heavily inspired by his collection of African masks and the works he saw in the Ethnographic Museum in Paris; however, others award the honour to Braque's *Houses at L'Estaque* (1908).

3 KEY ARTISTS

Pablo Picasso (1881–1973)

Spanish artist whose views on (and treatment of) women weren't brilliant; briefly an official suspect in the 1911 theft of the *Mona Lisa* from the Louvre.

Georges Braque (1882–1963)

French artist and one-time Fauve, he was injured during the First World War and temporarily lost his sight, requiring a trepanation (a hole drilled in the skull).

Marevna (1892–1984)

Russian painter thought of as the first female Cubist; developed her own style of 'Dimensionalism' by combining Cubism with Pointillism.

3 KEY ARTWORKS

Jean Metzinger, *Two Nudes* (1910–1911)

This work was displayed at the 1911 *Salon des Indépendants* where the Cubists caused a stir when their 'in' at the Salon – French Cubist Henri Le Fauconnier – used his position on the board to ensure that all the Cubist works were hung together, rather than in the usual alphabetical order.

Juan Gris, *Portrait of Pablo Picasso* (1912)

Gris was in awe of Picasso and first met his idol in 1906 after selling all of his belongings in Spain in order to move to Paris, but sadly the feelings weren't mutual and Picasso apparently wished that Gris would back off a bit.

Fernand Léger, *Soldier with a Pipe* (1916)

Also part of the key Cubist exhibition at the 1911 Salon, Léger's work was characterised by the use of cylindrical forms, which led to Louis Vauxcelles describing Léger's style as more 'Tubism' than Cubism.

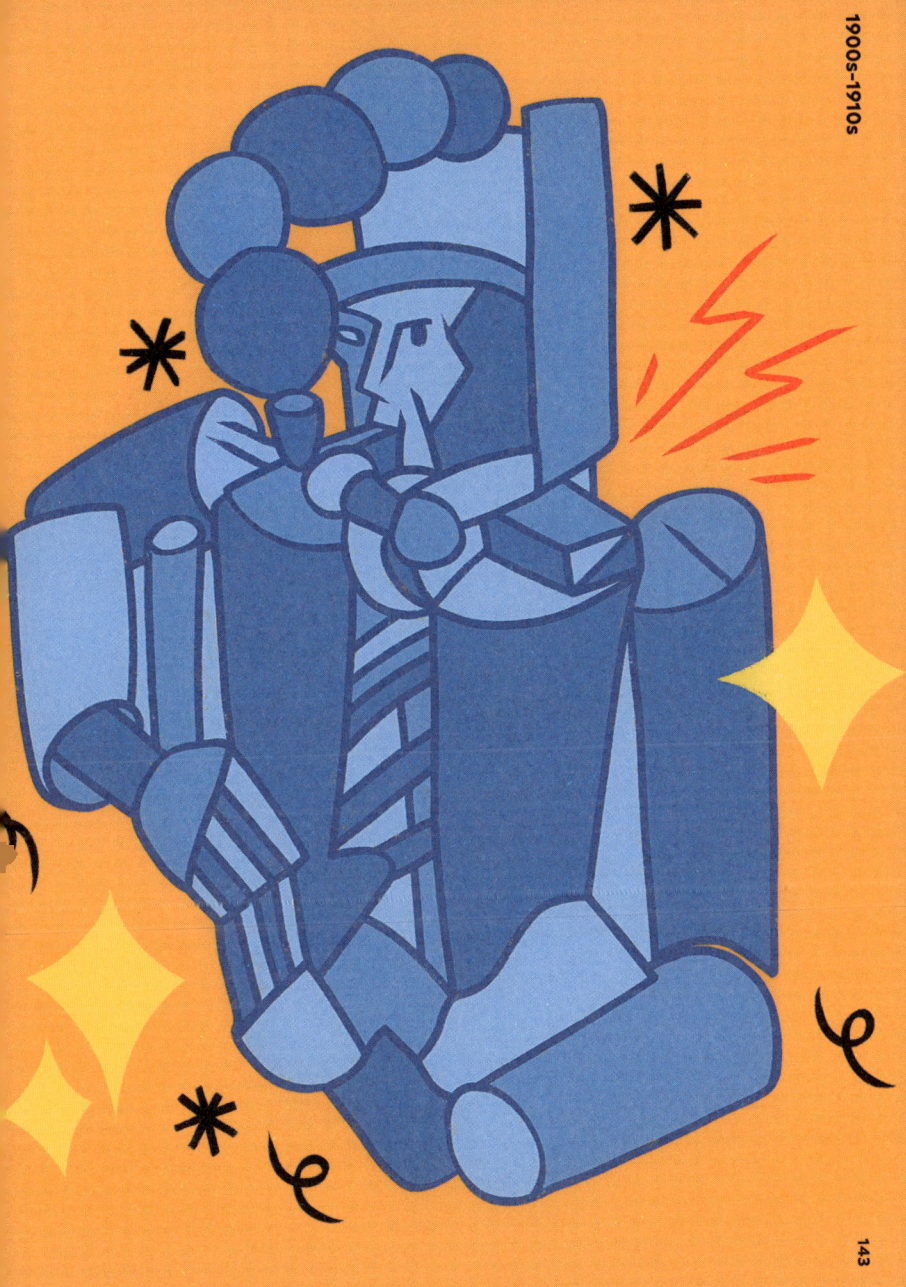

WHAT WAS FUTURISM?

Guided by the philosophy of the writer and theorist Filippo Tommaso Marinetti, Futurists wanted to create an entirely new art world focused purely on contemporary life in a new machine age.

Futurism
1900s–1910s

ITALY

WHAT INSPIRED THEM?

The Futurists thought society was too preoccupied with the past (in Italy, the main cultural things still being celebrated were ancient ruins and artefacts from the long-gone Roman Empire); instead they wanted to create a new culture focused on technological innovation, modernity and speed.

WHAT KIND OF THINGS DID THEY PAINT?

Futurists worshipped technological progress so painted scenes from life in fast-growing metropolitan cities, urban landscapes and machines in motion including bicycles, cars (new tech at that point) and aeroplanes (even newer, and the inspiration for a Futurist spin-off movement called *Aeropittura*).

HOW DID A CAR ACCIDENT KICK IT OFF?

In 1908, Marinetti drove his car into a Milan ditch when he swerved to avoid hitting two cyclists, an event that left him inspired to develop his theories about modern technology, rather than being completely traumatised, which is good, probably?

AH, A MOVEMENT ABOUT BICYCLES AND PLANES; THAT MUST BE NICE?

Disprezzo della donna (scorn for women) was literally in the Futurists' manifesto, with the movement being one of history's most openly misogynistic, so maybe 'nice' isn't the word.

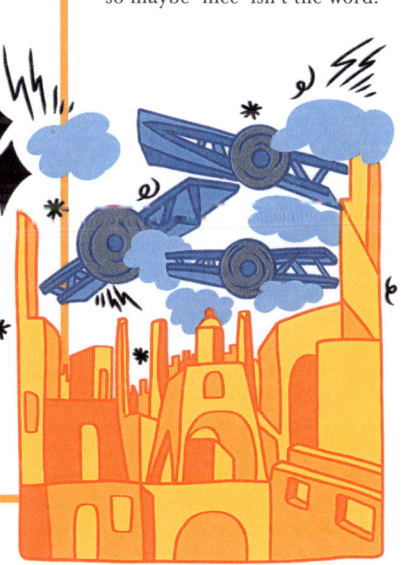

AH WELL, THEY WERE PROBABLY ALL RIGHT OTHERWISE?

The Futurists were pro-war and into violence, and when they received a poor review for their first exhibition in Milan in 1911, a group of artists promptly responded by assaulting the critic who wrote it when they found him sitting outside a café.

WHAT SECURED FUTURISM'S BAD BRAND IMAGE?

Given that war was one of the Futurists' favourite things, it's not surprising that, during the First World War, Marinetti merged his Futurist political party with the Fascist party of Benito Mussolini, forever tying Futurism's legacy to fascism.

SO HOW BIG WAS THEIR BEEF WITH THE PAST?

In a 1909 manifesto (the Futurists produced over 50 manifestos on all sorts of things from smells to lust), Marinetti called for all libraries and museums to be destroyed, allowing the country to break free from its obsession with the past and lose what he called the 'foetid gangrene of archaeologists' (ew).

WHY DID THE FUTURISTS HATE PASTA?

In the 1930 Manifesto of Futurist Cooking (I told you there were a lot

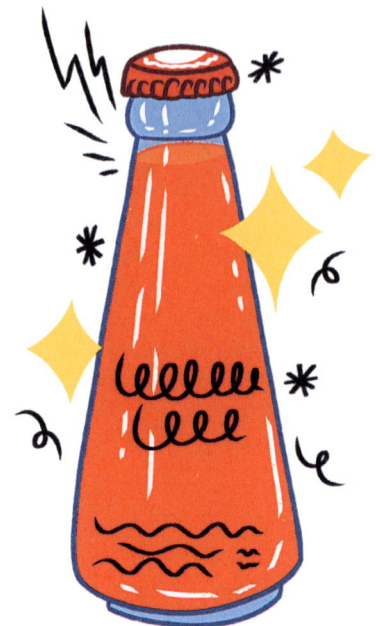

of manifestos), Marinetti called for the abolition of pasta, which he called a ludicrous religion that only slowed people down.

HOW DID RUSSIAN FUTURISM DIFFER FROM THE ITALIAN VARIETY?

Russian Futurism was the other major Futurist movement (there were Futurist goings-on in England and Belgium, too) and in comparison to the Italian version, artists generally used more angular lines, less blurriness and were more willing to incorporate the artistic past into their vision of the future.

3 KEY ARTISTS

Fortunato Depero (1892–1960)
Italian artist, writer and creator of toys designed to keep children imaginative (and actively dangerous toys to encourage children to be pro-war); also designed the Campari Soda bottle.

Umberto Boccioni (1882–1916)
Italian painter and sculptor, massive patriot who died in active service (as he would have wanted), from injuries sustained when his horse got spooked by a car (as he probably would not have wanted).

Benedetta Cappa (1897–1977)
Italian artist, married to Marinetti despite the whole Futurists-hate-women thing; co-creator of Tactilism, a Futurist spin-off incorporating different textures, which she and Marinetti came up with while skinny dipping.

3 KEY ARTWORKS

Giacomo Balla, *Dynamism of a Dog on a Leash* (1912)
Dynamism is one of Balla's best-known works, significantly more popular than the 'anti-neutralist' outfit he designed during the First World War (a wrap-around suit with matching beret and shoes designed for kicking neutralists – people against Italy joining the war).

Gino Severini, *Dynamic Hieroglyphic of the Bal Tabarin* (1912)
Showing the inside of a Paris nightclub (not very Italian, but Severini did recognise France's importance as the home of cutting-edge Modernist art), this work was painted entirely from memory.

Natalia Goncharova, *Cyclist* (1913)
Painted by a Russian Futurist and one of the movement's most famous artworks, the shop signs that the cyclist is passing are fragmented to demonstrate quite what a lick he's going at.

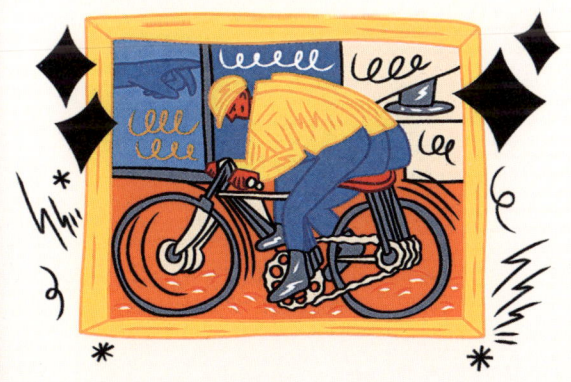

WHAT WAS *DER BLAUE REITER?*

Meaning 'the Blue Rider', DBR was a group of Expressionist artists based in Munich, led by Wassily Kandinsky, Franz Marc and Gabriele Münter.

Der Blaue Reiter

1910s

GERMANY

WHO INSPIRED THEM?

Members of DBR had been part of the *Neue Künstlervereinigung München* – an Expressionist group that met at Marianne von Werefkin's (see page 122) Munich home which she called her 'pink salon' (oo-er) – and just two weeks after they left that group, the first *Blaue Reiter* exhibition was held.

WHERE DOES ITS NAME COME FROM?

In a letter to the German art historian Paul Westheim, Kandinsky wrote that he and Marc chose the name because they both liked the colour blue: Marc liked blue horses, and Kandinsky liked blue horse riders – sorted.

WHAT WAS SO IMPORTANT ABOUT BLUE?

For the leaders of DBR, blue had a special spiritual quality, and a particularly masculine one at that (its feminine counterpart was yellow), which they believed drew viewers towards the infinite.

SO, WHAT WAS THE DEAL WITH ALL THOSE HORSES?

Marc was a deeply spiritual man who had originally planned to become a priest and who saw animals as the embodiment of the world's purity and innocence, believing that horses in particular had a special closeness to God.

WHY DID KANDINSKY DITCH THE HORSES AND START PAINTING ABSTRACTLY?

One story tells of how Kandinsky went into his studio and was struck by the sight of the most amazing painting (which turned out to be one he had painted earlier but left upside-down),

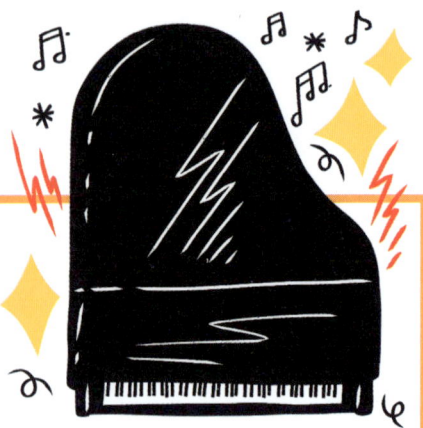

IN WHAT WAY IS ART LIKE A PIANO?

In 1919, Kandinsky published his book *Concerning the Spiritual in Art,* in which he compared the soul to a piano: the soul-piano has lots of soul-y strings, colours are the keys on the piano and the eye is the hammer that hits the strings.

but generally it's accepted that Kandinsky went more and more abstract as an exercise in exploring spiritual (and musical) harmony in his works.

WAS KANDINSKY THE FIRST ABSTRACT PAINTER?

Despite the fact that Kandinsky made a watercolour in 1910 called *First Abstract Painting*, more than a decade earlier the spiritual Swedish painter Hilma af Klint was already making large-scale abstracts (and in her world, blue was for the feminine and yellow the masculine – huh!)

HOW DID THE FIRST WORLD WAR CHANGE THEIR LOOK?

As the horrors of a global war approached, Marc's innocent, docile-looking animals started to become darker and more distressed.

WHAT ENDED THE MOVEMENT?

The First World War saw Marc (who created camouflage for artillery out of tent canvas onto which he often painted homages to Kandinsky's abstract designs) killed in action and Kandinsky forced back to Russia, and in one of the saddest letters in art history, Kandinksy wrote that now that his friend was dead, he didn't want to carry on alone.

3 KEY ARTISTS

Wassily Kandinsky (1866–1944)

Russian painter who didn't think America got abstract art so never bothered going there (literally choosing Nazi-occupied Paris instead); got engaged to Gabriele Münter probably to the surprise of his wife, from whom he separated a swift eight years later.

Gabriele Münter (1877–1962)

German painter, she captured key Expressionist moments and gatherings with her trusty camera, and hid a significant collection of DBR artworks in her home during Nazi rule.

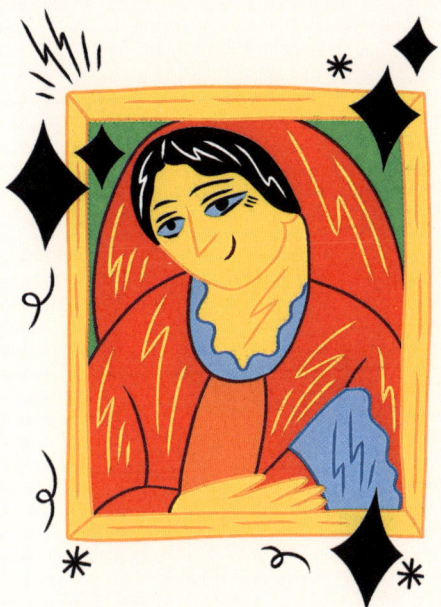

Franz Marc (1880–1916)

German painter and printmaker, apparently such an ugly baby that his father fainted at his baptism; Van Gogh-y vibe with the whole religious-but-super-sad thing.

3 KEY ARTWORKS

Alexej von Jawlensky, *Red Veil* (1912)

It was during his time as a member of DBR that von Jawlensky whacked up the colour intensity of his works and created vivid portraits like this one, inspired by the Orthodox religious icons he saw as a child in Russia.

Auguste Macke, *Greeting* (1912)

This linocut (featuring a horse – classic) was made by Macke who, aged 27, was the first *Blaue Reiter* member to be killed in the First World War, just two months into the conflict.

Maria Franck-Marc, *Girl with Toddler* (1913)

This piece, like much of Franck-Marc's work, focuses on the world of children – such subjects, along with the female artists who often painted them, have been largely overlooked by art history.

It was a short-lived Post-Impressionist (see page 88) group working in London, made up of sixteen male members (not **male members** – stop laughing), led by Walter Sickert.

Camden Town Group

1910s

BRITAIN

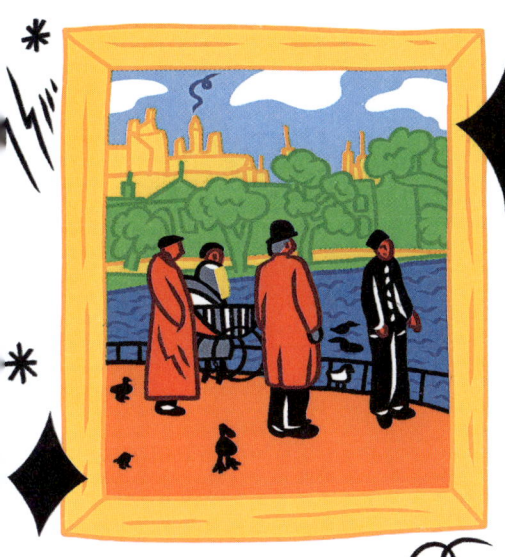

WAIT, IS THAT ANOTHER PISSARRO?

Lucien Pissarro, the oldest son of Camille Pissarro (see page 75) was one of the original members of the group, and was a strong guiding force for the deeply Impressionist-inspired artists.

WHAT WAS THE NEW ENGLISH ART CLUB?

The club was set up in 1886 – including future Camden Town Group members like Sickert – with the aim of giving artists the opportunity to exhibit when their work hadn't been admitted for display at the Royal Academy (taking a leaf out of the Impressionists' book).

WHERE WERE THE LADIES?

No women were admitted into the Camden Town Group for fear that they would bring down the reputation of the group, even though women **were** allowed in Sickert's earlier Fitzroy Street Group.

WHY CAMDEN?

Some of the group lived near Camden in north London and would often meet in Sickert's Camden studio, but the name was also chosen as a gag because the area at the time was a bit underwhelming and rough-around-the-edges, so an unlikely place to have an avant-garde movement named after it.

WHO WERE THEY INSPIRED BY?

Big influences for the Camden Town Group included the work of Paul Gauguin and Vincent van Gogh (see page 93), and the goings-on they saw around them in north London.

WHO WAS MRS MOUNTER?

Starring in several masterpieces by Harold Gilman, Mrs Ann Emma Mounter lived in the same building as Gilman and was previously identified as his landlady although now it is thought more likely that she was his housekeeper (or 'charlady').

WHO WERE THE THICKEST PAINTERS IN LONDON?

The Camden Town Group had their issues, one of which being that Sickert didn't like the impasto (see page 72) of some members' works, leading him to write a particularly passive-aggressive article in *The New Age* magazine in which he referred to Harold Gilman and Charles Ginner as 'the thickest painters in London'.

WHAT BROKE THEM UP?

Tensions grew within the group, partly over the exclusion of women, and also because their three exhibitions hadn't been very successful and the Carfax Gallery refused to hold another one.

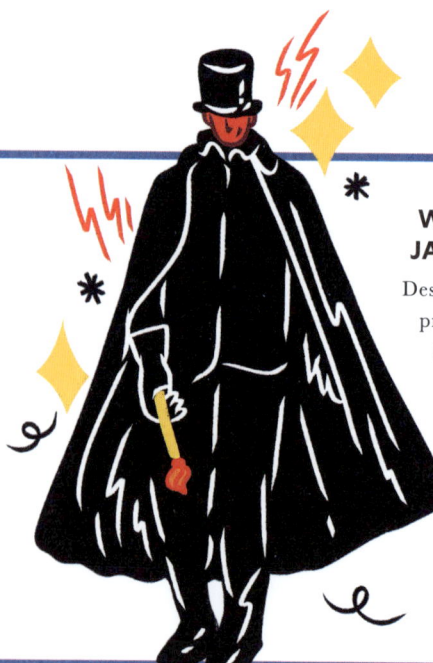

WAS WALTER SICKERT JACK THE RIPPER?

Despite speculation, Walter Sickert probably wasn't Jack the Ripper, but he didn't try very hard to make himself not look like him, creating a series of creepy paintings about the murder of Emily Elizabeth Dimmock in Camden in 1907, and calling a painting of his own bedroom *Jack the Ripper's Bedroom*.

3 KEY ARTISTS

Walter Sickert (1860-1942)

German-born British painter who originally wanted to be an actor, and thought the English obsession with niceness was holding art back.

Spencer Gore (1878-1914)

English painter, the first elected president of the Camden Town Group and son of the first Wimbledon tennis champion.

James Bolivar Manson (1879-1945)

English painter, director of the Tate for eight years and probably the worst one (mostly drunk, liked hardly any modern art); secretary for the Camden Town Group.

Charles Ginner, *Piccadilly Circus* (1912)

Showing the bustling centre of modern London, Ginner created this work when the number of cars in the capital had only just overtaken the number of horse-drawn carriages.

Stanisława de Karłowska, *Swiss Cottage* (c.1914)

De Karlowska was married to Camden Town Group member Robert Bevan (who painted a lot of horses – a lot of the men in this book painted a lot of horses), and her work has only recently been brought into conversations about the CTG.

3 KEY ARTWORKS

Malcolm Drummond, *In the Park (St James's Park)* (1911)

This work demonstrates Drummond's signature approach of painting from unusual angles, often depicting the backs of people's heads.

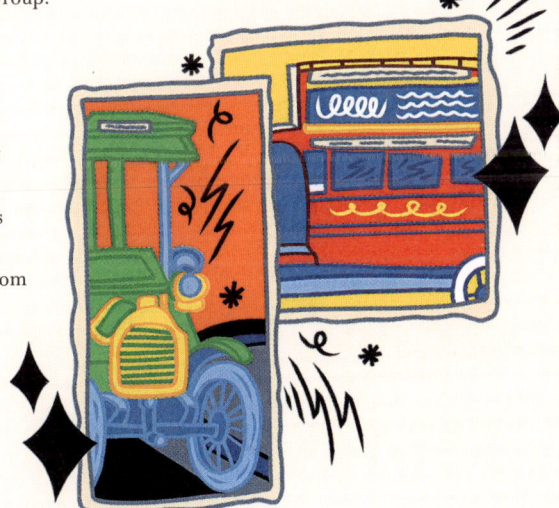

WHAT WAS ORPHISM?

It was an offshoot of Cubism (see page 138) that used vivid colours and concentric circles to create a visual harmony comparable to musical harmony.

Orphism
1910s

FRANCE

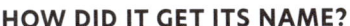

HOW DID IT GET ITS NAME?

French poet Guillaume Apollinaire named Orphism in 1912 after Orpheus, the musician in Greek mythology who used his music to save the Argonauts (of 'Jason and the…' fame), and who was seen as the embodiment of true artistry.

WHO WAS AT THE CENTRE OF ORPHISM?

One of art history's power couples, Sonia and Robert Delaunay were the founders of Orphism, marrying in 1910 after Sonia's amicable split from her marriage of convenience with closeted art dealer Wilhelm Uhde.

HOW WAS IT RELATED TO CUBISM?

The Orphists used the abstracted viewpoints and fractured perspectives of Cubism as their foundation, but added their deep interest in colour – something OG Cubism hadn't really bothered with.

WHAT INSPIRED THE ORPHISTS?

They drew inspiration from innovations in technology and city life, so several Orphist works feature big developments of the day including electric street lamps, early aeroplanes and a young Eiffel Tower.

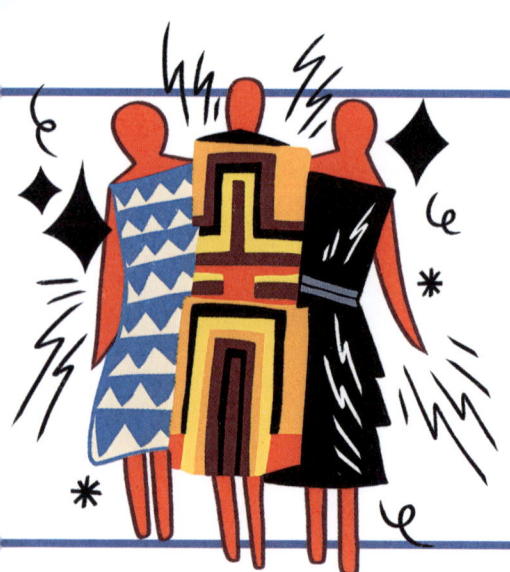

WHAT ELSE DID THE DELAUNAYS DESIGN?

As well as painting, the Delaunays created costumes (Sonia) and stage designs (Robert) for ballets including the 1917 Ballets Russes *Cleopatra*; Sonia's geometric designs were also used on textiles and to make high-fashion outfits.

WAS ORPHISM APPRECIATED?

For an exhibition catalogue in 1936, the art historian Alfred H. Barr created a flowchart demonstrating how each art movement from the 1890s onwards influenced and was influenced by one another; Orphism was the only movement that Barr showed as a dead-end – brutal.

WHAT WAS THE SNUGGLIEST ORPHIST ARTWORK?

A quilt made by Sonia Delaunay for her newborn son, Charles, made from irregular sections of colourful fabric and inspired by the peasant-style quilts she saw growing up in the Russian Empire, is considered the first (and certainly cosiest) Orphist artwork.

WHAT WAS SIMULTANISM?

The term the Delauneys used for their own brand of Orphism, it was a Cubist-influenced method that focused on colour relationships and combining multiple viewpoints in a single image.

WHERE DID IT GO?

Orphism was a short-lived movement that had fallen out of vogue by the First World War, but both Delaunays continued to make visually Orphist works for the remainder of their art-making lives.

3 KEY ARTISTS

František Kupka (1871–1957)

Czech painter, apprenticed as a teen to the local saddlemaker who was also the local medium (typical freelance career); formed some of the first theories about Orphism so wasn't just a third wheel.

Robert Delaunay (1885–1941)

French painter considered a Neo-Impressionist for a bit; too colourful for some of the Cubists.

Sonia Delaunay (1885–1979)

Ukrainian-born Russian painter and designer, orphaned and adopted by her uncle whose successful law career afforded her a childhood of travel and cultural education; the first female artist to have a retrospective show at the Louvre during her lifetime.

3 KEY ARTWORKS

František Kupka, *Disks of Newton (Study for Fugue in Two Colours)* (1912)

Ever-interested in colour theory and astronomy, Kupka made this work as a homage to Sir Isaac Newton's seventeenth-century discovery that light is made up of a spectrum of seven colours.

Robert Delaunay, *Homage to Blériot* (1914)

Dedicated to pioneering aviator Louis Blériot, Delaunay included symbols of mechanical progress in this composition, including a large propeller, a biplane and the Eiffel Tower.

Sonia Delaunay, *Prismes Électriques* (1914)

An interpretation of the chromatic effects of electric street lamps, Delaunay's painting namedrops her friend, the poet Blaise Cendrars (who influenced many other artists) and 'Jeanne de France' (a fifteenth-century saint and queen of France).

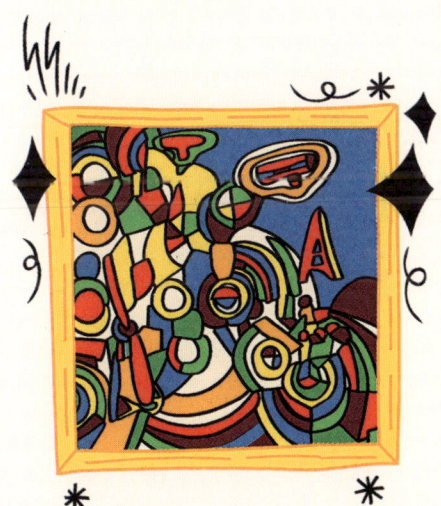

WHAT WAS VORTICISM?

It was a London-based movement founded by writer and artist Wyndham Lewis, characterised by the use of abstract geometric forms and the desire for art to reflect the industrial world.

Vorticism

1910s

BRITAIN

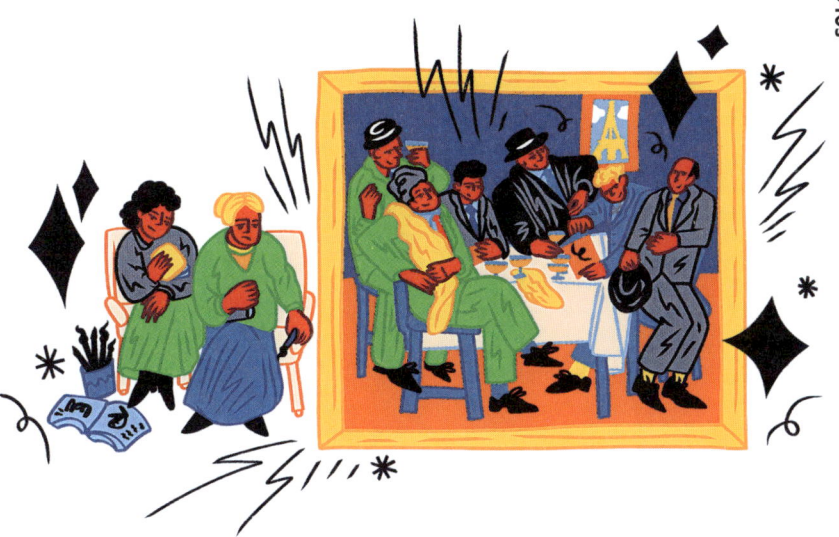

WHAT INSPIRED VORTICISM?

The Vorticists were deeply inspired by Cubism (see page 138) and Futurism (including some of its fascist tendencies – see page 144) but sought to go a step further and abandon recognisable figures entirely (although sometimes figures are still suggested).

WHAT WAS 'BLAST'?

Published only twice (the first just a month before war on Germany was declared), *BLAST* was the Vorticist magazine that members of the group can be seen reading in William Roberts' 1961–1962 painting, *The Vorticists at the Restaurant de la Tour Eiffel, Spring 1915*.

WHY 'VORTICISM'?

The poet Ezra Pound developed the artistic concept of 'the vortex' – a moment of extreme energy – which Lewis adopted, giving the movement's first manifesto the title *Long Live the Vortex!*

WHAT WERE THEIR DEMANDS?

As laid out in their first manifesto, Vorticists wanted to create art that was rooted in the present, they wanted artists to follow their own unique visions regardless of their class, and they also noted that they didn't want to make men wear pink and blue trousers – which is, well, fair enough.

WHAT WAS IN (OR OUT) FOR THE VORTICISTS?

In another manifesto in *BLAST*, they made their own Hot or Not list; 'Blasted' things included humour, the Post Office, aperitifs and English weather, while 'Blessed' were English ships, hairdressers and Scottish politician R. C. Bontine Cunninghame Graham (but specifically 'not his brother' – ouch).

WHAT WAS THE REBEL ART CENTRE?

The Rebel Art Centre in London was founded by Lewis as a meeting place for radical artists, with the hope of rivalling the Bloomsbury Group's Omega Workshops (see page 131) less than half-an-hour's walk away, but it only lasted a few months before internal disagreements shut it down.

HOW AND WHEN DID VORTICISM END?

The First World War changed the public's appetite for art – avant-garde fell by the wayside in favour of a return to realism – and also many key Vorticist artists were drafted, some of whom would be killed in action.

WHAT WAS GROUP X?

Like going back to your ex because it'll definitely work out this time, Group X was Wyndham Lewis' second go at creating a radical group of artists in 1920, but – like going back to your ex because it'll definitely work out this time – it didn't stick.

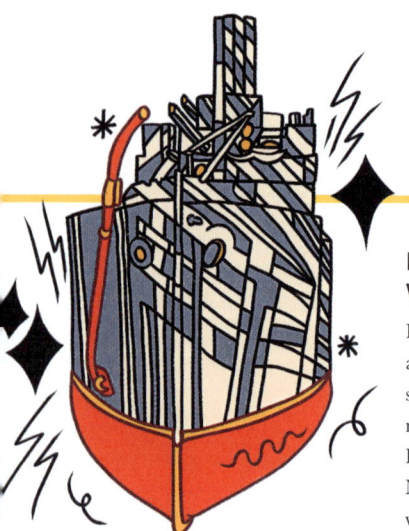

HOW DID THEY HELP THE WAR EFFORT?

In 1917, a method for disguising ships at sea was invented in which abstract shapes would be painted onto boats to make them harder to detect, and Vorticist Edward Wadsworth, serving in the Royal Navy at the time, was one of the artists who painted these 'dazzle ships'.

3 KEY ARTISTS

Wyndham Lewis (1882–1957)
American-British writer and painter who fell out with loads of people and said he was born on a yacht.

Helen Saunders (1885–1963)
English painter who rarely signed her works so as not to embarrass her family; seen with Jessica Dismoor in the Roberts' portrait of the Vorticists but the girls are practically being pushed out of the door.

Edward Wadsworth (1889–1949)
English painter of groovy boats; sent to Munich by his dad to do an engineering degree but learned woodcut printing instead (whoops).

3 KEY ARTWORKS

Henri Gaudier-Brzeska, *Red Stone Dancer* (c.1913)
Made two years before his death in the First World War at the age of just 23, this sculpture was heavily inspired by the carvings Gaudier-Brzeska saw at the British Museum's ethnographic gallery.

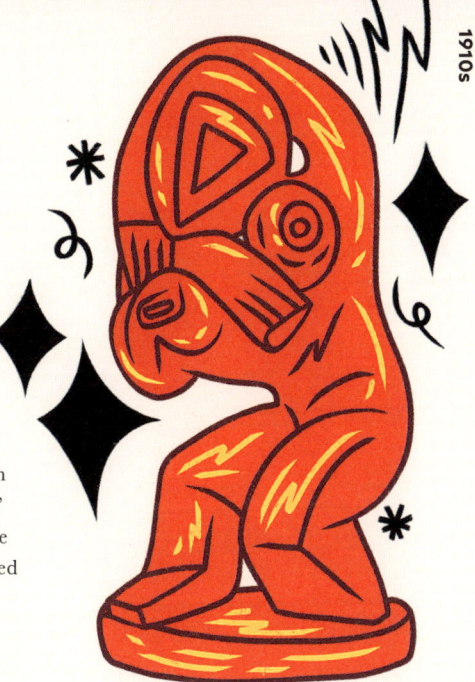

William Roberts, *Two-Step II (study)* (c.1915)
Inspired by dance (there are two boogieing figures hidden here), the finished painting was exhibited at a Vorticist exhibition in June 1915 but was then lost.

Jessica Dismorr, *Abstract Composition* (c.1915)
Dismorr's abstract works have a distinctly architectural quality and she also wrote about cityscapes for *BLAST* (as well as about a sexy guy called Rodengo).

WHAT WAS DADA?

Reacting against the
horrors of the First World
War, Dada was a
movement that rejected
the value of logic and
reason, and had major
bases in Zurich, Berlin,
Cologne and New York.

Dada
1910s–1920s

SWITZERLAND, GERMANY, US

WHAT WERE THEY RALLYING AGAINST?

The Dadaists had witnessed how 'rational' civilisation had led itself into the bloodiest war of all time, and so became entirely against civility and the rules of the past, even turning against language itself and creating a lot of unintelligible poetry.

WHAT DOES 'DADA' MEAN?

Lots of things: 'Rocking horse' in French, 'Yes, yes' in Romanian and Russian, and 'The tail of a sacred cow' in the Kru language of West Africa; but the mystery of its name (and the fact that it sounds like a baby's babble) played into Dada's reputation for being playfully nonsensical.

HOW SHOCKING WAS IT?

The Dadaists were deliberately controversial: Rudolf Schlichter and John Heartfield created *Prussian Archangel* in 1920, which was a dummy in German military uniform with a papier-mâché pig's head, and Duchamp challenged the art world in 1919 with his moustachioed Mona Lisa with 'L.H.O.O.Q.' written beneath her (which, said out loud in French, sounds like 'she has a hot ass').

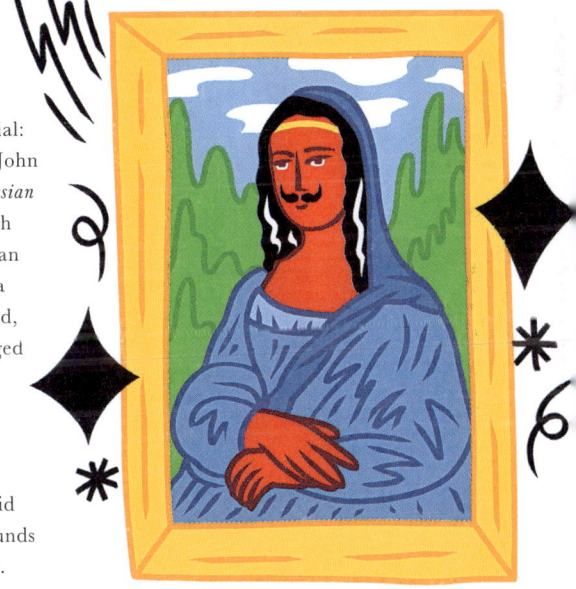

WHAT IS ICONOCLASM?

It's the destruction of sacred images, and the Dadaists were taking part in their own cultural iconoclasm by tearing apart old values and creating something entirely new with their wild performances, politically critical collages and use of invented languages.

WHAT WAS CABARET VOLTAIRE?

A Zurich nightclub founded by the cabaret performers and poets Hugo Ball and Emmy Hennings in 1916, Cabaret Voltaire was the location of several key Dada performances including Ball's nonsense poem *Karawane,* which he performed wearing a strange priest's costume made from paper.

WHO WAS THE CABARET'S MOST FAMOUS NEIGHBOUR?

For more than a year, the exiled Russian agitator and future leader of the 1917 Russian Revolution, Vladimir Lenin, lived right across the road from Cabaret Voltaire and was probably able to hear their bizarre performances.

WHO WERE THEY INSPIRED BY?

Turning away from Western culture, many Dadaists took 'inspiration' from African cultures, but they often drew on problematic stereotypes and the idea that African societies (which Dadaists saw as a homogeneous whole) were free from rationality (as the Dadaists aspired to be).

WHAT WAS THE SIGNIFICANCE OF PHOTOMONTAGE?

Photomontage, the art of combining photographic and printed images, was pioneered by Hannah Höch (one of the few women celebrated within the group), and allowed Höch to directly challenge the stereotypes of women promoted by mainstream media.

HOW DO YOU GET GOOD PRESS?

Dada artists often fed fake or sensationalist stories to Swiss newspapers in order to drum up a bit of attention and undermine the authority of the press, including in July 1912, when the press received a report that two Dadaists held a pistol duel in which Jean Arp was grazed on the thigh.

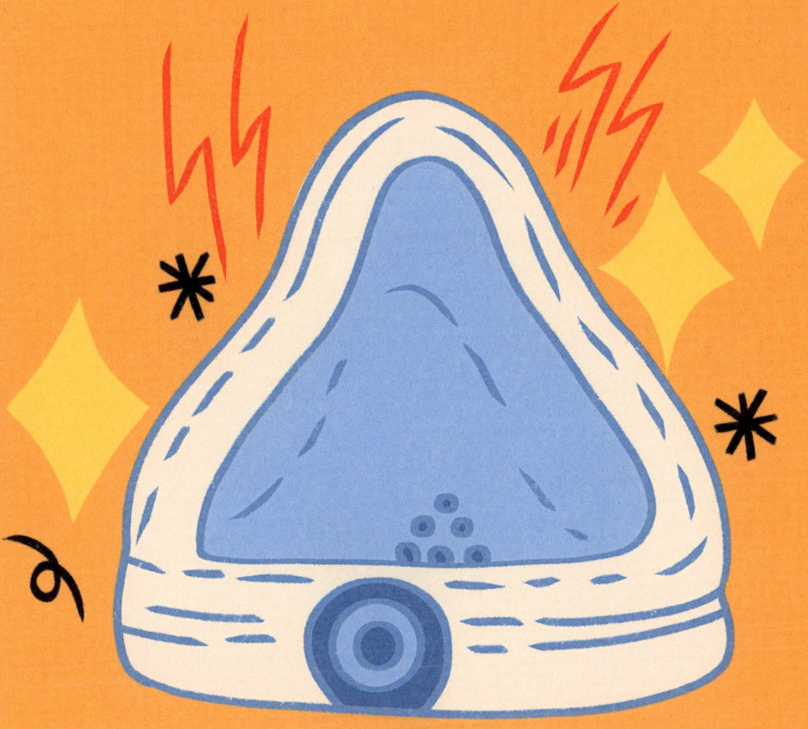

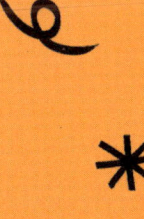

WHY DID THAT URINAL CAUSE SUCH A FUSS?

Marcel Duchamp's *Fountain* was submitted to New York's Society of Independent Artists exhibition in 1917, made from a pre-purchased urinal from J. L. Mott Iron Works, and it sent shockwaves through the art world because for the first time, an artist was claiming that any object could be 'art' simply because he said it was.

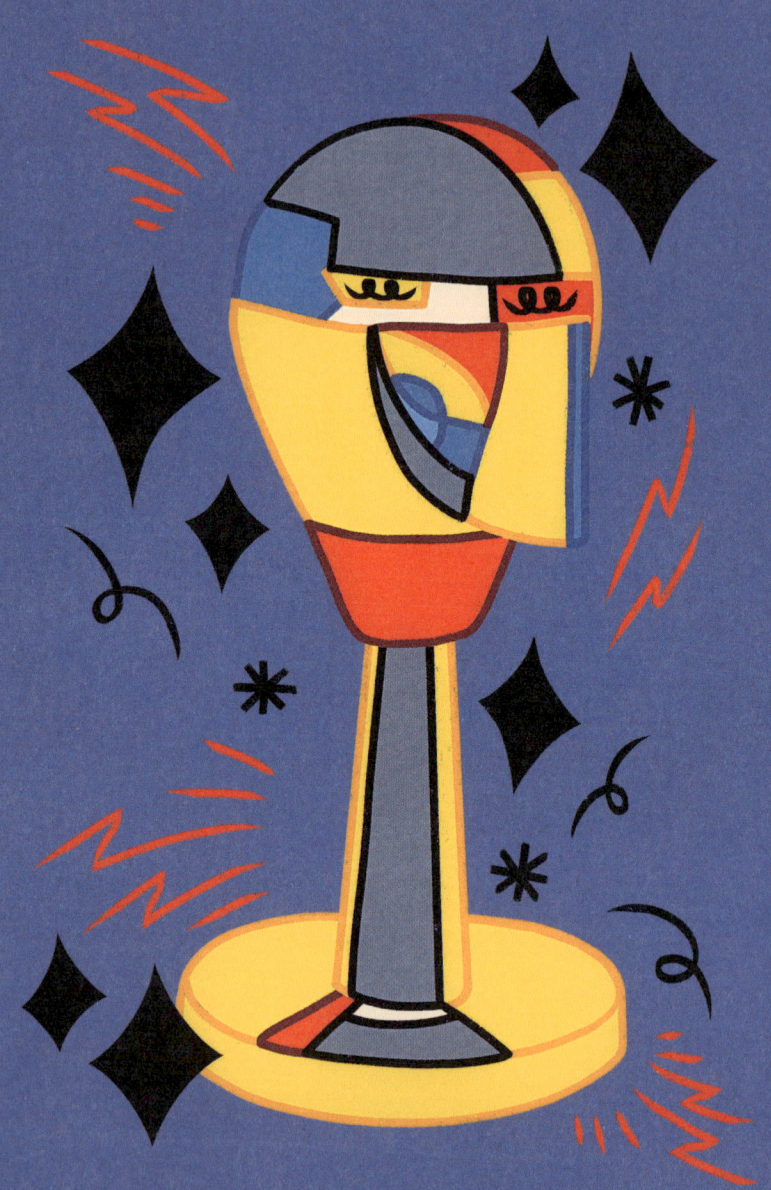

3 KEY ARTISTS

Johannes Baader (1875-1955)

German artist who represented Dada ideals as leader of Dada's political party and who believed he might be the reincarnation of Jesus Christ.

Hans/Jean Arp (1886-1966)

French-German painter and sculptor (Hans when German and Jean when French); got out of the German draft by pretending to be insane (getting undressed, adding up all the numbers on the draft form and making the sign of the cross whenever he saw a portrait of Field Marshal Hindenburg).

Man Ray (1890-1976)

American artist and photographer, he thought that New York was already so crazy that there was no way that Dada could compete there; made Dadaist 'rayographs' – photographic prints taken without a camera.

3 KEY ARTWORKS

George Grosz, *A Victim of Society (Remember Uncle August, the Unhappy Inventor)* (1919)

Kitted out with a bicycle tube, a razor in the neck, a brioche forehead and five real buttons glued to the canvas, *Uncle August* is Grosz's embodiment of a society gone wrong.

Sophie Taeuber-Arp, *Dada Head* (1920)

Taeuber-Arp was known for her Dada puppets and heads like this one, which blurred the lines between traditional crafts and avant-garde art.

Marcel Duchamp, *Fresh Widow* (1920)

Thought to be a dark pun on 'French window' (becoming 'Fresh Widow' perhaps as a reference to the French casualties of the First World War), this was the first work that Duchamp signed Rose Sélavy, his female alter ego.

Founded and guided by Kazimir Malevich (spoiler: a **lot** of this chapter is about Kazimir Malevich), it was an abstract art movement determined to find out what was at the core of art, discarding the goal of representation and starting afresh, focusing purely on colour and shape.

Suprematism
1910s

RUSSIA

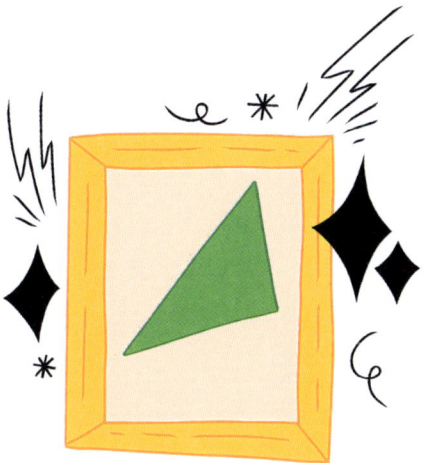

WHY WERE THEY CALLED SUPREMATISTS?

The name was coined by Malevich because, for him, the mission of creating art that is fully focused on pure feeling was more important (supreme) than artworks that try to recreate something from the real world (even the Cubists – see page 138 – were making pictures, however unusual, *of* something).

WHAT WAS GOING ON IN RUSSIA AT THE TIME?

Times were hard: in 1913, when Malevich first began his love affair with squares, Russia was still reeling from its First Revolution of 1905 and its defeat in the Russo-Japanese War that same year, and by the time of the first Suprematist exhibition in 1915,

Russia was experiencing colossal casualties in the First World War.

WHAT WERE THEY TRYING TO SAY WITH THEIR WORK?

With his monochromatic paintings, Malevich was trying to draw attention to the foundation of painting – shape and colour – and to create something universal and eternal; a pure form of art.

WHAT DID IT HAVE IN COMMON WITH POETRY?

The Russian poet Aleksei Kruchenykh was also trying to break art forms down to their very core, and in 1913 he coined 'Zaum' poetry, which used an invented, untranslatable language with its own syntax and rules (and Malevich even wrote some himself).

WHAT WAS THE 0.10 EXHIBITION?

The Last Futurist Exhibition of Paintings 0.10 in Petrograd 1915 was the first time the Suprematists exhibited their work, with '0' representing Year Zero – a new beginning for art – and '10' after the ten artists originally billed to exhibit (in the end there were 14, but maybe they'd already printed the posters...)

WHAT WAS THE POINT OF THE BLACK SQUARE?

Malevich's masterpiece *Black Square* (1915) announced a clean break from the art that had come before because it was in no way trying to reflect society, it wasn't even trying to reflect squares or the colour black (because it was neither a perfect square nor perfectly black).

HOW SPECIAL DID MALEVICH THINK HIS SQUARE WAS?

Malevich referred to it as a 'royal infant' and at the 0.10 exhibition, he hung it on the wall in a position usually reserved for religious icons in Russian Orthodox households: so, pretty special.

WHY COULDN'T HE JUST PAINT SOMETHING NICE?

Malevich went through various styles and phases in his career, but he came to the conclusion with Suprematism that true artists are those who can create something new rather than copy from nature; he compared painting what we see around us in nature to being like an imprisoned thief.

WHAT ENDED SUPREMATISM?

Suprematism was dissed as elitist by the up-and-coming Constructivists (see page 174); then, in the 1920s, all avant-garde art in the Soviet Union was squashed by Stalin – but even when Malevich adopted the state-approved Socialist Realist style (see page 204) he sneakily signed some works with a tiny black square.

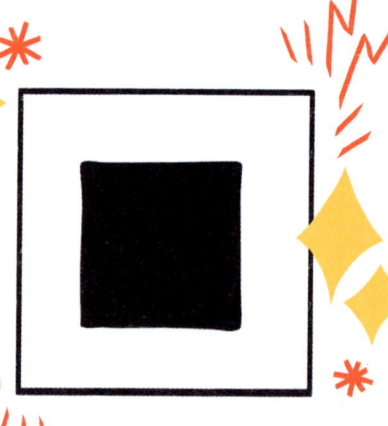

3 KEY ARTISTS

Kazimir Malevich (1879-1935)

Ukrainian-born artist who identified as both Ukrainian and Polish; when he died his urn was buried beneath a monument of *Black Square* created by felllow Suprematist Nikolai Suetin.

Olga Rozanova (1886-1918)

Russian artist and the only true Suprematist according to Malevich; secretary for the Suprematists' journal which – despite having articles written for it and being a year in the making – was never published.

Ilya Chashnik (1902-1929)

Latvian-born Russian artist and loyal student of Malevich, he applied Suprematist thought to various media, including his designs for Saint Petersburg's Imperial Porcelain Factory.

3 KEY ARTWORKS

Kazimir Malevich, *Black Square* (1915)

Haven't you read this chapter?

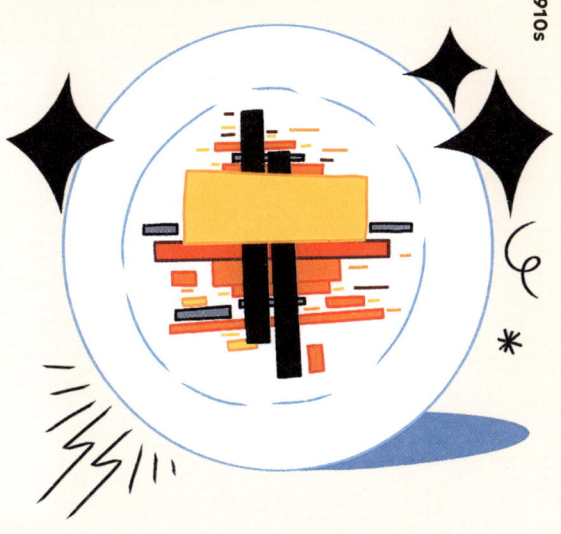

Ivan Kliun, *Composition* (1917)

Colour mattered more for Kliun than for Malevich, and in *Composition*, a lone green triangle takes centre stage (although underneath it are several other shapes from previous works that he decided to paint over).

Liubov Popova, *Painterly Architectonic* (1917)

As suggested by the title, the shapes have an architectural, three-dimensional vibe that suggests they aren't quite as flat as they first appear, something Popova would develop further during her work as a Constructivist.

WHAT WAS CONSTRUCTIVISM?

Founded by Vladimir Tatlin and Alexander Rodchenko in 1915, Constructivism aimed to create art that served a practical social purpose, using industrial materials and geometric shapes to make artworks that everyone could understand.

Russian Constructivism
1910s–1930s

RUSSIA

WHY THE NAME?

First calling themselves 'Productivists', Constructivists saw industrial labour as the beating heart of the newly formed Soviet Union and named their artworks 'constructions' rather than 'compositions', positioning artists as more like engineers.

WHAT'S SO ACCESSIBLE ABOUT SHAPES?

In 1917, fewer than 40 percent of men and 13 percent of women in Russia were literate, so the Constructivists primarily used shapes and colours to get their messages across to as many people as possible, sometimes incorporating words and photographs into their work, too.

HOW DID IT INTERACT WITH SUPREMATISM?

Both Suprematists (see page 170) and Constructivists focused on the use of geometric forms, but the groups were fundamentally opposed in their beliefs about the purpose of art: Suprematism was all about the philosophy of art-making, whereas Constructivists thought art had a job to do in society.

DID THEY GET ON?

Several Suprematists became Constructivists, and despite their shared love of shapes, the groups didn't transition neatly, with Tatlin and Kazimir Malevich apparently having a nasty public row at the 0.10 exhibition (see page 172).

WHAT WERE THEY INSPIRED BY?

The Russian Revolution (recreated geometrically in El Lissitzky's *Beat the Whites with the Red Wedge*) and the foundation of the Soviet Union on Marxist principles placed the working classes at the centre of society (at least on the surface), and Constructivism aspired to be an accessible artform for them.

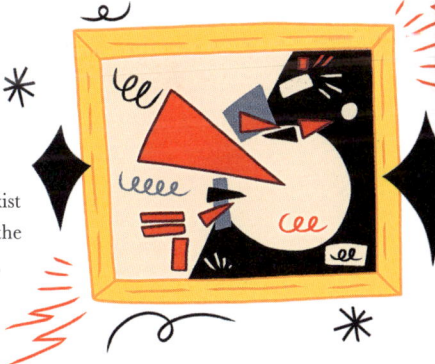

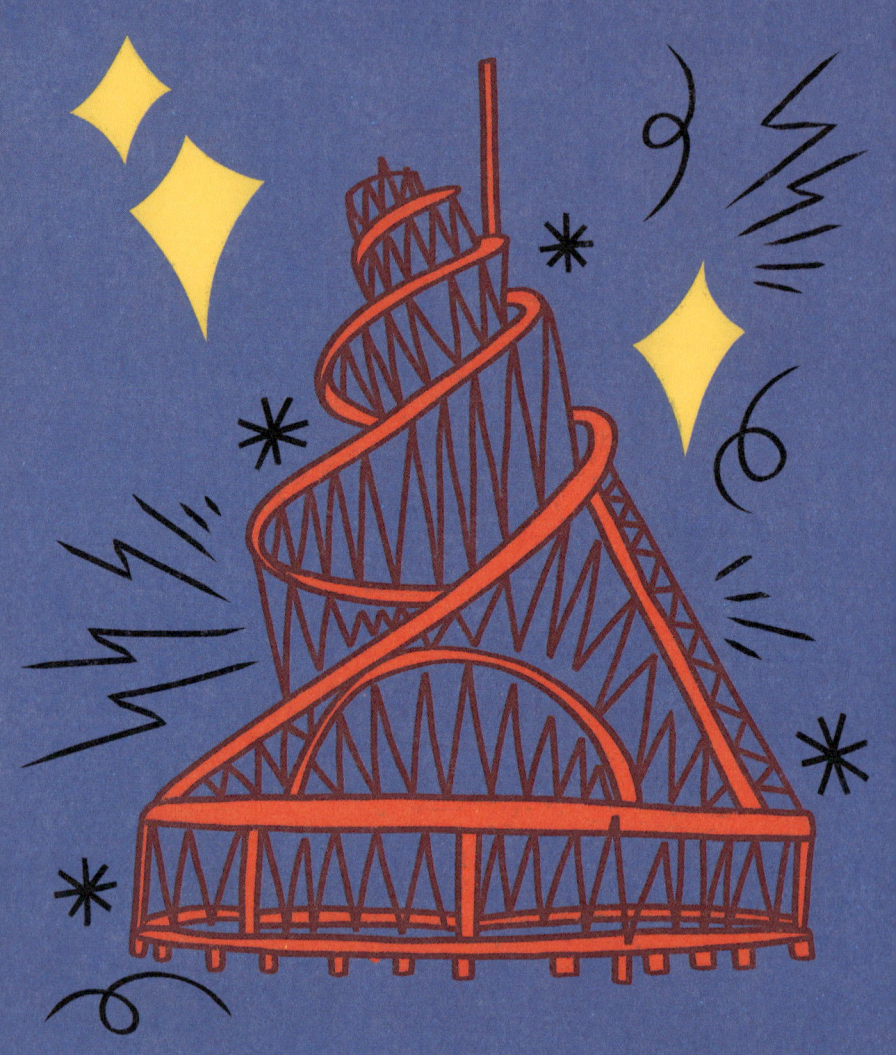

WHAT WAS SO SPECIAL ABOUT TATLIN'S TOWER?

Tatlin's *Monument to the Third International* was a proposed building for the St Petersburg HQ of the Communist International organisation, designed to be almost twice as tall as the Eiffel Tower and made of complex rotating structures, but the plan never came to fruition because it would have been incredibly expensive and near-impossible to build.

OTHER THAN GOOD MATHS, WHAT WAS 5 × 5 = 25?

It was the title of a 1921 exhibition held in Moscow, where Alexander Rodchenko first displayed his seminal Constructivist paintings *Pure Red Colour*, *Pure Yellow Colour*, and *Pure Blue Colour*, canvases filled with just one colour, which he saw as the logical conclusion of painting.

WHAT WAS THE LETATLIN?

In the 1930s, having spent more than a decade dismantling the lines between fine art and functional objects, Tatlin set out to create a flying machine (the 'Letatlin'), which was powered entirely by the person pedalling inside the bird-like structure – sadly, it didn't take off (literally).

WHAT ARE PROUNS?

'Prouns' were what El Lissitzky began to call his geometric paintings in 1919 – PROUN being a Russian acronym for 'Project for the Affirmation of the New'.

WHAT ENDED CONSTRUCTIVISM?

One of Constructivism's staunchest supporters had been Leon Trotsky, the People's Commissar for Military Affairs; when he fell out of favour and was exiled in 1929 by Josef Stalin, Constructivism became suspect by association and Socialist Realism (see page 204) took hold.

3 KEY ARTISTS

Vladimir Tatlin (1885–1953)
Russian artist who had a beef with Malevich (one tale includes him kicking Malevich's chair from under him to demonstrate that abstract concepts of forms aren't that comfy); designed loads of stuff like tea cups without handles (handles get in the way of pure form – get with it).

El Lissitzky (1890–1941)
Russian artist and architect, originally turned away from the St Petersburg Art Academy because they had exceeded their quota of Jewish students for the year; wrote a book with Hans/Jean Arp about each of the 'isms' of art (but please keep reading this one).

Varvara Stepanova (1894–1958)
Lithuanian-born Russian artist, collaborated with husband Alexander Rodchenko who photographed her extensively; designed some incredibly snazzy sports outfits for the Soviet Union.

3 KEY ARTWORKS

Naum Gabo, *Head No. 2* (1916)
Gabo was interested in how you could get across a sense of volume without creating something bulky or heavy; this figurative bust is made of multiple thin, flat planes to fill out the space.

Mikhail Kaufman, *Alexander Rodchenko in the Studio* (1924)
In this photograph, we can see how Rodchenko fashioned himself not as a typical artist but more like an engineer, with metal shapes stacked up behind him like a worker's tools.

Alexander Rodchenko, *Books (Please)!* (1924)
Created as a nationwide advert to promote reading, Rodchenko's design features the glamorous Russian socialite Lilya Brik, who was a muse for many Russian avant-garde artists of the day.

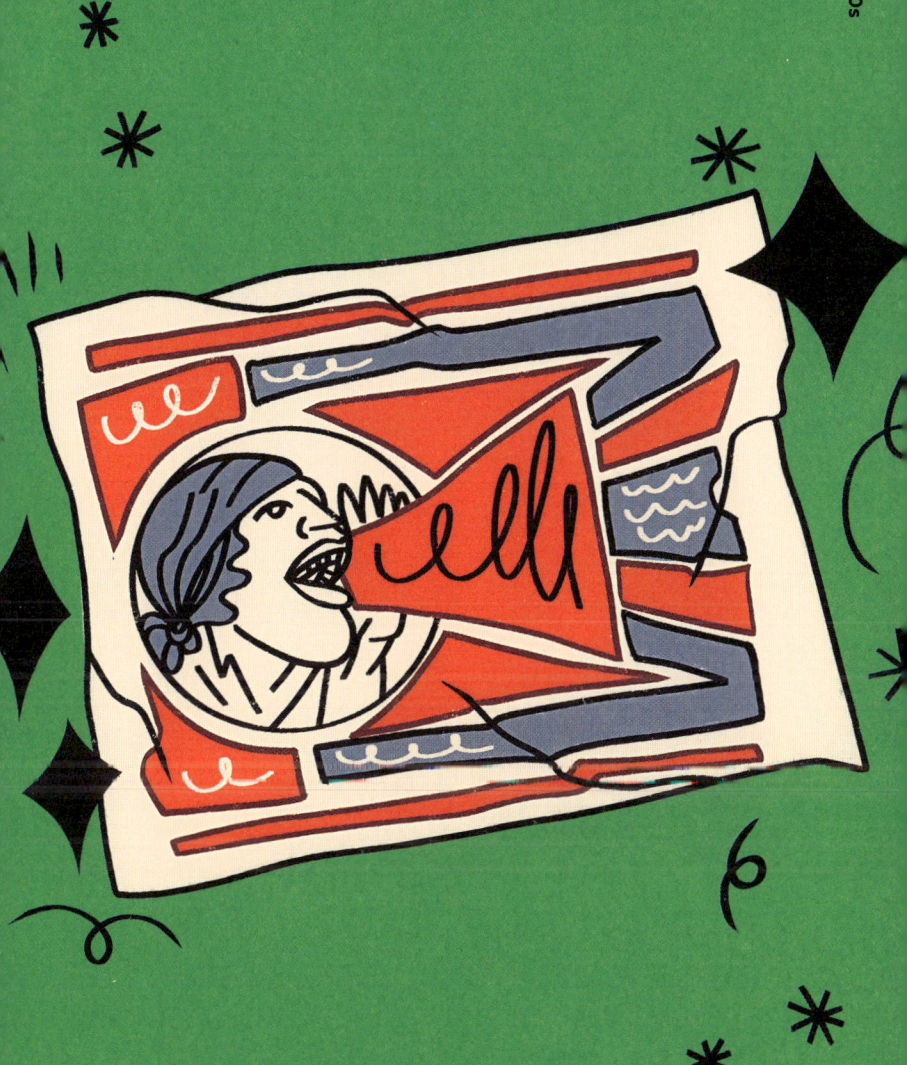

It was an abstract artistic endeavour by Dutch artists and architects, led by Theo van Doesburg, who wanted to boil compositions down to their most essential parts.

De Stijl
1910s–1930s

THE NETHERLANDS

WHAT WAS NEOPLASTICISM?

The core idea of *De Stijl*, Neoplasticism was all about reducing the world to its fundamental elements – lines and flat colour – in order to reveal the true underlying harmony of the universe (you know, straightforward stuff).

WHAT WAS ALL THE FUSS ABOUT PRIMARY COLOURS?

De Stijl artists, including Piet Mondrian, believed that the real colours of nature could never be properly replicated in art, so they saw the primary colours (red, yellow and blue – not magenta, cyan and yellow like your printer tells you) as the 'pure' building blocks of art.

AND ALL THOSE SQUARES?

It was less about rectangles and squares per se and more about the intersection of vertical and horizontal lines, which make up the world around us and form a fundamental visual language that can be understood from anywhere in the world.

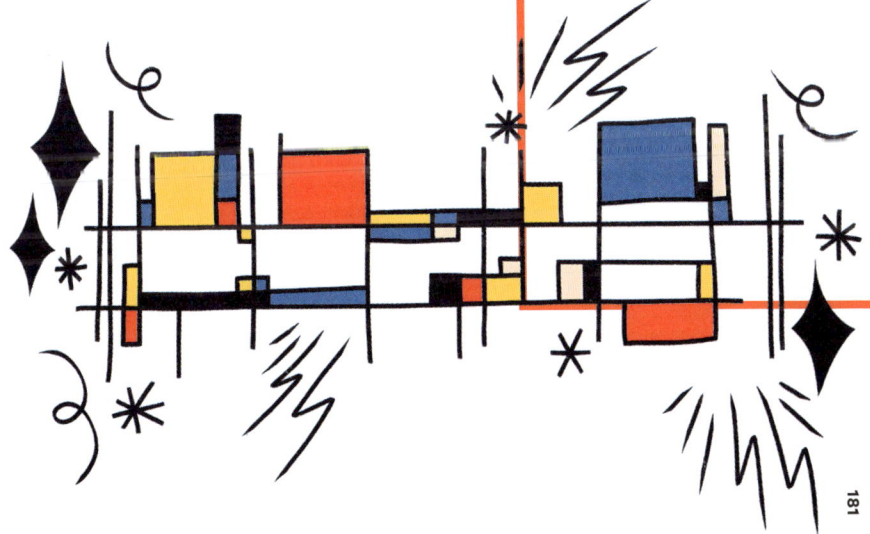

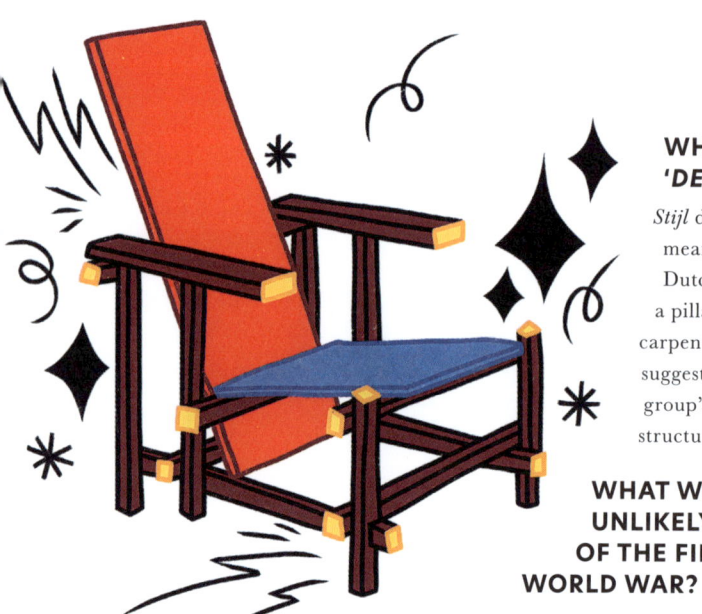

Stijl didn't just mean 'style' in Dutch, but also a pillar or jamb in carpentry, which is suggestive of the group's focus on structure.

WHAT WAS AN UNLIKELY PERK OF THE FIRST WORLD WAR?

The Netherlands remained neutral throughout the war, effectively cutting the Dutch off from the art movements occurring in neighbouring France and Germany; this spurred van Doesburg to create his own movement in his home country.

WHAT IS VERTICALITY?

It was a key element in *De Stijl* artworks, and it means an emphasis on vertical-ness.

WHAT IS HORIZONTALITY?

Guess.

WHAT INSPIRED IT?

De Stijl was influenced by abstraction and the Bauhaus school (see page 188) in Germany (where several *De Stijl* artists worked at one point or another), which placed a similar emphasis on geometrical form.

WHAT ENDED *DE STIJL*?

In 1923, van Doesburg began using diagonal lines, which Mondrian considered a betrayal of *De Stijl*'s principles, leading to him leaving the movement and digging deeper into Neoplasticism, while van Doesburg continued to publish the *De Stijl* journal until his death in 1931.

3 KEY ARTISTS

Theo van Doesburg (1883–1931)
Dutch artist and *De Stijl* leader,
intense personality, wanted
De Stijl out there in as many
formats as possible so created
all sorts of things including *De
Stijl* flowerpots.

Vimos Huszár (1884–1960)
Hungarian artist and co-founder of
the *De Stijl* magazine who created
a brilliant design to promote Miss
Blanche Egyptian cigarettes.

Gerrit Rietveld (1888–1964)
Dutch furniture designer and
architect, contributor to the *De
Stijl* journal, and creator of the
famous *Red and Blue Chair,* which
wasn't necessarily *De Stijl* to begin
with, but then he painted it red
and blue to match the aesthetic.

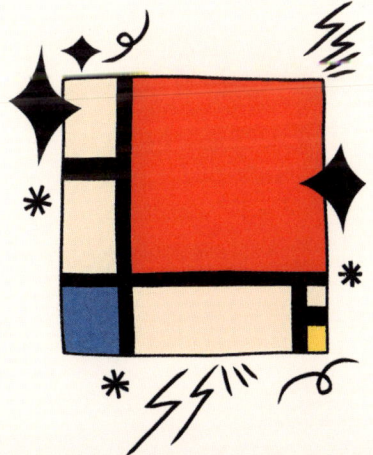

3 KEY ARTWORKS

**Bart van der Leck,
Composition No.3 (1917)**
At first, this work looks like a
typical abstract *De Stijl* design,
but it is actually a DeStijlified
version of his 1910 naturalistic
painting, *Leaving the Factory*.

**Georges Vantongerloo,
Construction of Volume Relations
(1921)**
Brought into *De Stijl* by van
Doesburg with the hope that his
works would bridge a gap between
the group's architects and painters,
Vantongerloo's sculptures,
including *Construction*, were heavily
influenced by mathematics.

**Piet Mondrian, *Composition II
in Red, Blue, and Yellow* (1929)**
Mondrian's designs may seem
straightforward, but the artist
didn't make life easy for himself:
he always mixed his own colours
rather than using them straight
from the tube, and he also never
used a ruler.

**WHAT WAS
THE HARLEM
RENAISSANCE?**

It was a hugely creative
period in the US, when
African American artists,
musicians and cultural
movers and shakers were
shining a light on and
celebrating the role
Black culture played
in cosmopolitan life.

Harlem
Renaissance

1910s–1930s

US

WHY HARLEM?

The neighbourhood, in northern Manhattan, New York, had the highest concentration of Black people in the world at the time, after more than 175,000 African Americans moved there during the Great Migration.

WHAT WAS THE GREAT MIGRATION?

Between 1916 and 1970, around six million African Americans moved from the segregated southern states to the Northeast, West and Midwest where racism was still prevalent but living conditions and economic opportunities were somewhat better.

HOW WAS IT LIKE THE ITALIAN RENAISSANCE?

Like the Italian version, the Harlem Renaissance was named in hindsight – artists at the time knew it as the New Negro Movement.

WHAT WAS THE *NEW NEGRO*?

It was a compendium of essays, poetry and prose, compiled by Black philosopher Alain Locke, which discussed how the new generation of African Americans must demand the same rights and respect as their white peers and get their art appreciated on a global scale.

DID IT JUST HAPPEN IN HARLEM?

Nope, other areas with large Black populations, including the South Side of Chicago, saw New Negro art bloom; also, several New Negro artists lived and worked abroad in Europe, making the impact of the Harlem Renaissance felt internationally.

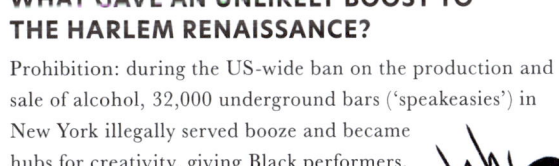

WHAT GAVE AN UNLIKELY BOOST TO THE HARLEM RENAISSANCE?

Prohibition: during the US-wide ban on the production and sale of alcohol, 32,000 underground bars ('speakeasies') in New York illegally served booze and became hubs for creativity, giving Black performers, including jazz musicians, opportunities to showcase their work.

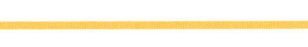
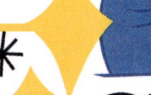
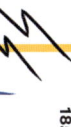

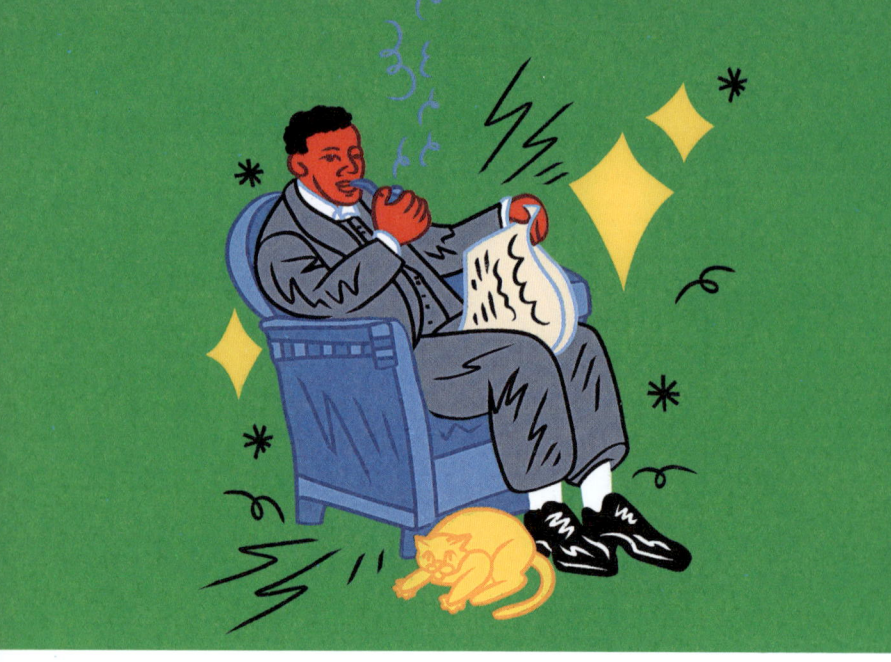

WHAT HAPPENED AT THE 1900 PARIS EXPOSITION?

This huge international showcase was a key moment in the development of the Harlem Renaissance when the sociologist W. E. B. Du Bois curated an award-winning exhibition of 363 images of middle-class African Americans living fulfilling modern lives, which challenged racist stereotypes.

WHAT ENDED THE RENAISSANCE?

The 1929 Wall Street Crash, the subsequent Great Depression and the end of Prohibition were all death knells for the nightlife scene that was the lifeblood of the Harlem Renaissance, draining the energy – and money – that fuelled the New Negro movement.

WHAT DID IT INSPIRE?

The Harlem Renaissance was a key influence for the *Négritude* movement in Paris in the 1930s that celebrated African and Caribbean artistic culture, led by Martinican poet Aimé Césaire, French Guianese poet Léon Damas and the poet and future first president of Senegal, Léopold Sédar Senghor.

3 KEY ARTISTS

Meta Vaux Warrick Fuller (1877–1968)

American sculptor, many of whose early works were destroyed in a tragic fire; won a lot of prizes.

James Van Der Zee (1886–1983)

American photographer who used elaborate props and multiple exposures to create complex compositions; came out of semi-retirement in his nineties to photograph Black celebrities including Muhammad Ali and Jean-Michel Basquiat.

Richmond Barthé (1901–1989)

American sculptor, exhibited his artwork publicly aged 12 (which doesn't make the rest of us feel like feckless underachievers **at all**); his excellent memory meant he could save money on actual models.

expensive so some copies are actually plaster casts, painted by the artist to look like bronze.

Archibald Motley, *Black Belt* (1934)

Depicting Chicago's historically Black Bronzeville neighbourhood with the aim of showcasing the vibrant street life in the area, *Black Belt* shows Motley's interest in the effects of moonlight and electric light.

Aaron Douglas, *Aspects of Negro Life: From Slavery to Reconstruction* (1934)

In his four mural panels made for the New York Public Library, Douglas used radiating circles to highlight significant objects – in this, the second panel, the focus is on a copy of the Emancipation Proclamation of 1863.

3 KEY ARTWORKS

Augusta Savage, *Gamin* (c.1929)

Modelled on Savage's nephew, *Gamin* was reproduced many times and is one of Savage's most popular works, but bronze was

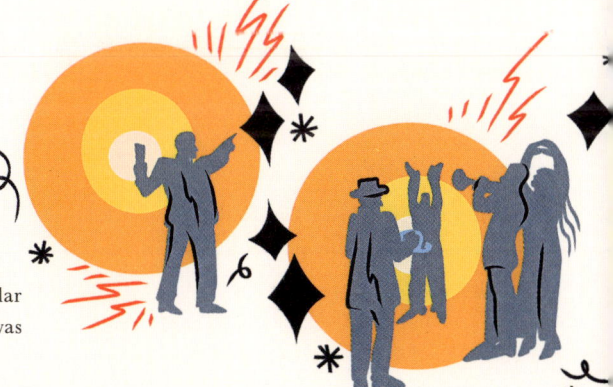

WHAT WAS BAUHAUS?

It was a radical school of art and design established by the architect Walter Gropius in Weimar (later moving to Dessau and Berlin), by combining the Weimar Academy of Fine Art and the School of Arts and Crafts.

Bauhaus

1910s–1930s

GERMANY

WHAT WERE ITS KEY PRINCIPLES?

The Bauhaus wanted to create a society in which all art forms interacted with and informed each other (see page 107 for *Gesamtkunstwerk*), where form followed function – meaning its creations were useful as well as beautiful – and where teachers (called 'masters') lived among and exhibited with the students.

WHY DID IT MOVE TO DESSAU?

After the conservative local government of Weimar got fed up with the Bauhaus' radical young art students (radical young art students are tiresome, to be fair), they demanded that the school put on an exhibition to show what they were doing with their funding; the officials were so unimpressed with what they saw that they slashed the school's grant, forcing it to move.

HOW WAS BAUHAUS DIFFERENT UNDER ITS THREE DIRECTORS?

Gropius set up the conceptual foundations of the Bauhaus, his successor Hannes Meyer was focused on bringing Bauhaus designs to more people on an industrial scale and was considerably more political than Gropius, and Mies van der Rohe kicked out several politically outspoken students and refocused the school on architecture.

WHAT WAS THE *VORKURS*?

The Bauhaus encouraged its students to forget everything they'd been taught before at other arts institutions, and the mandatory six-month *Vorkurs* (foundation course) did away with specialities, giving all students an introduction to a variety of media and theories.

WAS IT TRULY AN EQUAL UTOPIA?

In its first year, women made up fifty-one percent of the Bauhaus student body, which Gropius feared would mean the school would be taken less seriously; also while men could choose their speciality 'workshop' after completing the *Vorkurs*, almost all women were required to enter the weaving workshop.

HOW DID THE LOOMING SECOND WORLD WAR CHANGE THINGS?

In 1932, Nazi politicians in Dessau declared the Bauhaus a Bolshevik, Jewish-led establishment and closed it down, using the building as the local party HQ; the school moved again – to an old telephone factory in Berlin – before van der Rohe closed the Bauhaus in 1933, rather than see it shut down by force.

I GUESS THAT WAS THE END FOR BAUHAUS, THEN?

Due to the closure of the school and the impending war, many key Bauhaus figures (including Gropius, Meyer, and Josef and Anni Albers) moved to the US, helping to spread Bauhaus ideas and aesthetics more widely than if the school had never been closed (yay! maybe…)

HOW DID THEY SMELL?

Johannes Itten, the creator and master of the original *Vorkurs*, was a passionate follower of the Mazdaznan religion, which included a strict vegetarian diet that he also pushed onto his students, leading to the group gaining a reputation that they all stank of garlic.

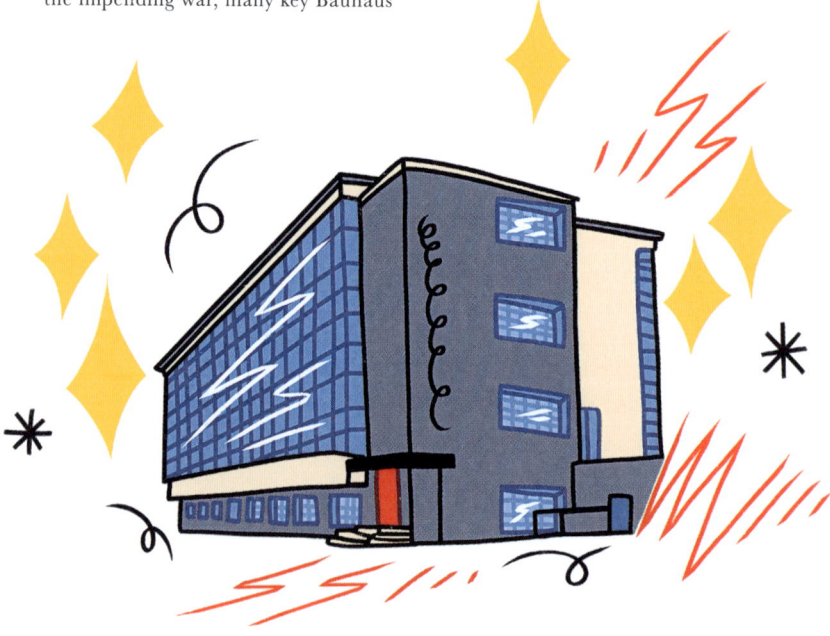

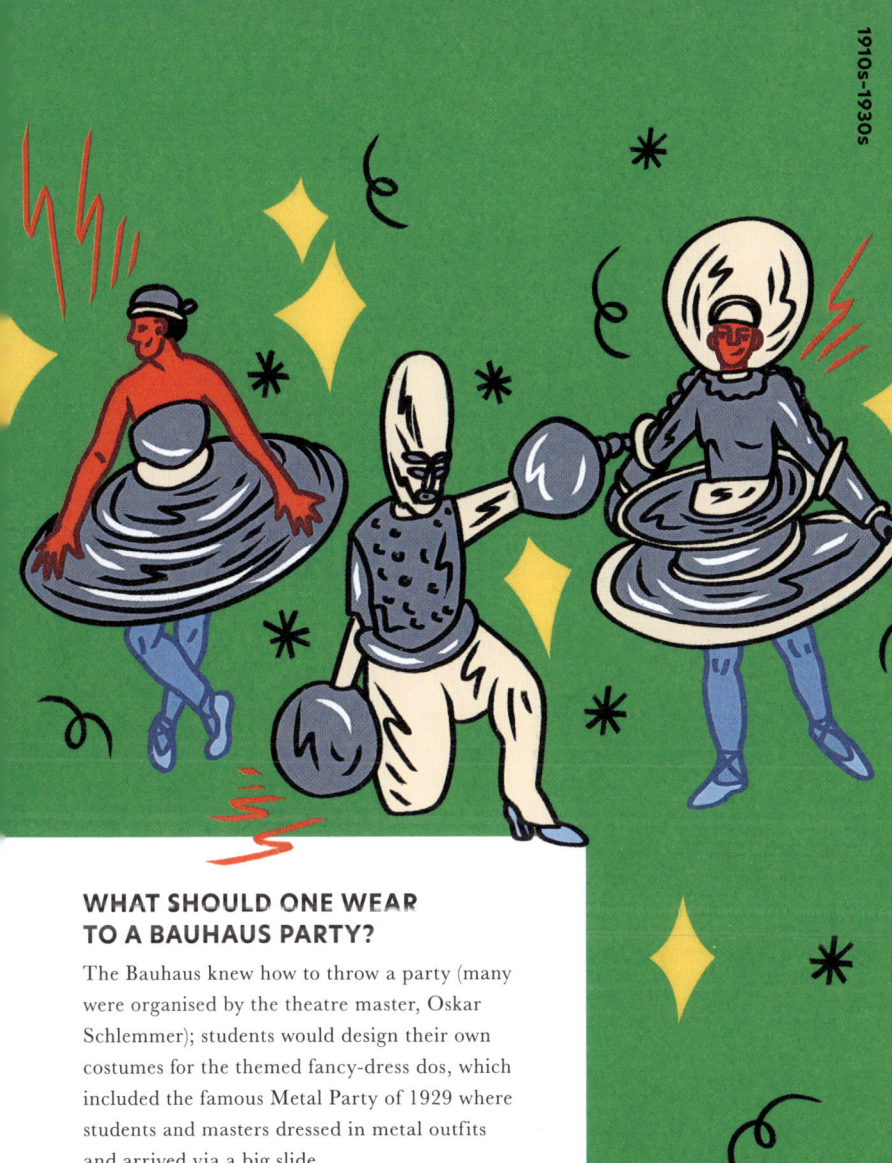

WHAT SHOULD ONE WEAR TO A BAUHAUS PARTY?

The Bauhaus knew how to throw a party (many were organised by the theatre master, Oskar Schlemmer); students would design their own costumes for the themed fancy-dress dos, which included the famous Metal Party of 1929 where students and masters dressed in metal outfits and arrived via a big slide.

3 KEY ARTISTS

Paul Klee (1879-1940)

Swiss-born German artist who taught art theory and was the head of the glass-painting workshop in Weimar and Dessau; tended to be wherever Kandinsky (see page 151) was at the time.

László Moholy-Nagy (1895-1946)

Hungarian painter and photographer invited by Gropius to teach the *Vorkurs* and also headed the metal workshop; key figure in the *Neues Sehen* (New Vision) photography movement, which believed cameras had a unique ability to view the world.

Anni Albers (1899-1994)

German textile artist, initially a reluctant weaving student in Weimar but later head of the workshop in Dessau; after moving to the US, she became a passionate collector of pre-Columbian textiles.

3 KEY ARTWORKS

Joost Schmidt, *Poster for the Bauhaus Exhibition in Weimar* (1923)

Schmidt created several iconic pieces of Bauhaus graphic design, including this poster for their first official exhibition – made two years before he began to teach the lettering course at the school.

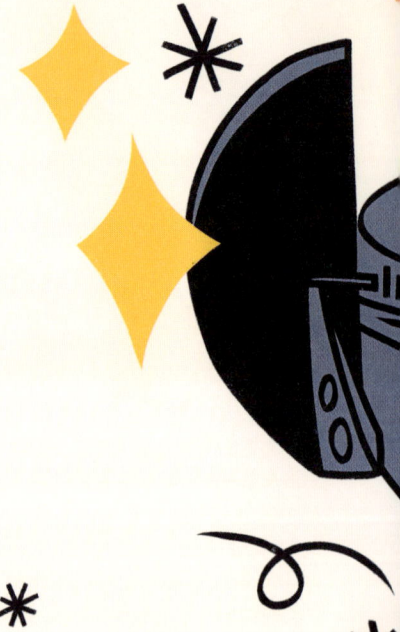

Marianne Brandt,
Tea Infuser (1924)
Brandt was the only woman to
gain a degree at the Bauhaus metal
workshop – which she would later
lead – and she created this tea
infuser at the end of her first year,
(what did **you** achieve by the end
of **your** first year, other than a
terrible situationship?)

Takehiko Mizutani,
Material Study (1927)
One of the very few non-European
Bauhaus students, Japanese artist
Mizutani created this work as part
of the *Vorkurs* run by Josef Albers,
creating an airy, shell-like
composition from brass sheeting.

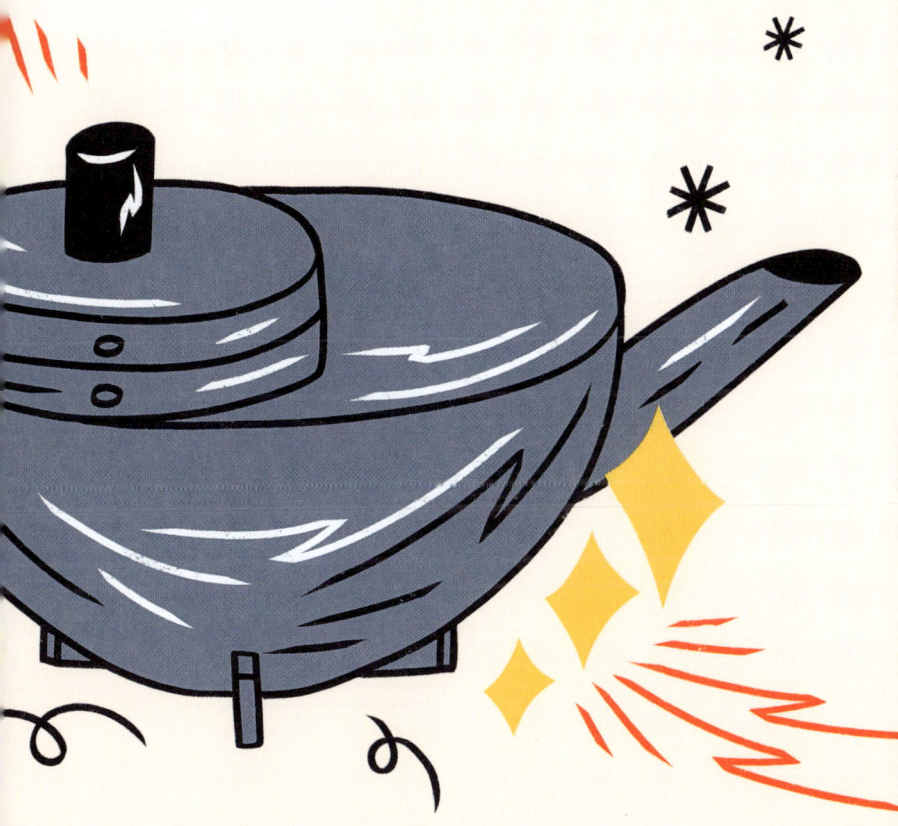

WHAT WAS SURREALISM?

It was an artistic and literary movement that explored the unconscious mind, creating works that have a dreamlike quality (but not always in a fun way).

Surrealism

1920s–1960s

WESTERN EUROPE

WHO CAME UP WITH SURREALISM?

French poet André Breton and French-German poet Yvan Goll wrote rival Surrealist manifestos in 1924, but Breton ultimately won the battle to be considered the founder of Surrealism (even though Goll wrote his a month earlier – life's unfair).

WHY DID SURREALISTS NEED THEIR 40 WINKS?

In his manifesto, Breton described a key belief of 'surreality' (*sur* meaning 'beyond' in French) that the life we lead in our dreams is just as real (if not more real) as the one we experience in our waking lives.

WHY DID SURREALISM OCCUR WHEN IT DID?

Like Dada (see page 164), of which Breton was one of the original members, Surrealism came as people were trying to deal with the trauma and horror of the First World War, leaning into absurdity as a reaction against the 'rationality' that they saw as leading to devastation in Europe.

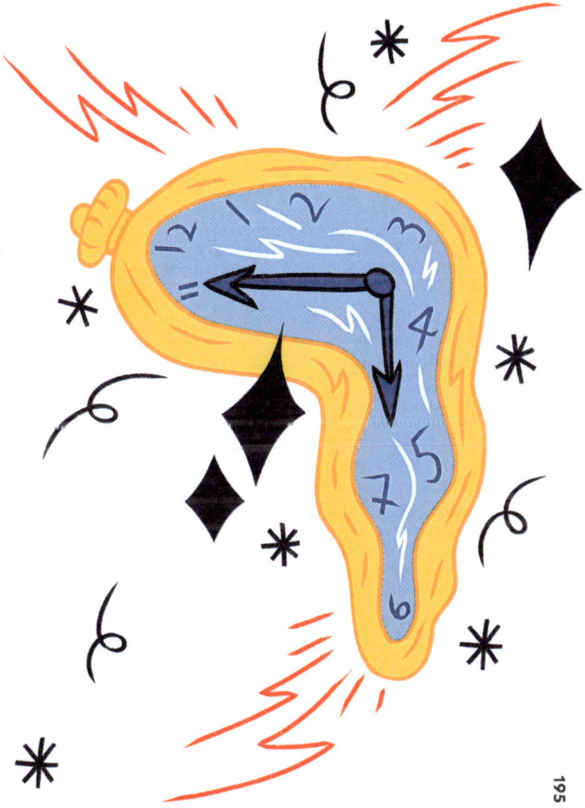

WHAT WAS AUTOMATISM?

It was the Surrealists' idea that they could better access what was going on in their unconscious mind by drawing and writing without any set plan and letting their hands move across the page without thought, an idea first developed by Austrian psychoanalyst Sigmund Freud.

WERE THEY INTO FREUD?

In his 1900 book *The Interpretation of Dreams*, Freud posited that dreams were the expression of things buried in our unconscious, revealing our deepest desires, fears and thoughts; the Surrealists longed to tap into these hidden layers of our minds, and saw Freud as a kind of patron saint.

OH, SO FREUD AND THE SURREALISTS GOT ON, THEN?

Freud was initially incredibly sceptical about the Surrealists, but was quite impressed by Salvador Dalí when he met him in 1939, although the young Spanish artist thought the meeting had gone terribly, writing that Freud hadn't paid any attention to the magazine he had brought to show him (never meet your heroes, kids).

WHY DID IT COME TO AN END?

Some put the end of Surrealism at 1947 with the Surrealism retrospective at Paris' Galerie Maeght, while other say it lasted until 1966 when Breton died, but in either case, Surrealism's darling Dalí was already long gone, having been expelled in 1939 for his political fascination with Hitler.

WAS FRIDA KAHLO A SURREALIST?

The Mexican artist has been on-and-off categorised as a Surrealist for almost 100 years but she couldn't stand the French Surrealists, seeing them as pretentious 'artistic bitches' who did nothing but warm their arses in cafés, banging on about their theories.

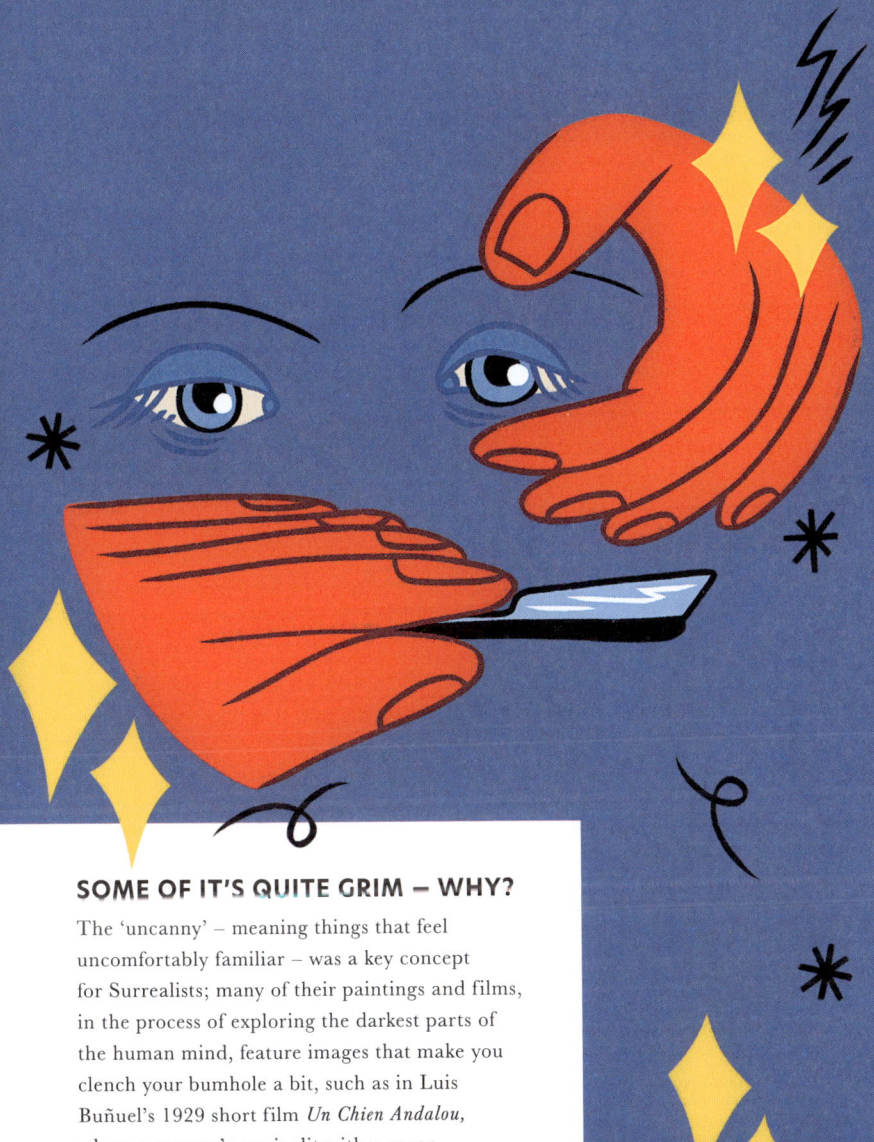

SOME OF IT'S QUITE GRIM – WHY?

The 'uncanny' – meaning things that feel
uncomfortably familiar – was a key concept
for Surrealists; many of their paintings and films,
in the process of exploring the darkest parts of
the human mind, feature images that make you
clench your bumhole a bit, such as in Luis
Buñuel's 1929 short film *Un Chien Andalou*,
where a woman's eye is slit with a razor.

3 KEY ARTISTS

Max Ernst (1891–1976)

French painter, previously Dada, he was romantically associated with three of Surrealism's key women – Peggy Guggenheim, Dorothea Tanning and Leonora Carrington.

Yves Tanguy (1900–1955)

Self-taught French painter, inspired by proto-Surrealist Giorgio de Chirico, whose work he saw in a gallery as he passed by in a bus; commissioned by Breton to create twelve artworks (but cashed in and only did eight – whoops).

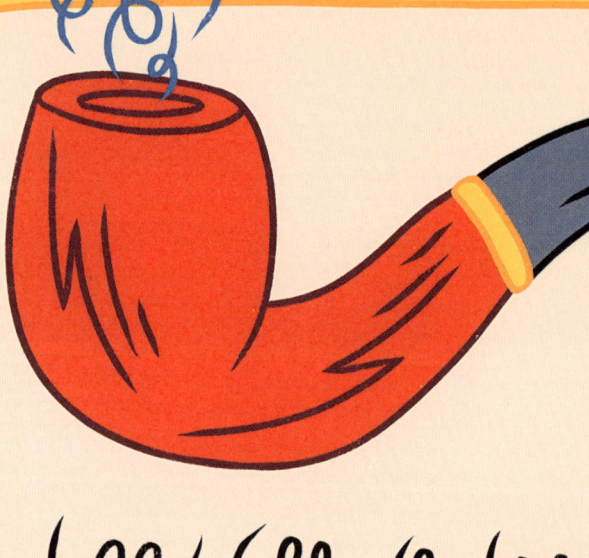

Dora Maar (1907-1997)
French photographer and artist, major influence on (but overshadowed by) her boyfriend Picasso; collaged photos together seamlessly to create Surrealist combos for magazine adverts.

3 KEY ARTWORKS

René Magritte, *The Treachery of Images* (1929)
Reminding us of the inherent deception of all images, yes, it's a picture of a pipe, but it's not an *actual* pipe, hence its inscription, '*Ceci n'est pas une pipe*' ('This is not a pipe').

Salvador Dalí, *The Persistence of Memory* (1931)
This painting is filled with symbols that come up frequently in Dalí's works including ants as symbols of decay, inspired by the time, as a child, Dalí saw a half-dead bat crawling with the little bastards.

Meret Oppenheim, *Object* (1936)
By covering a teacup, saucer and teaspoon with fur, Oppenheim created a work of art that is both deeply uncomfortable to view (can you imagine having to drink out of that?) and erotically charged (what else is covered in hair that you might put your lips to?)

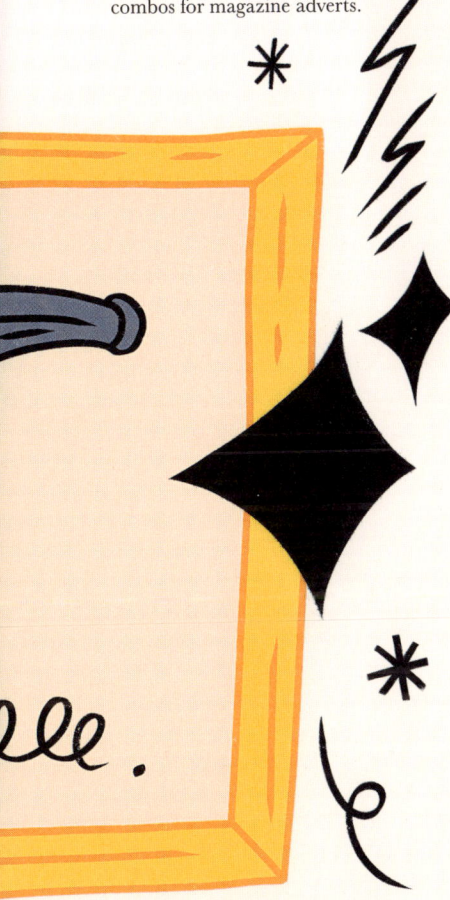

**WHAT WAS
AMERICAN SCENE
PAINTING?**

It was an umbrella term for
two styles – Social Realism
and American Regionalism
– that captured a distinct
American-ness following the
Great Depression of 1929.

American Scene Painting

1930s–1940s

US

WHAT WAS REGIONALISM?

Regionalist art focused on scenes and figures from the rural American Midwest and South.

WHAT WAS IT INSPIRED BY?

City life had been the inspiration for artists for a generation, but Regionalist artists turned their attention to their own rural areas, and rather than looking to European modernists for style inspiration, they drew more on conservative Academic traditions.

WHAT WAS SOCIAL REALISM?

Social Realist art attempted to document American life through realist paintings and documentary photography.

WHAT WAS IT INSPIRED BY?

The Social Realists were heavily influenced by the Mexican Muralists of the 1910s, who made government-funded public artworks following the Mexican Revolution, creating murals celebrating the honourable toil of the modern working classes.

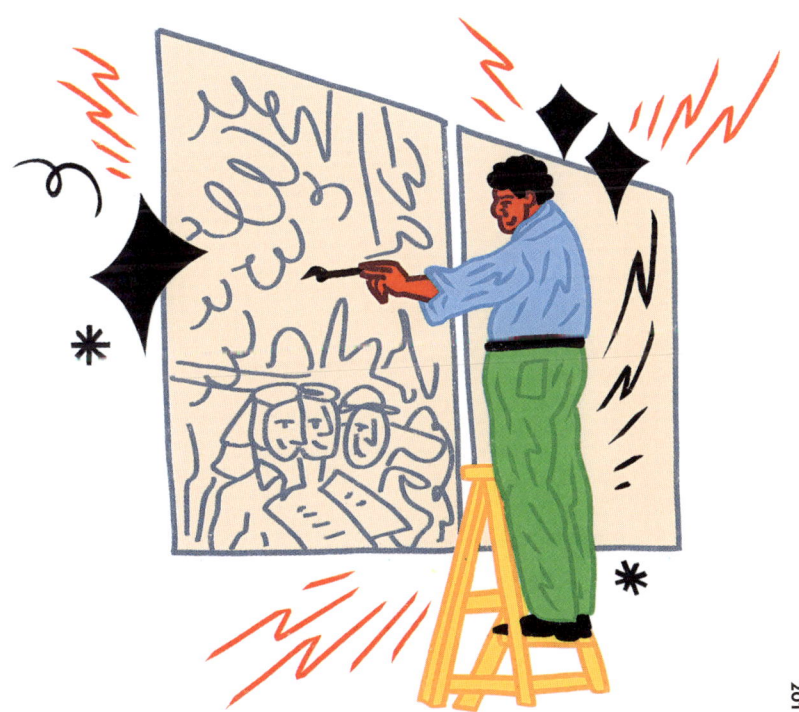

HOW WAS IT DIFFERENT FROM SOCIALIST REALISM?

While both Social Realism and Socialist Realism (see page 204) claimed to be capturing the spirit of their nation, Social Realism was able to criticise the US in a way that would have, well, ended badly for a Socialist Realist artist.

WHAT WAS THE NEW DEAL?

It was a set of initiatives created by President Franklin D. Roosevelt in 1933 in response to the Great Depression, which included several public programmes that employed American Scene artists.

HOW COULD I FIND OUT WHERE GRANT WOOD WAS?

A busy man, Grant Wood installed a moveable dial on the door of his studio to let people know his whereabouts, with options including 'Taking a Bath' and 'Having a Party'.

CAN A PAINTING BE TOO AMERICAN?

Norman Rockwell's *Freedom from Want* (1943), which shows a family sitting down to Thanksgiving dinner (massive turkey, uncomfortably intense eye contact between family members, you know the drill) was inspired by a speech by the US President, but many Europeans found the design distastefully opulent while they were suffering wartime shortages.

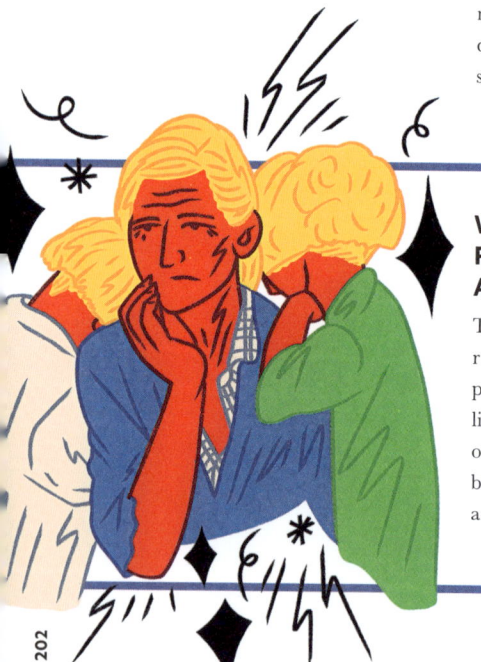

WHAT WAS THE FARM SECURITY ADMINISTRATION?

The FSA was created to tackle rural poverty and employed photographers to document the lives of impoverished farm workers; one such photo, *Migrant Mother*, by Dorthea Lange, has become an iconic American image.

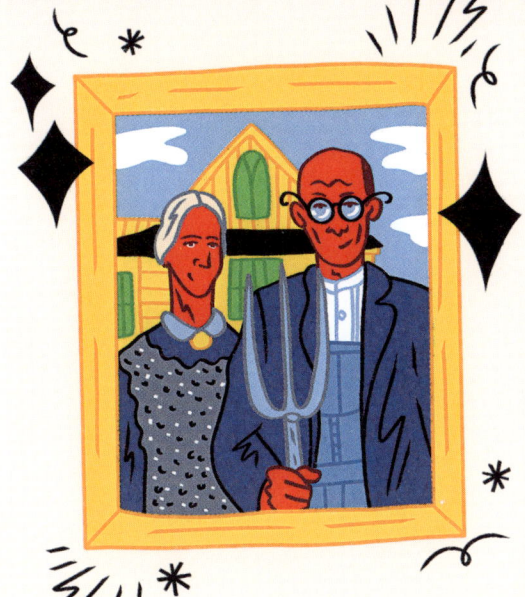

3 KEY ARTISTS

Thomas Hart Benton (1889–1975)

American artist, Regionalist painter of controversial murals, and *TIME* magazine cover boy.

John Steuart Curry (1897–1946)

American Regionalist painter of Kansan scenes who didn't always go down well with Kansans.

Ben Shahn (1898–1969)

Lithuanian-born American Social Realist painter of scenes of oppression and injustice, pals with Diego Rivera (of the Mexican Muralists).

3 KEY ARTWORKS

Grant Wood, *American Gothic* (1930)

Wood used his sister and his dentist as models for the farmer and his daughter in *American Gothic,* which Wood was inspired to paint after seeing the farmhouse in the painting (still standing today) in Iowa.

Edward Hopper, *Nighthawks* (1942)

Considered an American Realist (and, at a push, a Regionalist who preferred the city to the countryside), Hopper and his wife Josephine modelled for *Nighthawks*, which may have taken its title from the beak-like nose of the bloke with the cigarette.

Andrew Wyeth, *Christina's World* (1948)

Wyeth's inspiration came from watching a disabled woman, Anna Christina Olson, pull herself through a field near her home in Maine, although he used his much younger wife, Betsy, as the model.

WHAT WAS
SOCIALIST REALISM?

It was the state-sanctioned
artistic style of the USSR
from the 1930s through to
the late 1980s (with its
beginnings in the 1920s,
following the 1917 Russian
Revolution), which created
artwork celebrating Soviet
socialist living.

Socialist
Realism
1930s–1980s

RUSSIA

WHAT WERE THE KEY PRINCIPLES?

Socialist Realist work was meant to tick certain boxes, including *narodnost* (nationalistic), *partiinost* (in line with Communist party ideology), *dostupnost* (accessible for all audiences), *opora na klassiku* (inspired by classical traditions), *klassovost* (speaks to class issues) and *pravdivost* (truthful).

WHAT SORT OF THINGS WERE BEING MADE?

Socialist Realist artists painted USSR landscapes and scenes from 'typical' Soviet life – healthy, hard-working people, all very smiley, all very not-showing-atrocities-y.

BUT RUSSIA WAS ALREADY HAVING A GREAT RUN WITH AVANT-GARDE ART; WHY WASN'T THAT ENOUGH?

With Suprematism (see page 170) and Constructivism (see page 174) Russia was at the cutting edge of modern art, but by the 1930s this art was seen by party leaders as elitist, even though those artists had been trying to create artwork for everyone (albeit in quite a headache-inducing, tricky, abstract way).

WHAT HAPPENED TO MODERNIST SOVIET ART?

Multiple avant-garde groups had been flourishing in Russia, and for a while after the Revolution they were allowed to continue their abstract art practices as long as they weren't actively anti-government; but in 1932, the Union of Arts – making only Socialist Realist works – was made the sole state-approved arts organisation.

WHAT HAPPENS WHEN BOY MEETS TRACTOR?

'Boy meets girl meets tractor' was a generalisation made about Socialist Realist artwork, literature and film plots, because loads of the storylines were about patriotic young people patriotically pairing up in between shots of people patriotically ploughing.

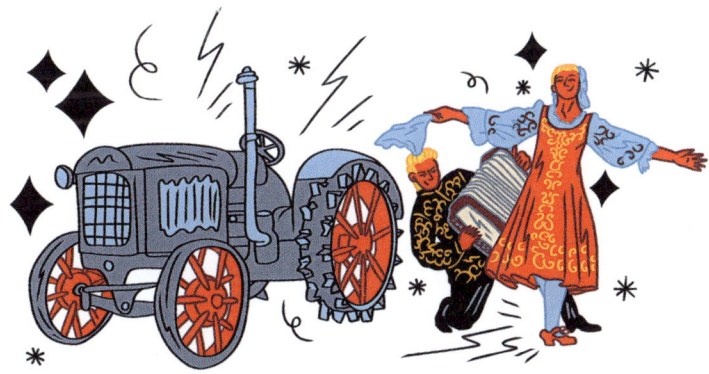

WHAT WAS THE BULLDOZER EXHIBITION?

It was a protest exhibition organised in 1974 by underground artists in a forest outside Moscow, which was violently shut down – artworks were destroyed with water cannons and bulldozers and artists were beaten and arrested.

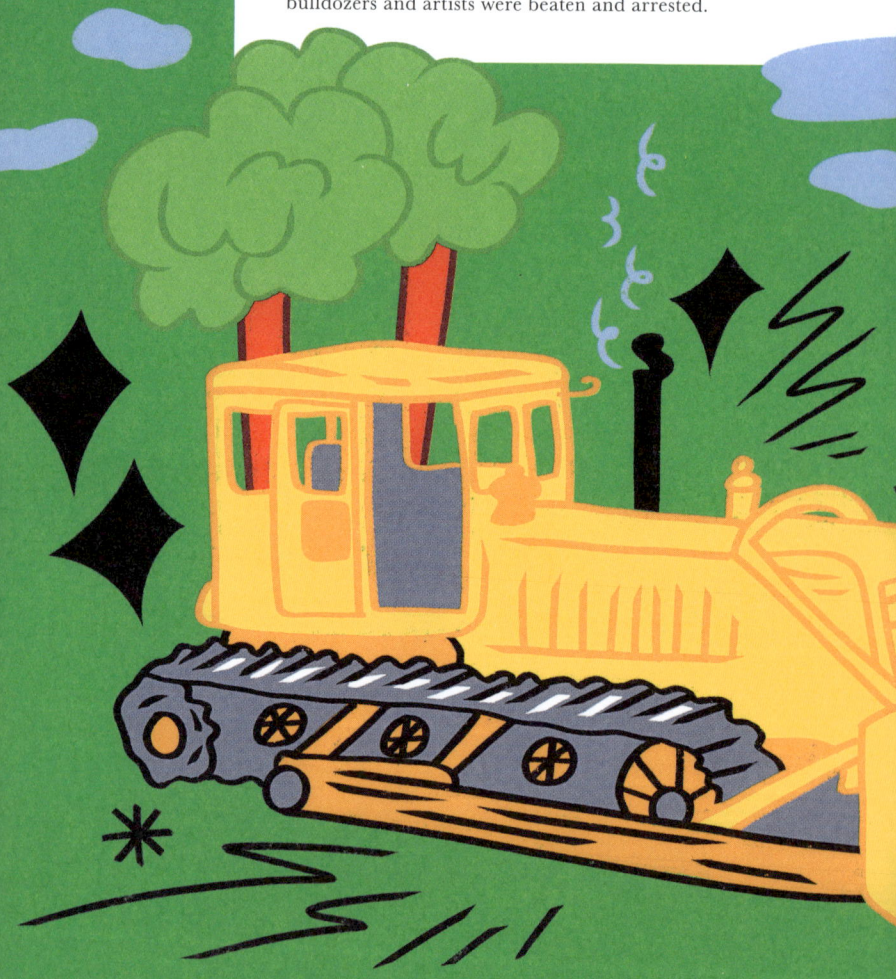

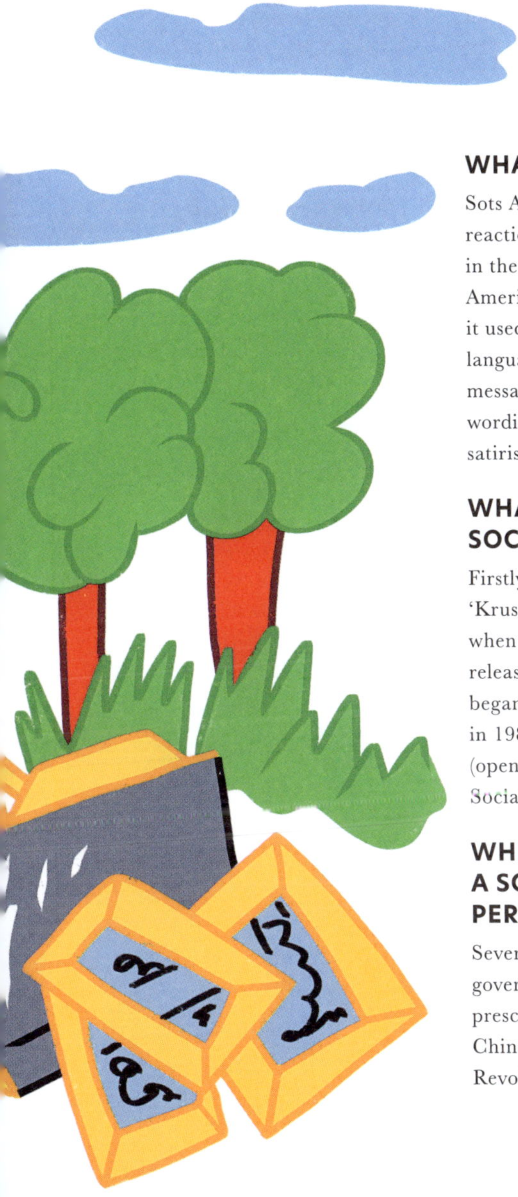

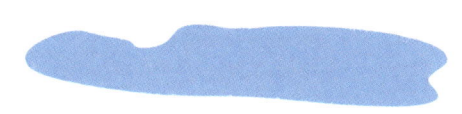

WHAT WAS SOTS ART?

Sots Art (Soviet Pop Art) was a
reaction against Socialist Realism
in the 1970s, and like British and
American Pop Art (see page 228),
it used bright colours and the visual
language of advertising to get across
messages, adopting the imagery and
wording of Soviet propaganda to
satirise Communist rule.

WHAT LOOSENED SOCIALIST REALISM'S GRIP?

Firstly, there was the short-lived
'Kruschev's Thaw' in the 50s and 60s,
when several imprisoned artists were
released and international artists
began to be exhibited again; then
in 1989, the new policy of *Glasnost*
(openness) permanently ended
Socialist Realism's monopoly.

WHERE ELSE HAD A SOCIALIST REALIST PERIOD?

Several countries with communist
governments have had similar, heavily
prescribed art movements, including
China, which called its version
Revolutionary Realism.

3 KEY ARTISTS

Aleksandr Gerasimov (1881-1963)
Russian painter and political hack who, unlike other artists, hadn't previously dabbled in abstraction so was a Socialist Realist poster boy.

Isaak Brodsky (1884-1939)
Ukrainian-born painter and head of the Russian Academy of Arts, whose flat was made into a national museum after his death.

Vera Mukhina (1889-1953)
Latvian-born sculptor, she created one of the world's first welded sculptures, *Worker and Kolkhoz Woman,* for the 1937 Paris International Exhibition (it's massive) and had a crater on Venus named after her.

3 KEY ARTWORKS

Aleksandr Deineka,
***Female Textile Workers* (1927)**
An early Socialist Realist painting with echoes of earlier geometrical abstract art in the pattern made by the rows of cylinders, Deineka presented new Russian factories as sleek and progressive.

Yuri I. Pimenov, *New Moscow* (1937)
In the 1930s, Pimenov destroyed many of his early artworks (including some that were already purchased by institutions) to ensure that all his existing work was in his new Socialist Realist style; this one depicts the cosmopolitan streets and vehicles of Moscow in an aspirational, utopian light.

Yuri M. Neprintsev, *A Rest after Battle* (1951)
Having fought in the Red Army during the Second World War, many of Neprintsev's paintings showed the Soviet military as a place of brotherly unity, and one version of *A Rest after Battle* was gifted to China's leader, Mao Zedong, in 1953.

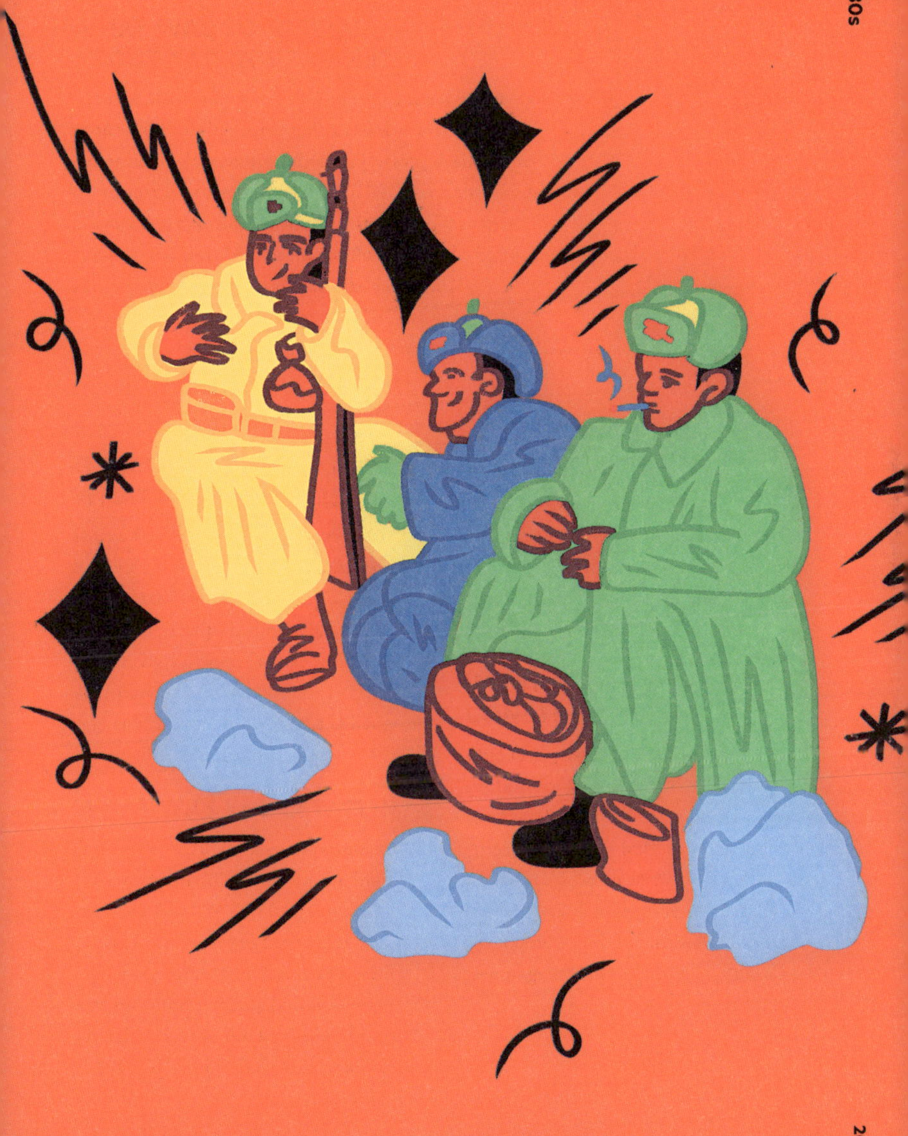

WHAT WAS THE ST IVES SCHOOL?

It wasn't an actual school (although there is also an actual school) but rather a term used for artists working in the Cornish town of St Ives during the mid-twentieth century.

St Ives School

1930s–1960s

BRITAIN

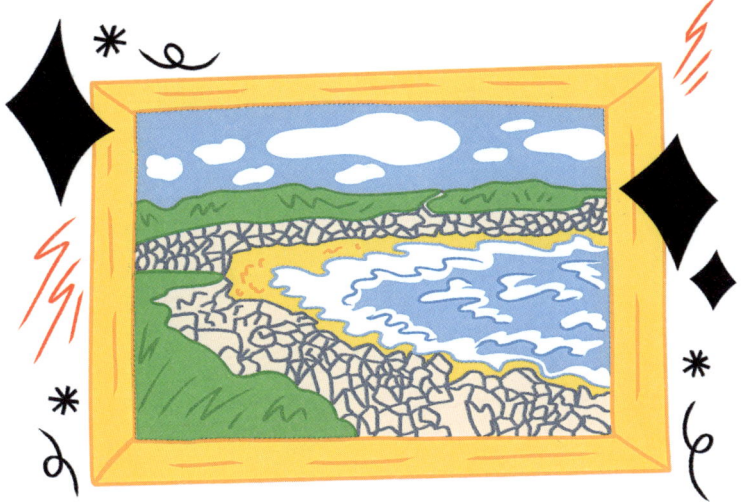

WHY ST IVES?

St Ives is beautiful but bloody ages away from most places in Britain, so when the first railway line opened there in 1877, artists began to flock to the town to enjoy its dramatic coastlines and incredible light caused by reflections off the sea.

WHAT SORT OF THING WERE THESE ARTISTS CREATING?

Artists in St Ives didn't necessarily share a style, and they each experimented with different levels of abstraction, but they all drew inspiration from the Cornish landscape and the people around them who were working in the fishing industry.

WHAT ELSE WAS HAPPENING IN ST IVES?

In 1920 the newly established St Ives Handcraft Guild invited Bernard Leach to become the Guild's potter; along with his friend Shōji Hamada, he set up the Leach Pottery, which boasted the very first Japanese *Noborigama* kiln in the West.

WHAT WAS A DRAWBACK OF ST IVES?

St Ives is notorious for narrow, winding lanes, and there are brilliant photos of Barbara Hepworth's *Winged Figure* – a 19-foot long sculpture – being manoeuvred through the town in 1962 on its way to London to be installed on the side of the new John Lewis building on Oxford Street (where it still is).

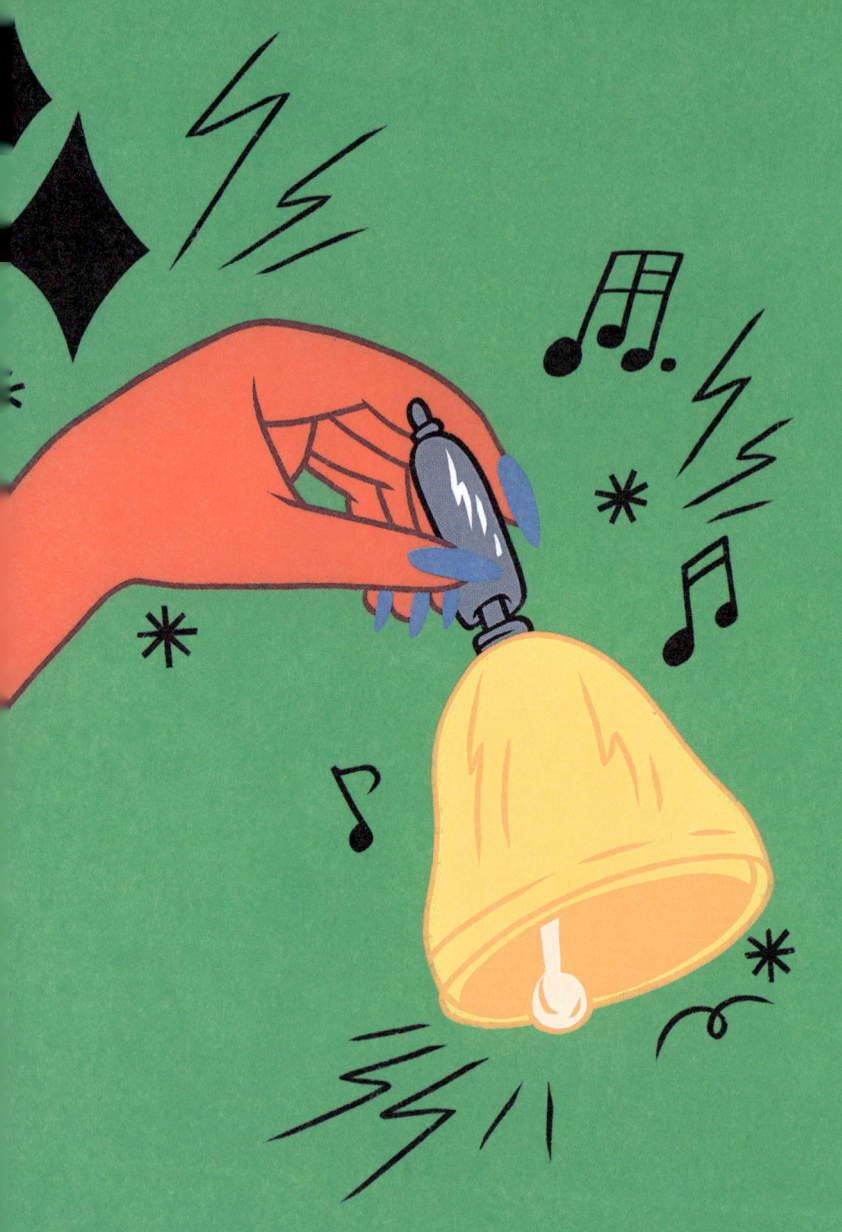

JUST HOW ARTY WAS IT?

St Ives isn't very big, but it was home to a **lot** of arts organisations including the St Ives Society of Artists (formed 1927), St Ives School of Painting (opened 1938), the Crypt Group (1947) and the Penwith Society of Artists (1949), as well as dozens of artists' studios.

WHAT DID HAMPSTEAD HAVE TO DO WITH ST IVES, 300 MILES AWAY?

Two of the most famous St Ives artists, Barbara Hepworth and Ben Nicholson, lived in Hampstead before moving to Cornwall during the Second World War and the inspirational London neighbourhood was also home to major artistic names, including art historian Ernst Gombrich, Bauhaus founder Walter Gropius, sculptor Henry Moore, *De Stijl* leader Piet Mondrian and the Constructivist Naum Gabo.

WHO HITCHED A RIDE?

At the start of the war, Hepworth and Nicholson drove to Cornwall together with Gabo and they apparently offered Mondrian a lift, but he turned them down because he didn't really like the countryside.

WHY IS IT NOT A GOOD IDEA TO TAKE CAREER ADVICE FROM POSH BOYS FROM LONDON?

In 1928 on a visit to St Ives, Nicholson and Christopher 'Kit' Wood (young cosmopolitan types) saw 77-year-old ex-fisherman Alfred Wallis painting at his kitchen table and encouraged him to try to sell his works in London; Wallis eventually found it all too much and spiralled into despair and poverty, ending up in the poorhouse.

WHAT SHOULD YOU DO WHEN BARBARA HEPWORTH RINGS A BELL?

Hepworth gained a local reputation as the 'Witch of St Ives' for her notoriously strict approach, ringing a bell to have her assistants hide away in the presence of guests, which on one occasion led the artist Terry Frost to have to wee in a plant pot while trapped in her garden studio.

3 KEY ARTISTS

Alfred Wallis (1855–1942)

English artist who used non-art materials like cardboard scraps and paint left over from the boatbuilding industry; rumoured to be the first person to sell pink ice cream in St Ives.

Ben Nicholson (1894–1982)

English artist and husband of two major artists, Winifred Nicholson and Barbara Hepworth (not at the same time); big sports fan who likened golf skills to those needed by artists.

Wilhelmina Barns-Graham (1912–2004)

Scottish artist, one of the 'second generation' St Ives artists after arriving with her friend from Edinburgh College of Art Margaret Mellis; disliked the competitive vibes in St Ives.

3 KEY ARTWORKS

Christopher 'Kit' Wood, *Cornish Fishermen, the Quay, St Ives* (1928)

A uniquely talented but troubled artist (hooked on opium, he spent a short time in Paris before alienating himself from some major contacts), Wood moved to Cornwall for fresh inspiration from fishing communities, which he captured in this work.

Barbara Hepworth, *Pelagos* (1946)

Taking its name from the Greek word for 'sea', Hepworth's elm and oak sculpture might appear to be totally abstract, but is actually an interpretation of St Ives' curving bay.

Peter Lanyon, *Porthleven* (1951)

Being **actually Cornish** was key to Lanyon's identity and he is best known for his abstracted coastal landscapes, like this one of Porthleven, including its famous (okay, not 'famous', but you might know it if you're Cornish) (okay, you'd know it if you were specifically from Porthleven) clock tower.

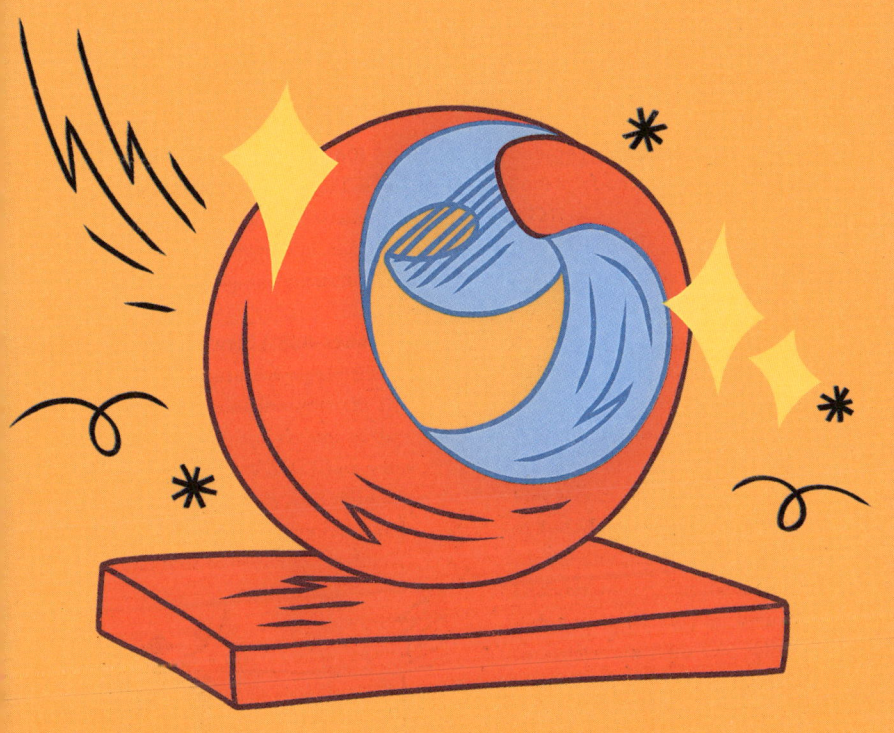

WHAT WAS *ART BRUT*?

Also known as Outsider Art, *Art Brut* is a term used for works created by those who exist outside of the traditional art world, including self-taught artists, psychiatric patients, prisoners, children and people who might not otherwise class themselves as artists.

Art Brut /
Outsider Art

1940s–1970s

INTERNATIONAL

WHY 'BRUT'?

Art Brut, meaning 'raw art', was named in 1945 by the artist Jean Dubuffet, and he saw it as in opposition to *art culturel* – art that had been born out of establishment art systems and mainstream culture.

WHAT WAS THE *COMPAGNIE DE L'ART BRUT*?

Together with André Breton (see page 195) and other writers, Dubuffet founded the group in 1948 as a way to scout out and showcase *Art Brut,* but he disbanded it four years later because no one else was doing any work (that's writers for you).

WHAT'S OUTSIDER ART'S CORE MESSAGE?

Outsider Art stands for the belief that artistic expression should not be the sole domain of formally trained artists using traditionally accepted art materials, and that these people don't have the monopoly on creating interesting and impactful work.

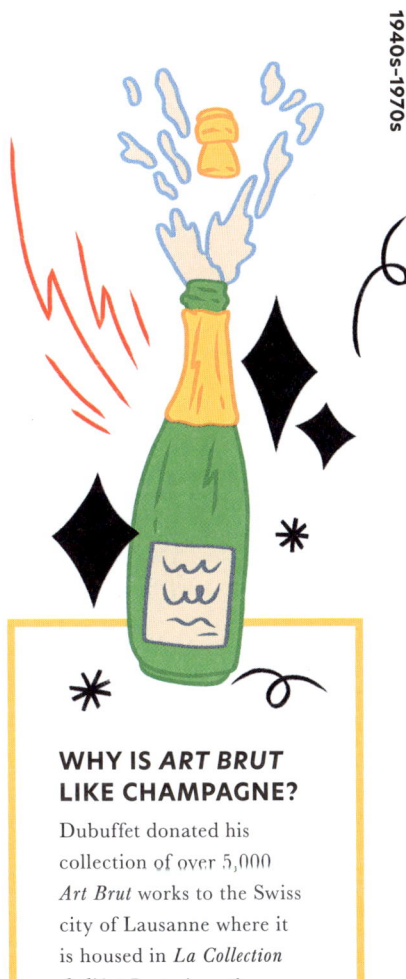

WHY IS *ART BRUT* LIKE CHAMPAGNE?

Dubuffet donated his collection of over 5,000 *Art Brut* works to the Swiss city of Lausanne where it is housed in *La Collection de l'Art Brut*; since then, technically only artworks in that collection can be called *Art Brut*, otherwise it's just sparkling Outsider Art.

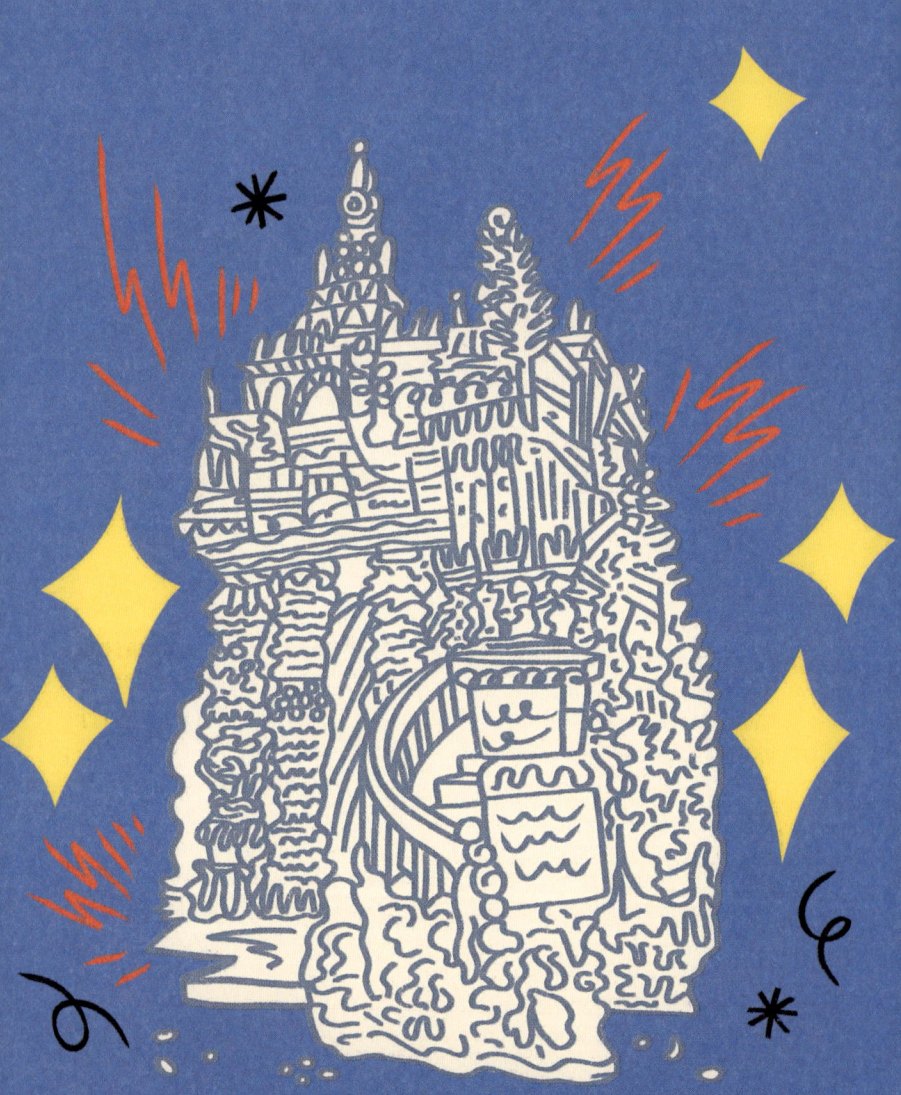

WHAT IS NAÏVE ART?

Naïve Art, *Art Brut* and Outsider Art all overlap, and Naïve Art is artwork that is simply and imperfectly executed (often described as childlike) but with more of an interaction with the traditional art world.

WHAT IS PRIMITIVISM?

Some Outsider and Naïve Art has historically been labelled 'primitive' – especially when the artist is from a Non-Western society – and when Western artists have intentionally mirrored this aesthetic (often in a voyeuristic, colonialist way) it has been called Primitivism.

WHAT IS *HORROR VACUI*?

Taken from the Latin for 'a fear of empty spaces', it's a quality often seen in Outsider Art, where the entire surface area is filled with tiny details, leaving no gaps.

WHERE IS THE GARDEN OF EDEN?

It's in Kansas: *The Garden of Eden*, a cabin made of stone in the town of Lucas and surrounded by over 150 cement sculptures sitting on 40-foot concrete trees, was created over a twenty-two year period by American Civil War veteran S. P. Dinsmoor.

WHAT WAS THE IDEAL PALACE?

Begun in 1879, it is a stone building created in Hauterives, France, by the local postman, Ferdinand Cheval, who worked on it (mostly at night) for thirty-three years, followed by another eight years making his own mausoleum, because a new law meant he couldn't be buried under his beloved Palace.

3 KEY ARTISTS

Adolf Wölfli (1864-1930)

Swiss artist who began drawing as a patient at Bern's Waldau psychiatric hospital, his work incorporated musical notation that looked made-up but which he actually played on a trumpet he'd made out of paper.

Jean Dubuffet (1901-1985)

French artist and founder of *Art Brut* even though he wasn't much of an outsider himself (he studied at Paris' prestigious Académie Julian); was on-again off-again with art, working as a wine merchant into his forties.

Judith Scott (1943-2005)

American sculptor who was born with Down's syndrome and became deaf as a baby; her prolific textile career – creating sculptures cocooned in colourful yarn – was supported through the Creative Growth Art Center in Oakland, California, which she joined in her forties.

3 KEY ARTWORKS

Abbot Fouré, *The Sculpted Rocks of Rothéneuf* (c.1894-1907)

A set of over 300 figurative sculptures carved directly into the rocks of the Brittany coast, the work was created by a local priest after he began to isolate himself from society, following a stroke.

Madge Gill, *Staircases* (c.1920-1960)

Filled with faces and patterns, this drawing is typical of the work of prolific self-taught artist Gill, who believed she was guided by a spirit called Myrninerest – and who never sold any works, in order to keep the spirit happy.

Aloïse Blanche Corbaz, *Napoléon III à Cherbourg* (1952-1954)

Corbaz's work, created at the Cery-sur-Lausanne asylum, often showed beautiful, semi-clad women with men in military uniforms, possibly inspired by the love affair she imagined that she was having with Kaiser Wilhelm II (which led to her diagnosis of schizophrenia).

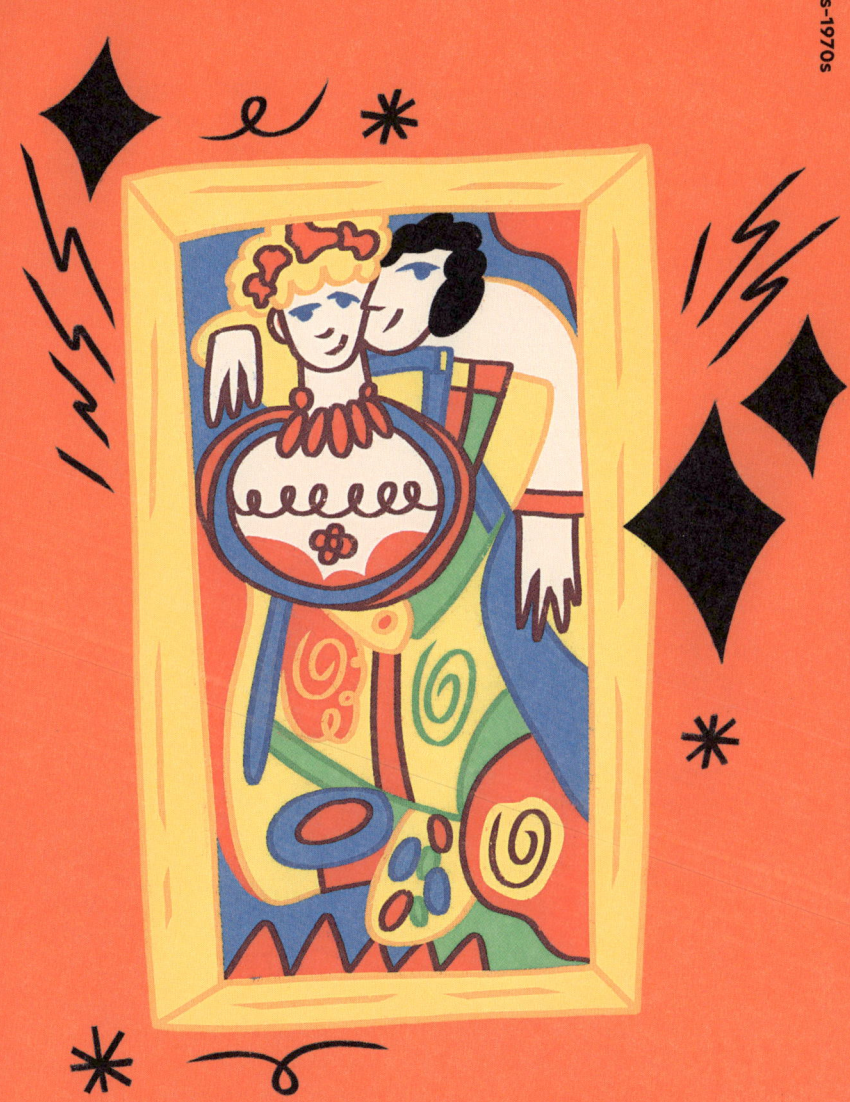

WHAT WAS ABSTRACT EXPRESSIONISM?

Abstract Expressionists wanted to (abstractly) express inner feelings through their artworks, finding new ways to create marks on their (often seriously big) canvases.

Abstract Expressionism

1940s–1950s

US

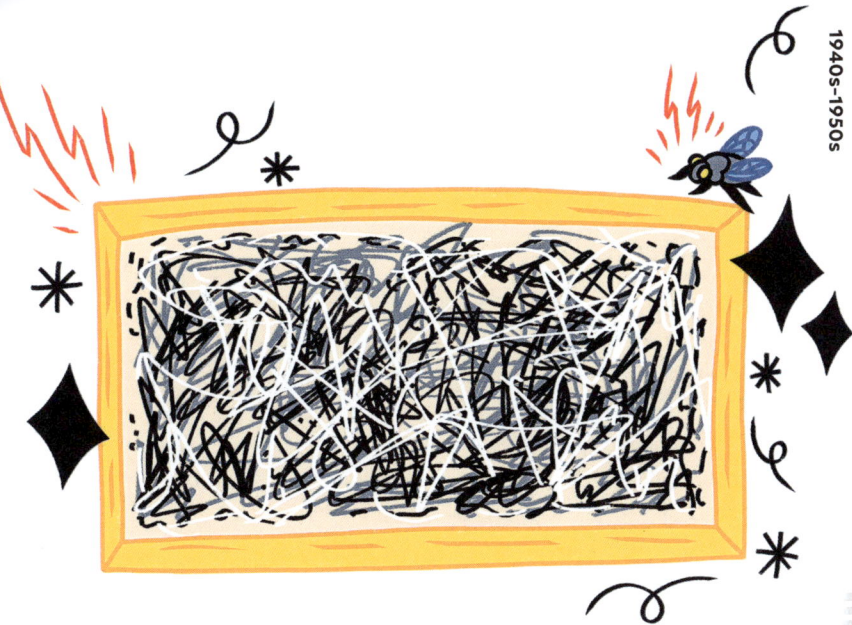

WHAT WERE THEY INSPIRED BY?

As well as the Automatism of the Surrealists (see page 194) and the improvisations of jazz music that inspired many AbEx artists, Jackson Pollock was influenced by the sand painting of Navajo artists, and Robert Motherwell drew inspiration from the traditional calligraphy of the Far East.

IN WHAT WAY WAS IT EXPRESSIONIST?

Like the Expressionist (see page 118) artists before them, the Abstract Expressionists were all about sensation and feeling, but this time they were set on pretty much entirely doing away with representations of the outer world, focused entirely on the inner world of the artist.

HOW DID THE CIA HELP TO PUT IT ON THE MAP?

Abstract Expressionism was devoted to freedom of expression, which was right up the US establishment's alley with their whole 'Land of the Free' thing, so the government, via the CIA, created the Congress for Cultural Freedom in 1950, which promoted the movement internationally (and wasn't revealed as a CIA intervention until 1966).

WHAT ARE COLOUR FIELD PAINTINGS?

One of the two 'branches' of Abstract Expressionism, the term 'colour field' was coined by the critic Clement Greenberg in 1970 to describe the work of Mark Rothko, Clyfford Still and Barnett Newman, who were using areas of flat (pure and unbroken) colour in their compositions.

WHAT IS ACTION PAINTING?

The second 'branch' of AbEx, sometimes called Gestural Abstraction; the term 'Action Painting' was first used by art critic Harold Rosenberg in 1952 to describe how artists like Jackson Pollock used the active, energetic force of their bodies to create bold marks on their canvas.

HOW DID ABEX DIFFER FROM MINIMALISM?

Minimalism (see page 238) aimed to reduce art to its most basic form and get rid of any emotional trace of an artist having been involved at all, whereas Abstract Expressionists – some of whom also created work deemed Minimalist – created wilder works with emotional expression at their core.

WHY ARE SO MANY WORKS UNTITLED?

By keeping an artwork untitled (or giving it an abstract title like *Zone, Red Painting* or *Last Piece,* all by Philip Guston) artists withheld their own interpretation of what viewers were meant to be seeing or feeling, handing power to viewers to make their own emotional connections.

WHERE COULD YOU HANG OUT IF YOU WANTED TO BUMP INTO AN ABSTRACT EXPRESSIONIST OR TWO?

The Cedar Tavern, a bar near Robert Motherwell's Greenwich Village studio, was a favourite haunt of the AbEx artists, although Pollock got himself banned for breaking the toilet door and throwing it at Franz Kline.

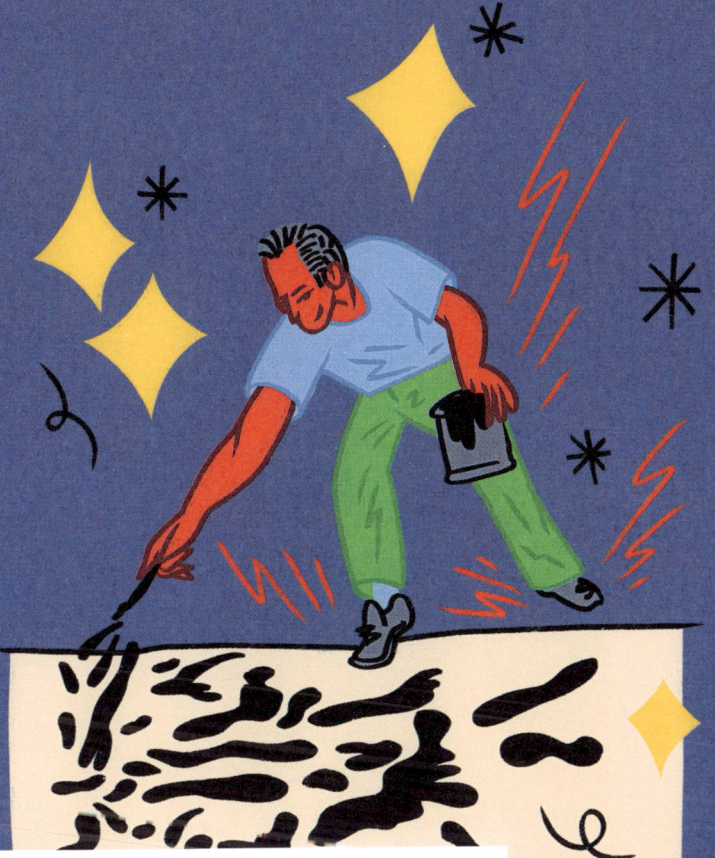

WHY DID JACKSON POLLOCK PUT HIS CANVASES ON THE FLOOR?

Pollock created work using his 'drip' method, flinging paint onto his canvas, which he laid on the ground in order to be able to walk all the way around it and to help him to feel like he was part of the painting itself.

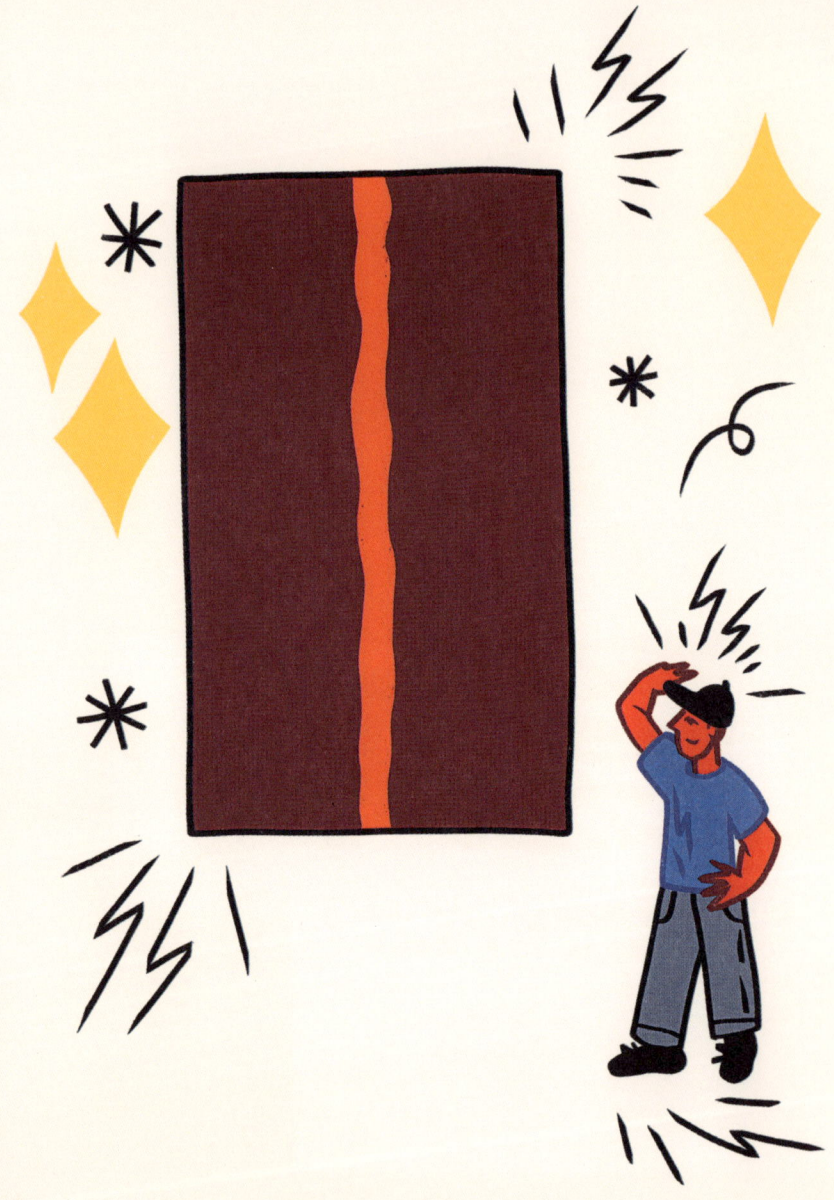

3 KEY ARTISTS

Mark Rothko (1903-1970)

Latvian-born American painter who paused making paintings for a year in order to properly study Freud (God, everyone loves Freud in this book, don't they?); he created a recipe for art which included the ingredients irony, hope and a preoccupation with death (mmm, delicious...)

Willem de Kooning (1904-1997)

Dutch-American painter who dropped out of school and stowed away on a ship to come to the US, he was uncomfortable with the 'Abstract Expressionist' label.

Lee Krasner (1908-1984)

American painter, employed by the Roosevelt administration to create public murals; historically overshadowed by her husband Jackson Pollock although she may have created 'allover' paintings (canvases entirely covered by abstract marks) before he did.

3 KEY ARTWORKS

Barnett Newman, *Onement III* (1949)

Newman's *Onement* paintings feature a 'zip' (a vertical line through the composition), which both divides and joins the space; this and his later, even larger works give a sense of the Sublime (see page 51) when viewed up-close because they seem to almost swallow you up.

Jackson Pollock, *One: Number 31* (1950)

Made using household- and industrial paints, Pollock created with such speed on his sticky surfaces that some works contain dried cigarette butts that had fallen onto the wet canvas; this work is known for the fly that's trapped in the right-hand corner.

Helen Frankenthaler, *Mountains and Sea* (1952)

This was the first example of Frankenthaler's 'soak-stain' technique, in which she allowed thinned oil paint to be absorbed by the canvas, resulting in fellow artist Joan Mitchell unkindly calling Frankenthaler the 'Kotex painter', after a brand of menstrual pads.

WHAT IS POP ART?

Pop Art, which began in
Britain before spreading
to the US, Europe and
Latin America, was a
movement that created
a new visual language for
art, using references and
objects taken directly from
popular culture.

Pop Art
1950s–1960s

BRITAIN & US

HOW DID IT START?

In 1952, a group of artists including Richard Hamilton and Eduardo Paolozzi met at London's Institute of Contemporary Arts under the name 'The Independent Group', creating readymades (existing objects presented as completed artworks) and discussing mass production in their work.

HOW DID IT GET ITS NAME?

The term 'Pop Art' takes its name from 'popular culture', but unlike pop music – where 'pop' describes the popularity of the music itself – the 'pop' in 'Pop Art' refers to the popular culture inspiring the artists, rather than the idea that the art itself is popular.

HOW DID BRITISH POP ART DIFFER FROM THE US VERSION?

In post-war Britain, Pop artists took inspiration from the ads, products, movies and TV shows that were pouring out of the US, to create playful artworks critiquing capitalism and consumerism; American Pop Art, on the other hand, was less ironic and a bit more 'God Bless America'.

WHO WERE THEY INSPIRED BY?

Pop Art was heavily inspired by Dada (see page 164), with Robert Rauschenberg and Jasper Johns initially seen as 'Neo-Dadaists', because of their inclusion of readymades and their playful, critical approach to capturing the world around them.

WHAT CEMENTED ITS POPULARITY?

The International Exhibition of the New Realists opened in October 1962 in New York City and confirmed Pop Art as the Next Big Thing – displaying, according to the *New York Times*, exactly the sort of things you would see if you just sat and watched telly adverts all day.

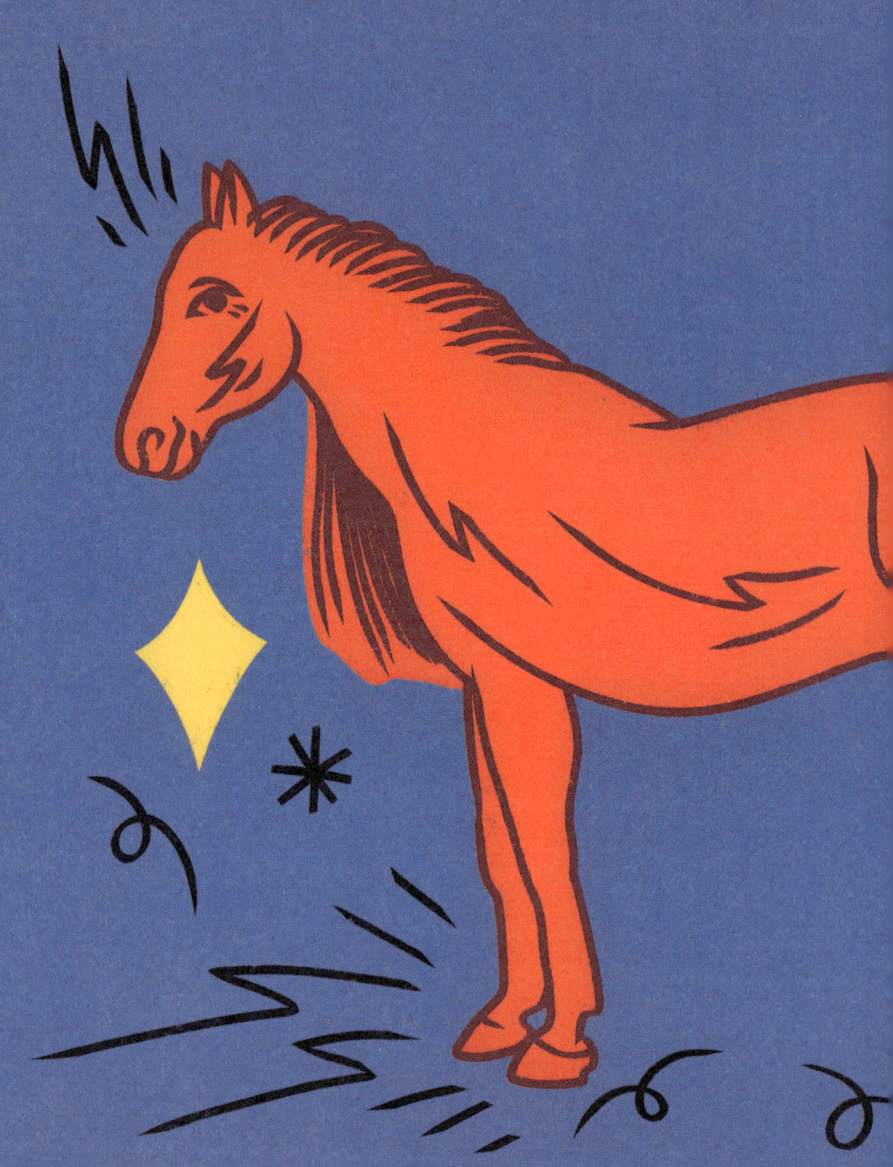

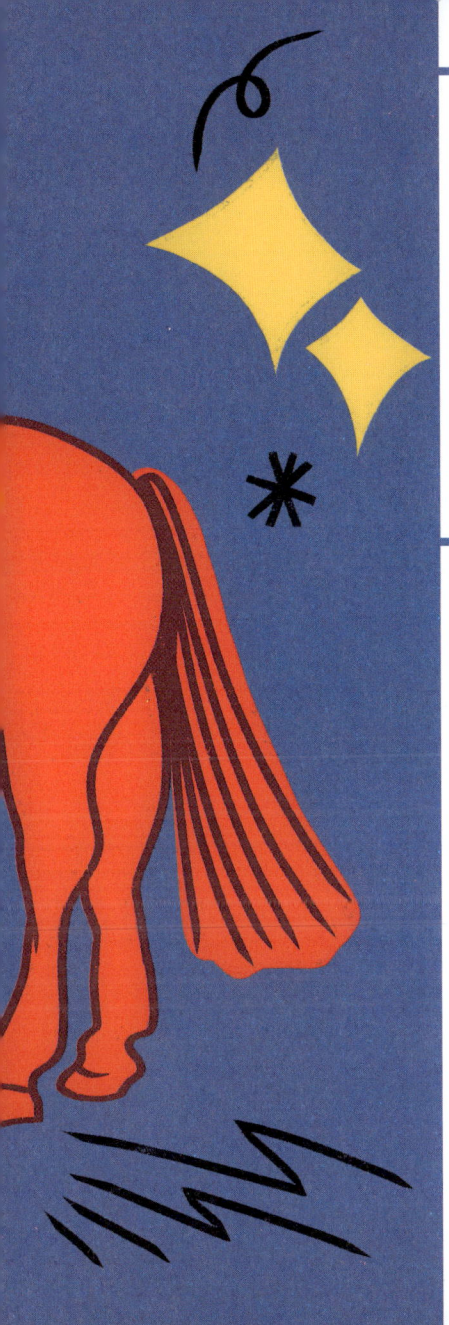

WHAT WENT DOWN AT THE FACTORY?

The Factory was Andy Warhol's silver-foil-covered studio in New York where his team of assistants helped him to create artwork, and also where he held raucous, celeb-filled parties; where he was shot; where he rented a horse for a film that kicked someone in the head; and where the photographer Billy Name lived for years in the toilet.

WHAT COULD YOU BUY AT THE STORE?

Claes Oldenburg opened The Store – part shop, part exhibition – in New York's Lower East Side in 1961, where he sold cheap, painted plaster sculptures of everyday items, including puddings, underpants and cigarettes.

WHAT IS *POP GOES THE EASEL*?

A 1962 documentary directed by Ken Russell, *Pop Goes the Easel* followed young Pop-Art pioneers Pauline Boty, Derek Boshier, Peter Blake and Peter Phillips, and featured a long clip of Blake sawing a door, Boshier talking about cornflakes, and everyone doing the twist because it was the sixties, so it was probably illegal not to.

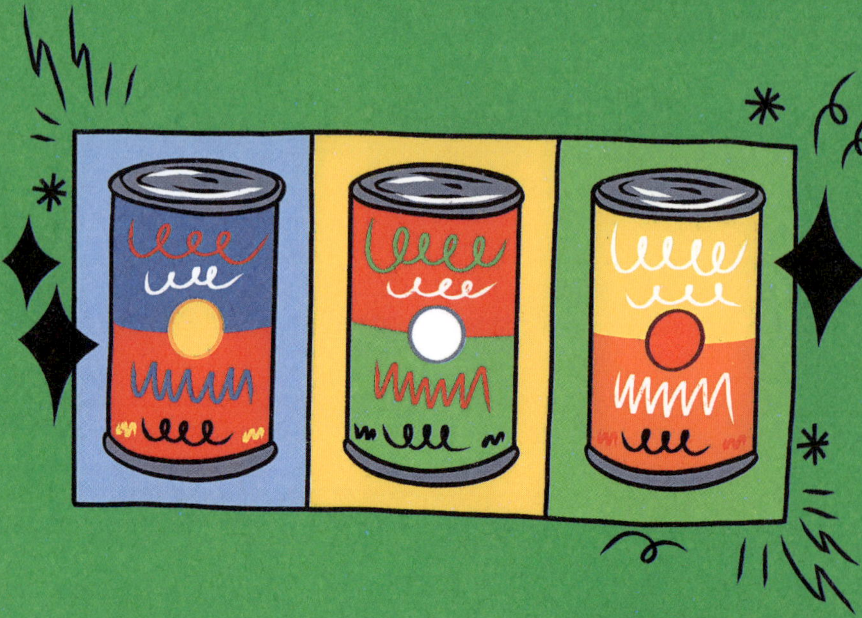

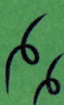

I FEEL LIKE I RECOGNISE MORE OF THESE ARTWORKS THAN IN OTHER CHAPTERS...

Many iconic Pop Art artworks were prints or sculptures, which meant they could be recreated many times, so you've likely seen a version of Robert Indiana's *Love* sculpture, one of Warhol's famous soup-can prints or Peter Blake and Jann Haworth's famous cover for the Beatles' 1967 album *Sgt. Pepper's Lonely Hearts Club Band*.

3 KEY ARTISTS

Marisol (1930–2016)
Venezuelan-American sculptor, inspired by pre-Columbian sculptures and best-known for her wooden sculptures including one of *Playboy*'s Hugh Hefner, which appeared on the cover of *TIME* magazine in 1967.

David Hockney (b.1937)
English artist who made a *Splash* in the pools of California, and who currently loves his iPad.

Pauline Boty (1938–1966)
English artist, stained-glass student turned model, dancer and actress; her artworks explored womanhood and sexuality in the era of the contraceptive pill.

3 KEY ARTWORKS

Richard Hamilton, *Just what is it that makes today's homes so different, so appealing?* (1956)
Like Scottish-Italian artist Eduardo Paolozzi's *I Was a Rich Man's Plaything* (1947), Hamilton's collage announced the dawn of the Pop Art age; made from images from American magazine adverts, it starred the US bodybuilder Irvin Koszewski.

Roy Lichtenstein, *Whaam!* (1963)
Lichtenstein created artworks in the style of (or directly copied from) comic strips, and *Whaam!* comes from an illustration in DC Comics' *All-American Men of War*.

Marcello Nitsche, *I Want You* (1966)
While a lot of Pop Art seems playful, Pop Artists in Brazil were creating work that addressed the violence Brazilians were facing from its US-backed regime, including this work, which takes Uncle Sam's iconic pointing finger and adds a stuffed-canvas drop of blood.

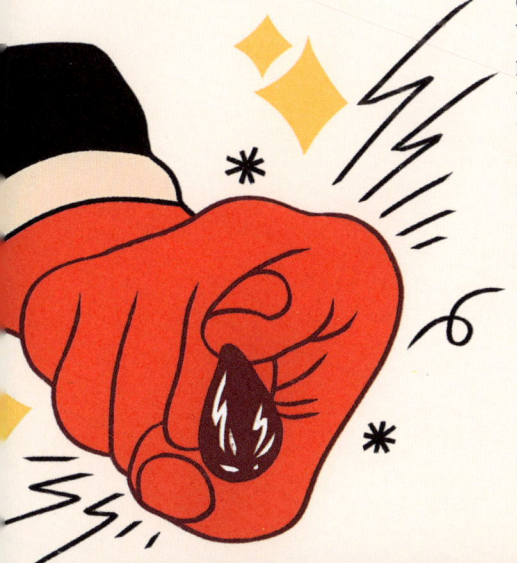

WHAT WAS OP ART?

Op (optical) Art – a term
first used in 1964 in *TIME*
magazine about the work
of Victor Vasarely – was a
movement in which artists
used patterns and colours
to create the illusion of
movement in a still artwork.

Op Art
1950s–1970s

INTERNATIONAL

DOES IT HAVE MUCH IN COMMON WITH POP ART, OR JUST THE RHYMING?

Both styles were popular during the 1960s but their goals were totally different: Pop Art (see page 228) wanted to create art that referenced modern life, whereas Op Art was all about how viewers experienced looking at the artwork (so yeah, pretty much just the rhyming).

WHO WERE THEY INSPIRED BY?

Op artists took inspiration from artists before them who had used and manipulated colour and perspective in order to create effects in the eye, including Pointillist Georges Seurat (see page 93), and M. C. Escher (tricky staircases).

WHAT WAS RESPONSIVE EYE?

It was a 1965 exhibition at MoMA in New York, curated by art historian William C. Seitz who believed art was all about the experience of viewing, and which showcased work by many major Op artists, really putting Op Art on the map.

BUT, LIKE, WHAT EVEN IS REAL, MAN?

At the end of the day, all art that attempts to depict something from real life is an illusion, because a canvas is just a flat surface and paint is just paint; Op Art played into this, believing that how it **feels** to **look** at an artwork is more important than the artwork's content.

WERE OP ARTISTS THE FIRST TO PLAY TRICKS ON OUR EYES?

Far from it – for centuries, details in *trompe l'oeil* ('trick of the eye') paintings have been executed so realistically that viewers would mistake them for reality; for instance, Carlo Crivelli's *St Catherine of Alexandria* (1491) appears to have a real fly sitting on its surface.

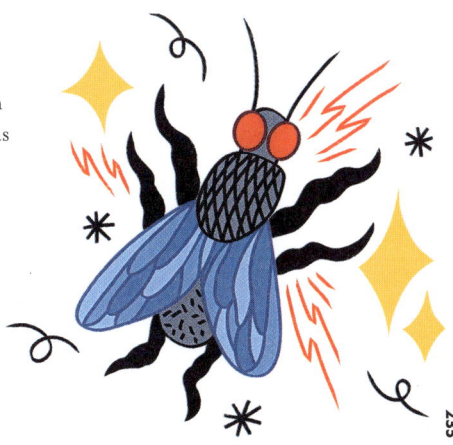

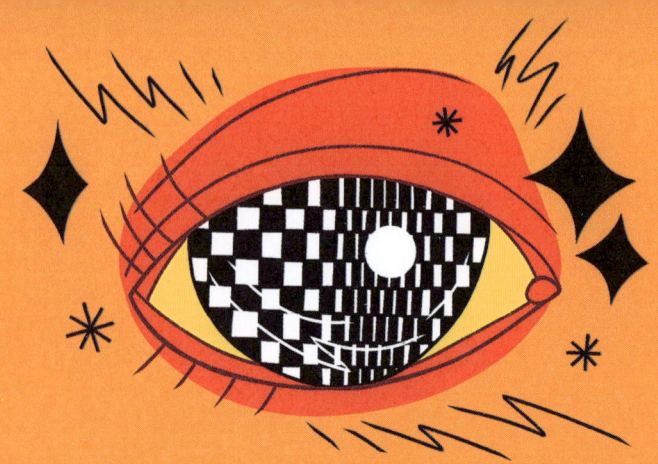

WHY DO THE PAINTINGS SEEM TO MOVE?

'Illusory motion' (when something that is still appears to be moving) is caused by several things, including the involuntary darting around of our eyes, our brains trying to helpfully fill in gaps in the visual information they receive, and the fact that our brains register light-coloured objects faster than darker ones.

HOW WAS IT RECEIVED?

Op Art was initially received poorly by critics who saw it as gimmicky, but it certainly did well commercially and inspired many fashion fabrics, to the extent that Bridget Riley had to take legal action against clothing companies using her designs without permission.

WHAT IS CHROMATIC TENSION?

This is the way in which colours placed next to each other seem to affect each other, and it's one reason why the colours in Op Art artworks seem to vibrate and warp.

WHAT ELSE MIGHT HAVE BEEN *COUGH* INFLUENCING *COUGH* OP ART AUDIENCES?

Hallucinogens, which intensified the user's perception of colour, were big in the sixties (LSD wasn't banned until 1966 in the UK and 1968 in the US), so looking at Op Art under the influence must have been **a lot**.

3 KEY ARTISTS

Carlos Cruz-Diez (1923–2019)
Venezuelan artist whose work was partly inspired by a childhood love of colourful kites; he didn't buy into the idea that to create art is to suffer.

Bridget Riley (b.1931)
British painter, initially monochrome; screwed over by the lack of copyright laws in the sixties.

Tadasky (b.1935)
Japanese painter, best known for his concentric circles, created a series using a lot of beige, which he referred to as his 'cheap American apartment series' (ouch).

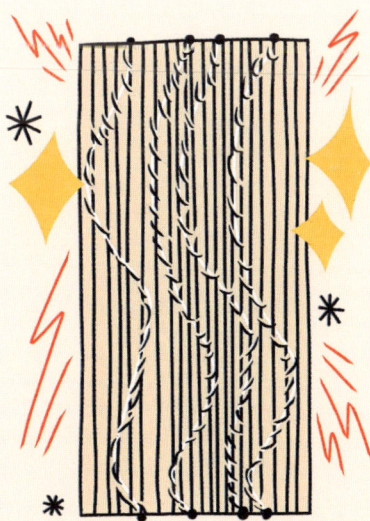

3 KEY ARTWORKS

Victor Vasarely, *Supernovae* (1959–1961)
A properly eye-hurty experience by the father of Op Art, *Supernovae* is made up of 1,161 black squares and is less about the sense of movement per se, than how heavy a punch it packs to your retinas.

Wojciech Fangor, *Number 17* (1963)
Originally creating Socialist Realist (see page 204) artworks in communist Poland, Fangor's work developed the characteristic blurry quality seen here after time spent with the Polish School of Posters allowed him to experiment with more abstract, conceptual imagery.

Julio Le Parc, *Form in Contortion over Thread* (1966)
Demonstrating the way that Kinetic Art (artworks that literally move) and Op Art (artworks that just seem to move) overlapped in the 1960s, this work's metal threads are powered by a motor hidden behind the wooden board.

WHAT WAS MINIMALISM?

It was a loose label that described artists using industrial materials to create purely abstract artworks, aiming to reduce their designs as much as possible and laying emphasis on how the audience interacts with the space surrounding an artwork.

Minimalism
1950s–1970s

US

WHO WAS MINIMALISM'S BIGGEST FAN?

Clement Greenberg, the superstar art critic of the day, was pro-Minimalism because he believed that art should always be moving on to the next thing and that each art form should be guided by its physical properties (e.g. painting is fundamentally flat and sculpture is fundamentally 3D), which Minimalism did – big time.

IF THERE'S NOTHING **IN** THE ARTWORKS, WHAT ARE THEY ABOUT?

Minimalist art isn't in any way narrative – instead it's about form, about material and experiencing what is directly in front of you.

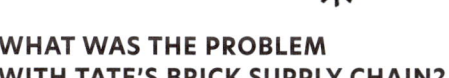

WHAT WAS THE PROBLEM WITH TATE'S BRICK SUPPLY CHAIN?

In 1972, London's Tate Gallery purchased the final artwork in Carl Andre's *Equivalent* series – in which he made different rectangles using 120 bricks – but after making the work in 1966, Andre had assumed that no one would buy it and sent the bricks back for a refund; he had to buy new bricks for the work, which were then sent to the UK.

WHY DOES SO MUCH OF IT LIVE ON THE FLOOR?

Many Minimalist masterpieces are sculptures, designed to make us think about the nature of three-dimensionality, and by displaying works on the floor, artists are forcing us to interact directly with the works, considering how they take up space as we walk around them.

HOW SIMILAR WAS IT TO ABSTRACT EXPRESSIONISM?

Unlike the Abstract Expressionists (see page 222) Minimalists removed any trace of the artist's hand from their works and didn't emphasise emotion, but like the AbEx lot they did often use *Untitled* for artwork titles, not because they wanted their works to be open to interpretation, but because they wanted no interpretation at all.

WHAT IS POST-PAINTERLY ABSTRACTION?

Several key Minimalists fit in the 'post-painterly abstraction' box, a term coined by Greenberg to identify a distinct movement that sat between the busy-ness of Abstract Expressionism and the practically-empty-ness of Minimalism.

TONY SMITH'S *DIE* IS JUST A BIG CUBE, COME ON!

You're right, the 1962 sculpture **is** a big cube, but exactly the **right** big: the piece was specifically made using the human body for its proportions, in order to prevent it seeming overwhelming or underwhelming for the viewer.

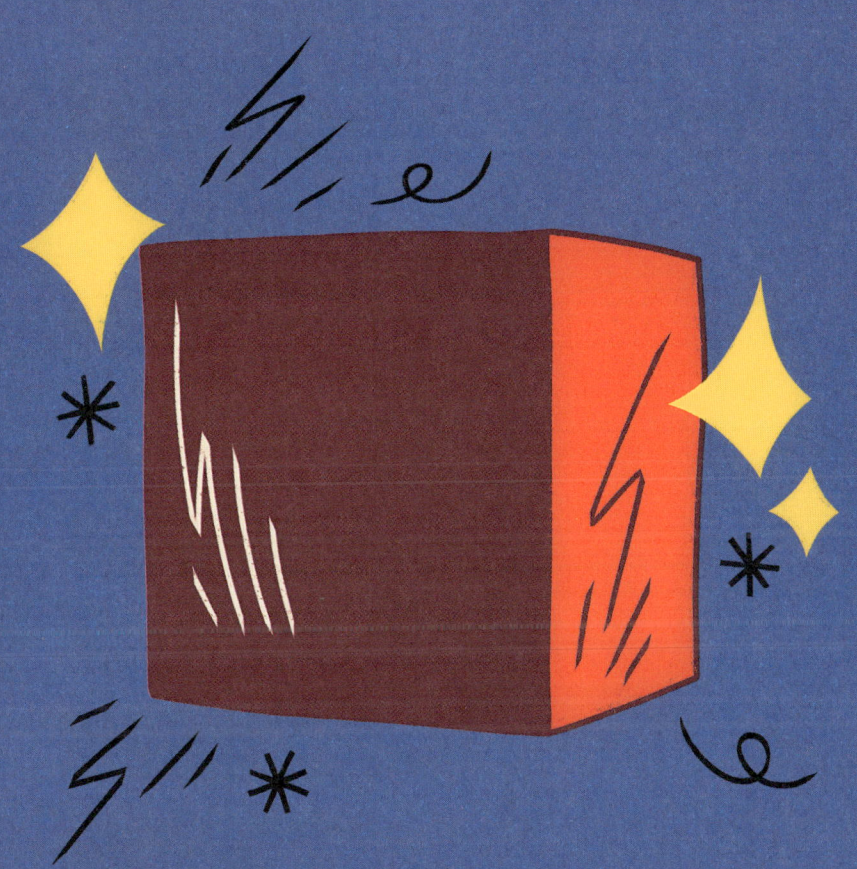

WHAT WAS HAPPENING OUTSIDE OF THE WEST?

Nasreen Mohamedi – often compared to her American Minimalist contemporaries – created Minimalist abstract line drawings, which earned her a reputation as one the most impactful artists in post-independence India.

WHAT WAS LIGHT AND SPACE?

Emerging in the 1960s and bridging Minimalism and Op Art (see page 234), Light and Space was a sculptural movement all about – you guessed it – light and space; but it's a doubly great name because one of its key artists, Fred Eversley, used to work at NASA (space, get it?)

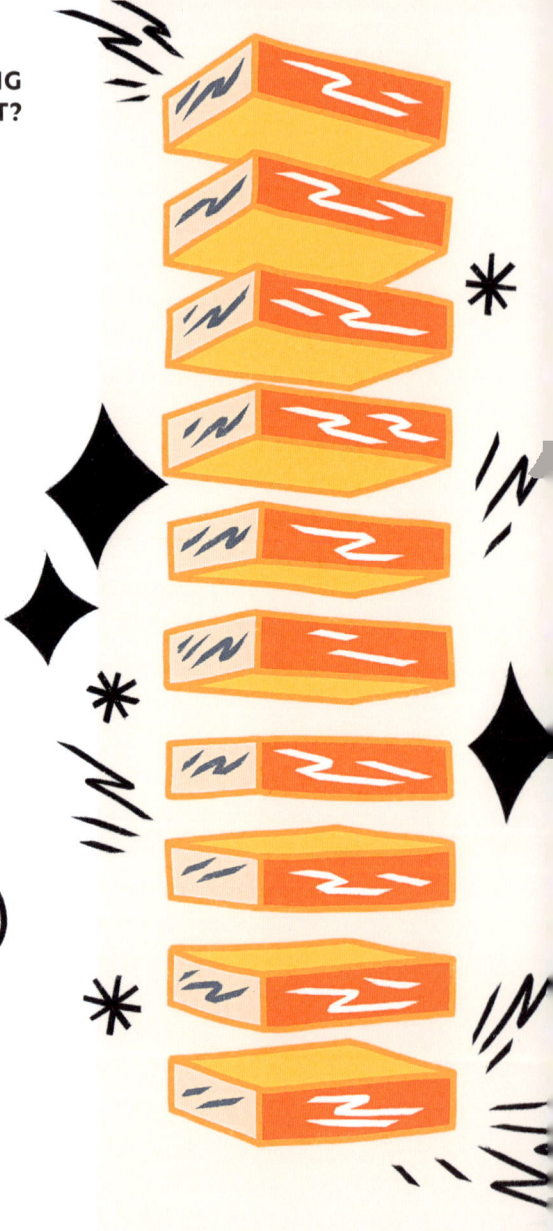

3 KEY ARTISTS

Agnes Martin (1912-2004)
Canadian-American painter who left New York to find peace in the New Mexico desert where she built her own houses; so anti-other people writing about her work that she cancelled a big Whitney Museum retrospective.

Ellsworth Kelly (1923-2015)
American artist known for his Colour Field painting (see page 224), served in the Second World War in the Ghost Army (a US tactical deception unit whose exploits included creating inflatable tanks).

Frank Stella (1936-2024)
American artist and jazz fan, his *Black Paintings* are seen as the first Minimalist artworks.

3 KEY ARTWORKS

Dan Flavin, *The Diagonal of May 25, 1963 (To Robert Rosenblum)* (1963)
The second of Flavin's iconic sculptures using fluorescent lights, this one is dedicated to US art historian Robert Rosenblum, who was a big supporter of modern art movements and also wrote a great book about dogs.

Mary Corse, *Untitled (First White Light Series)* (1968)
One of the only women associated with the Light and Space movement as well as Minimalism, Corse used glass microbeads mixed into paint in order to create works not just **about** but actually **made** of light.

Donald Judd, *Untitled* (1969)
This is one of Judd's 'Stack' vertical artworks, which he saw as straddling the boundaries between sculpture and painting because, like a painting, they're colourful and hung on a wall but, like a sculpture, if you get too close to it you'll bang your head.

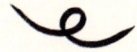

WHAT WAS
NOUVEAU
RÉALISME?

The Nouveau Realists
were a group of avant-
garde artists (initially the
nine signatories of their
1960 manifesto) creating
art about modern living,
who were particularly
keen on live performances.

Nouveau Réalisme

1960s–1970s

FRANCE

WHY 'NEW REALISM'?

Like the Realists (see page 58) more than a century earlier, the Nouveau Realists were interested in bridging art and real life, but this time they were going to literally bring real life into their artworks through performances and the use of readymades.

WHO WERE THEY INSPIRED BY?

The pioneering performance artists of the Japanese *Gutai* group in the 1950s were a major inspiration, especially their experimental performances, including Kazuo Shiraga's *Challenging Mud* (1955) in which the artist writhed in muck.

WHAT WAS ITS RELATIONSHIP TO POP ART?

Like Pop Artists (see page 228), Nouveau Realists were interested in experimenting with material and grounding their work in the present, but they were considerably less perky than the American and British Pop artists and visually, their work was more like Dada (see page 164).

WHAT WERE ASSEMBLAGES?

Many Nouveau Realists created sculptural works known as assemblages – 3D collages incorporating ready-made materials – and particularly famous are those by the French-American artist Arman, who created a series of assemblages using rubbish in clear Plexiglas containers which he called his *Poubelles* ('trash cans').

WHAT PART OF THE UNIVERSE DID YVES KLEIN OWN?

As a teenager, Yves Klein sat with two friends on the beach and decided to split the universe between them, with Klein taking the sky (a key moment in the development of his fascination with the colour blue, which would eventually lead him to invent his very own shade, called International Klein Blue).

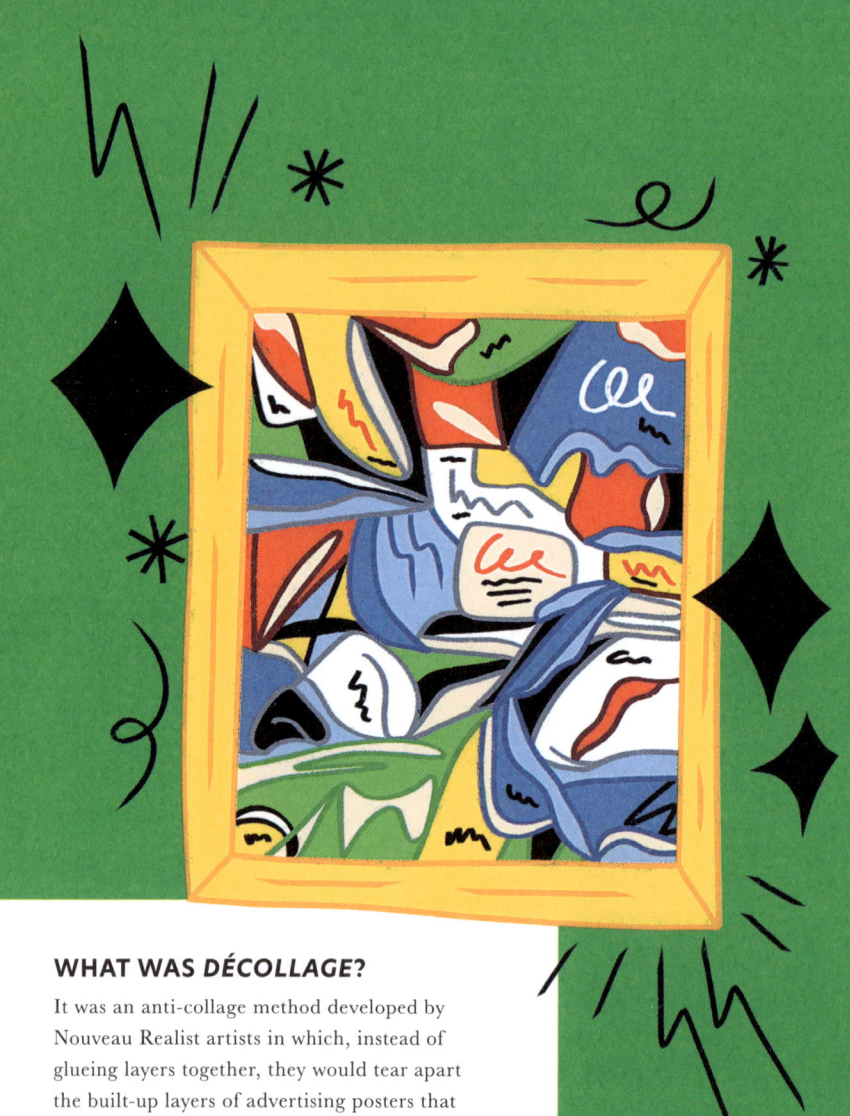

WHAT WAS *DÉCOLLAGE*?

It was an anti-collage method developed by
Nouveau Realist artists in which, instead of
glueing layers together, they would tear apart
the built-up layers of advertising posters that
they found in the street.

WHAT MIGHT CHRISTO AND JEANNE-CLAUDE HAVE GOTTEN YOU FOR CHRISTMAS?

The husband-and-wife duo are best known for their artworks in which they wrapped various items in fabric – Christo began doing this in 1958, possibly as a reference to his childhood as an Eastern European refugee – and in the 1960s, their wrapped items included furniture, trees, a motorcycle, a stretch of Sydney's coastline and a medieval Italian tower.

WHAT'S FOR DINNER?

Leftovers: Daniel Spoerri made a name for himself with his 'snare-pictures' in which he would take objects arranged as they already were in reality, fix them in place, and then display them; many of his most famous works included food, like *Kichka's Breakfast,* made of leftovers from his girlfriend's morning meal.

WHAT'S THE BEST PLACE FOR ART CRITICS?

In another food-focused work, Spoerri transformed the Galerie J gallery in Paris into the *'Restaurant de la Galerie J'* in which he cooked meals which were served to gallery-goers by art critics acting as waiters.

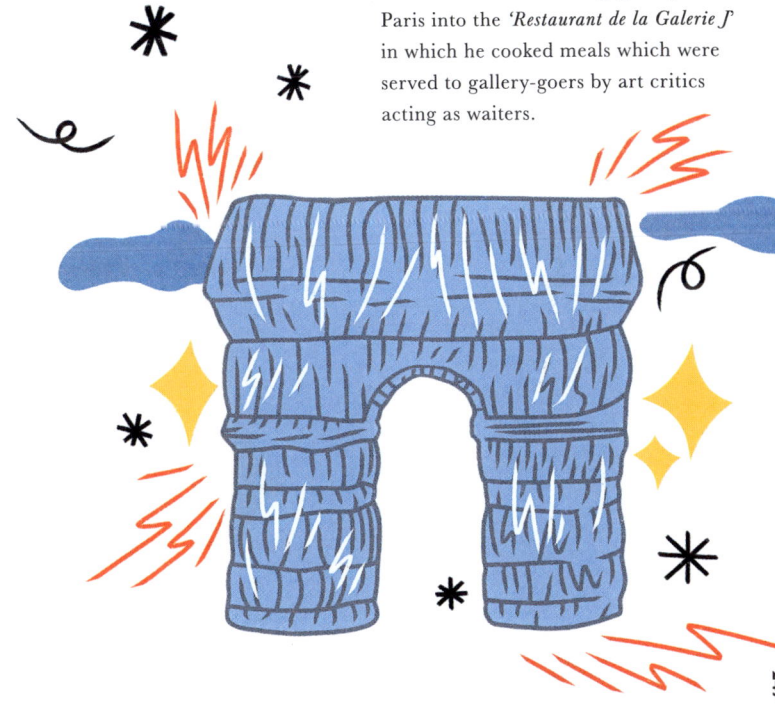

3 KEY ARTISTS

César (1921-1998)
French sculptor, interested in modern industrial materials like polyurethane and plastics, who was known for his *'compressions'* – artworks in which he crushed metal (particularly cars) – in a hydraulic press.

Jacques Villeglé (1926-2022)
French artist who was inspired by the typography in the work of Braque (see page 142); was also deeply interested in the urban environment, which sometimes has him labelled an early street artist.

Niki de Saint Phalle (1930-2002)
French-American artist and fashion model, also considered an Outsider Artist; known for shooting her work with guns.

3 KEY ARTWORKS

Yves Klein, *Large Blue Anthropometry [ANT 105]* (c.1960)
This series – named after the study of the measurements of the body – was made by Klein instructing nude female models, covered in International Klein Blue paint, to press their bodies onto sheets of paper as part of live performances where blue cocktails were also served.

Jean Tinguely, *(Fragment of) Homage to New York* (1960)
Tinguely is best-known for his kinetic (moving) sculptures which

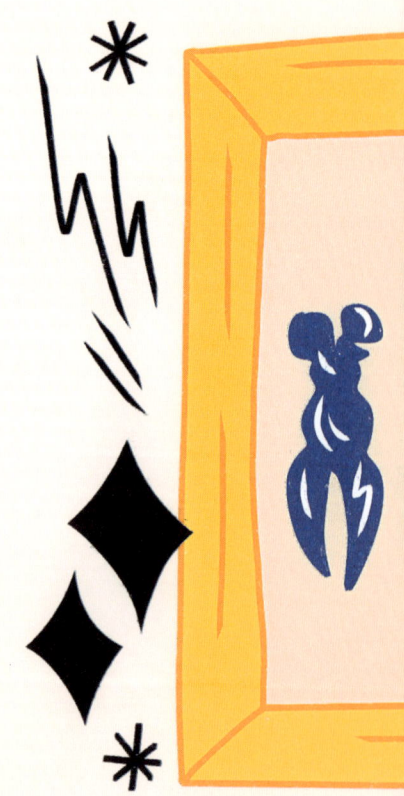

would self-destruct, and this one (originally a massive 7 × 8 metres) was made of found materials including a weather balloon, a bathtub and a piano, but a malfunction meant it didn't fully destruct.

Martial Raysse, *Made in Japan: La grande odalisque* (1964)
This version of an 1814 painting of the same name by Ingres (see page 49) comes from Raysse's *Made in Japan* series, which commented on beauty and overconsumption by luridly recreating artworks from art history.

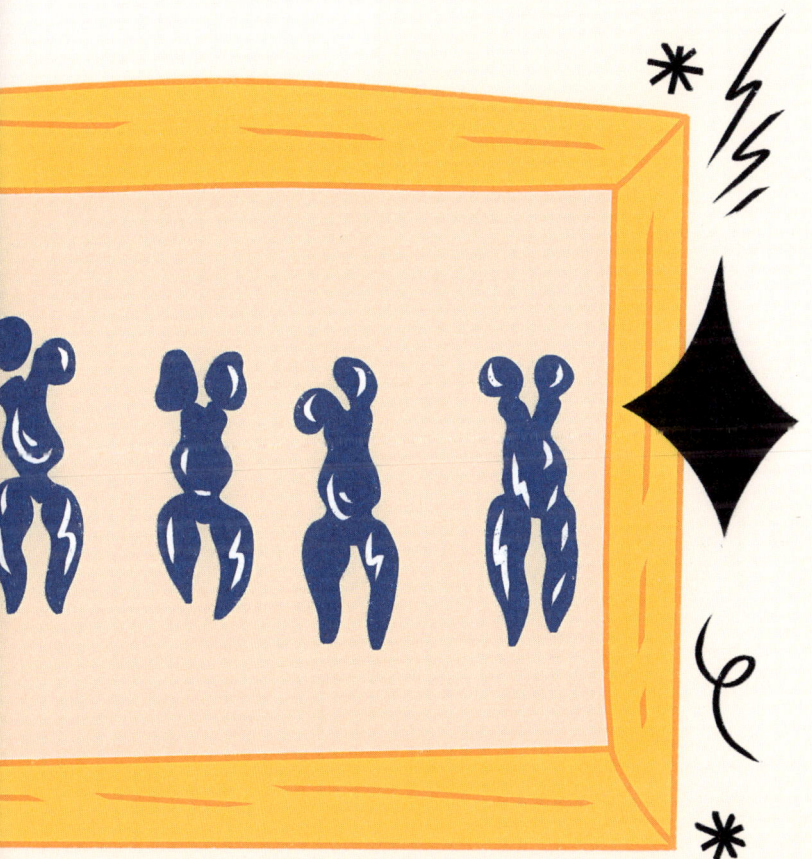

WHAT WAS FLUXUS?

Fluxus (from the Latin for 'flow') was an experimental international community of artists, informed by the philosophy that anything can be art and that the viewer should be an active participant in the work.

Fluxus
1960s–1970s
GERMANY & US

WHAT WERE THEY INTO?

Fluxus could probably be best defined by what it stood against: the commercialisation of art, the hierarchies that deemed some art forms as worthier than others and the way the traditional art market was run.

WHO WERE THEY INSPIRED BY?

Fluxus' inspirations were many, from Dada (see page 164) and Duchamp to Vaudeville and *Gutai* (see page 245), as well as the compositions of John Cage of *4'33"* fame – a completely silent piece of music lasting for four minutes and thirty-three seconds).

WHAT WAS A HAPPENING?

A Happening was a live artistic performance, a favourite medium for many Fluxus artists, as it got the audience directly involved.

HOW DID FLUXUS TRAVEL SO FAR?

Following the rise in global travel and international communications after the Second World War, artists from Asia, Europe and the US were all well represented within Fluxus (also, its leader George Maciunas moved from New York to Germany to avoid debt collectors).

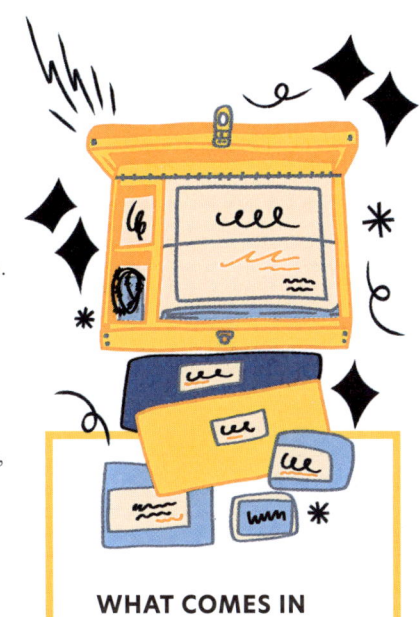

WHAT COMES IN A FLUXKIT?

Fluxkits (or Fluxboxes) were packages containing objects created and curated by Fluxus artists; one kit, *Flux Divorce Box* (1972–3), marked the divorce of the artists Geoffrey Hendricks and Bici Forbes and contained an album of their photographs cut in half, severed wedding invitations and pieces from their destroyed marriage bed.

WAS IT ALL SILLY?

A lot of Fluxus work was playful but also intensely political, like Valie Export's 1968 *Action Pants: Genital Panic* in which the artist walked through a cinema in crotchless trousers to comment on the gulf between real women and the reductive portrayals of women shown on the screen.

WHAT WAS JOSEPH BEUYS' FAVOURITE MATERIAL?

Beuys often used felt in his work; the legend being that when the artist was stationed in Crimea during the First World War, his plane crashed and he was saved from death by a group of nomadic Tatar tribesmen who kept his body warm by covering him in animal fat and wrapping him in felt.

WHO WAS BEUYS' HAIRIEST ROOMMATE?

In his 1974 performance *I Like America and America Likes Me*, Beuys was flown to the US from Germany, then transported in an ambulance (wrapped in felt, obviously) to SoHo's René Block Gallery, where he spent three consecutive days, eight hours at a time, locked in a cage with a live coyote (you could do worse for accommodation, in this economy).

WHAT WAS THE *OPERA SEXTRONIQUE*?

It was an invitation-only musical performance curated by Nam June Paik (who saw the lack of sex in classical music as its major drawback), meant to be played by the cellist Charlotte Moorman in different levels of undress, but the performance was interrupted during the second movement when Moorman was arrested for toplessness.

3 KEY ARTISTS

George Maciunas (1931–1978)

Lithuanian-American artist, leader of Fluxus and author of its '63 manifesto, he married Billie Hutching in a 'Flux Wedding' during which bride and groom swapped clothes.

Alison Knowles (b.1933)

American artist and founding Fluxus member whose best-known performances involved food (including *Make a Salad* in 1962, where she… made a salad).

Benjamin Patterson (1934–2016)

American musician, artist and founding Fluxus member, creator of *Paper Piece* performed using only – you guessed it – pieces of paper, and *Licking Piece* in which whipped cream was – you guessed it – licked – you probably didn't guess it – off a lady.

3 KEY ARTWORKS

Yoko Ono, *Cut Piece* (1964)

In *Cut Piece,* Yoko Ono invited members of the audience in Kyoto's Yamaichi Concert Hall to cut off pieces of her clothing and take the scraps away with them.

Ben Vautier, *Total Art Match-Box* (c.1965)

Vautier's box of matches was accompanied by directions on what to do with them (namely commit major arson); this was typical for Fluxus artworks, which often came with instructions.

Nam June Paik, *TV Buddha* (1974)

The first of several versions by the video art pioneer, this 1974 video sculpture featured a statue of Buddha facing a small television screen on which live closed-circuit footage of the statue was being broadcast.

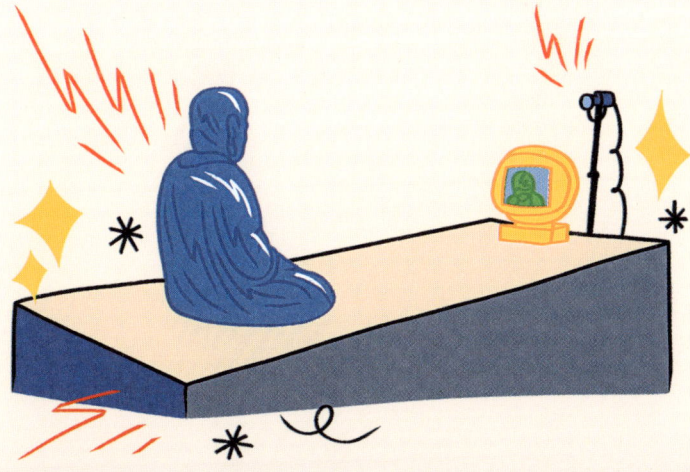

WHAT IS *ARTE POVERA*?

Meaning 'poor art', it was an Italian art movement that utilised natural and everyday materials as well as readymades (see page 229) to push against the traditions of the fine-art world.

Arte Povera

1960s–1970s

ITALY

WHY 'POVERA'?

'Poor Art' doesn't necessarily indicate cheapness (the non-art materials the artists used weren't always inexpensive) but rather humbleness, positioning the group in opposition to more extravagant art movements and styles, like Pop Art (see page 228) and Academicism (see page 36).

WHAT WAS HAPPENING IN ITALY AT THE TIME?

Arte Povera emerged during Italy's so-called Economic Miracle, a time of unprecedented levels of migration from southern Italy to the north (where *Arte Povera* got its start), with 1.7 million people moving from rural farms to take up factory jobs in the cities (particularly building Fiat cars in Turin).

WHAT WERE *ARTE POVERA* ARTISTS INSPIRED BY?

The artists were inspired by the 'poor theatre' of Polish director Jerzy Grotowski, who stripped theatre back to its basics (no expensive or extensive props or sets); the happenings of Fluxus (see page 250) and *Nouveau Réalisme* (see page 244); and the 'Spatialism' of Argentinian-Italian Lucio Fontana (the guy who made those slashes in canvases, which make people cross).

HOW DID IT DIFFER FROM LAND ART?

Occurring concurrently in the US, Land Art shared *Arte Povera*'s interest in using non-art materials and connecting art with nature, but the Land Artists created their works from natural materials and installed them outdoors, whereas *Arte Povera* artists brought natural materials indoors into the formal gallery space.

WHAT WAS *MONO-HA*?

Mono-ha, or 'The School of Things' was a loose art movement in Japan happening at the same time as *Arte Povera*, with a similar ethos and structure; its artists questioned the hierarchies of the traditional art world and debated the role of the artist.

THE ITALIANS HAVE SUCH A RICH ART HISTORY, LUCKY THEM!

That's not how the *Arte Povera* artists necessarily saw it, because, yes, Italy had been an artistic pioneer for well over 1,000 years, but *Arte Povera* saw no value in simply repeating what art had done already, seeking to create work that was deeply rooted in the here-and-now.

WHAT WAS DIFFERENT ABOUT PENONE'S POTATOES?

If you were going to chow down on Giuseppe Penone's 1977 installation of a pile of potatoes on the gallery floor, you might have lost some teeth because among the real spuds were bronze casts of potatoes that Penone had grown inside moulds of his ears, mouth and nose.

HOW MANY HORSES CAN YOU FIT IN A GALLERY?

As part of the opening of Rome's Gallery L'Attico in 1969, the Greek artist Jannis Kounellis moved twelve live horses into the gallery (looked after by proper grooms, chill out PETA), in a piece that posed questions about the purpose and nature of contemporary galleries (questions like, 'How many horses can I fit in here?')

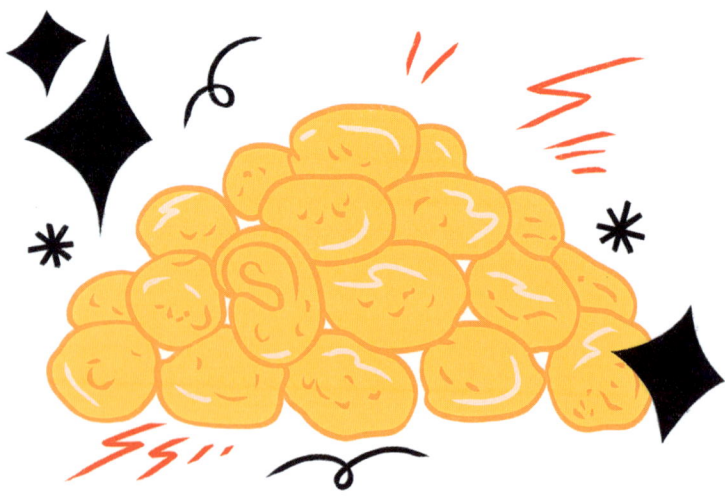

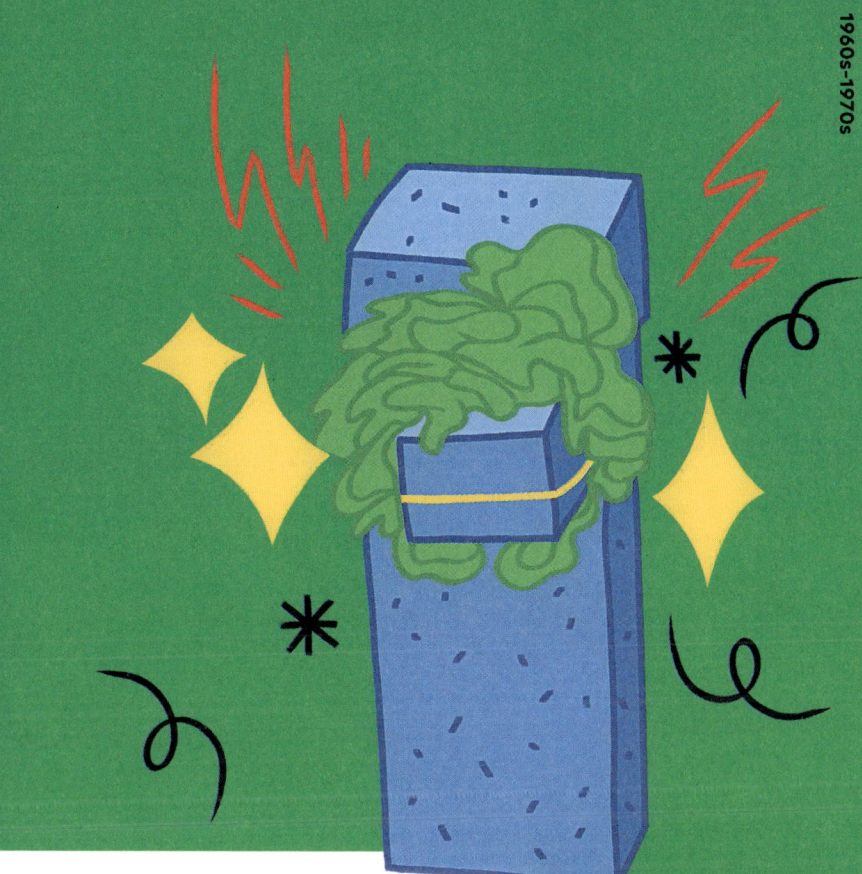

HOW HUNGRY IS GRANITE?

Giovanni Anselmo is probably best known for his 1968 sculpture *Structure That Eats*, in which a lettuce was wedged between two pieces of granite tied with copper wire, and the structure needed to be routinely 'fed' a new lettuce to prevent the piece from falling apart when the existing lettuce wilted.

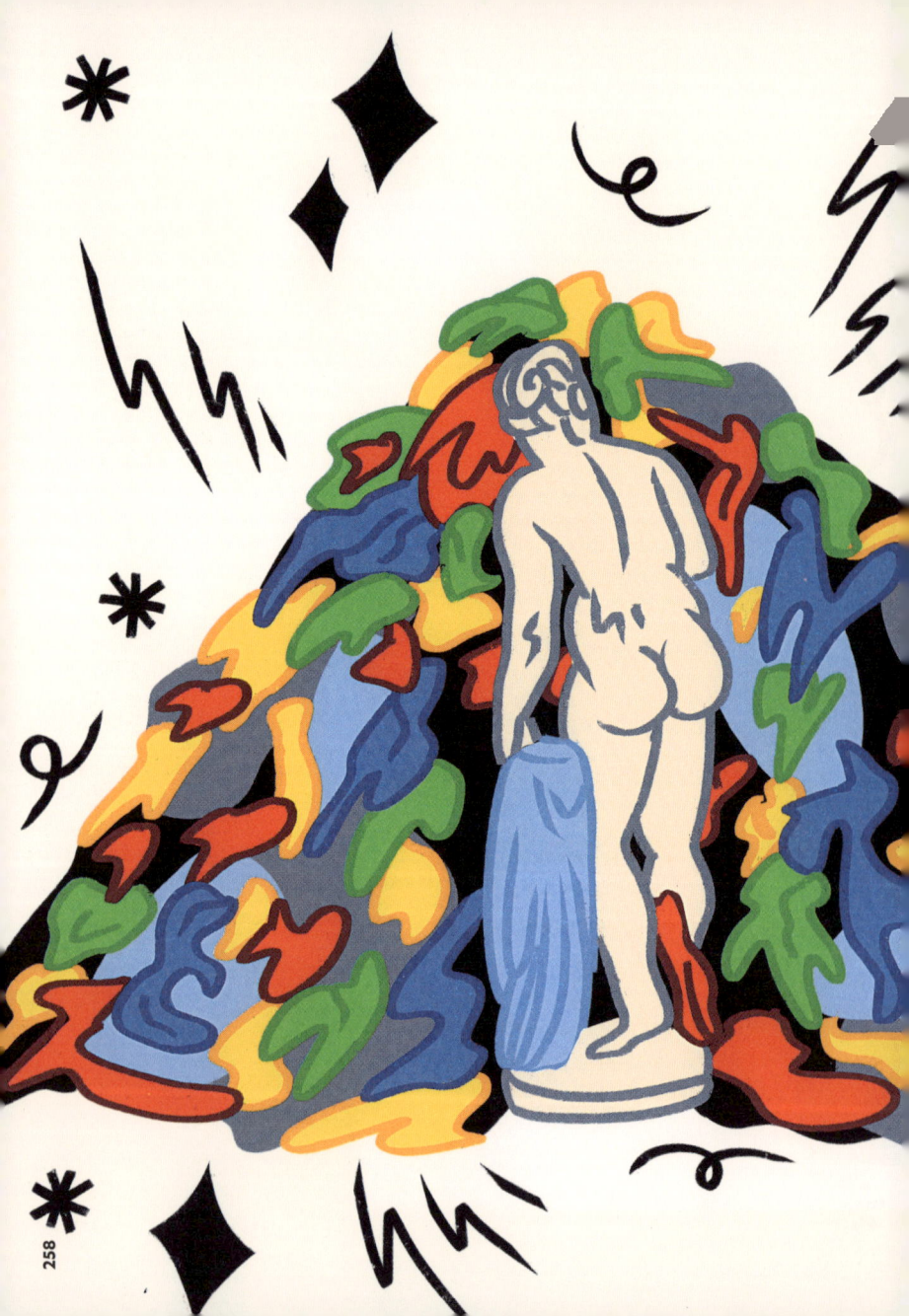

3 KEY ARTISTS

Marisa Merz (1926–2019)
Italian artist who was the only woman in the *Arte Povera* group; used a lot of aluminium foil.

Giovanni Anselmo (1934–2023)
Italian artist and big fan of granite, created a series of unreadable books (no, not like this one – shut up).

Luciano Fabro (1936–2007)
Italian artist interested in the relationships between artworks and the space around them; created a great video artwork of him falling on his bum (it's on YouTube).

3 KEY ARTWORKS

Alighiero e Boetti, *Lampada annuale* (1966)
This work lights up for eleven seconds once a year (but no one's sure when); the number eleven (written as two '1's) reflects Boetti's deep interest in pairs (he even added an 'e', meaning 'and', in his name to suggest that he is two people.)

Michelangelo Pistoletto, *Venus of the Rags* (1967)
In a piece that juxtaposes a symbol of Italy's traditional artistic past with modern overconsumption, *Venus of the Rags* was originally made using a statue of Venus bought in a garden centre, but later versions have been made from various materials, including marble (what a glow-up).

Mario Merz, *Igloo di Giap* (1968)
Igloos as a symbol of prehistoric and nomadic living came up frequently in Merz's practice and he created them from a range of materials including glass, stone and canvas.

The YBAs were a group of mostly London-based artists creating conceptual art that didn't shy away from messy themes (sex and death were on the agenda big time), often displaying their work in non-traditional venues.

Young British Artists

1980s–2000s

BRITAIN

WHEN DID THEY START?

The first exhibition of the YBAs' work was in 1988, but many of the artists already knew each other from university courses at London's Goldsmiths and the Royal College of Art.

DID THEY CHOOSE THEIR NAME?

The name didn't come about until 1992, first used either by the art historian Michael Corris in an *Artforum* article or by the mega-collector and gallerist Charles Saatchi for his exhibition Young British Artists I.

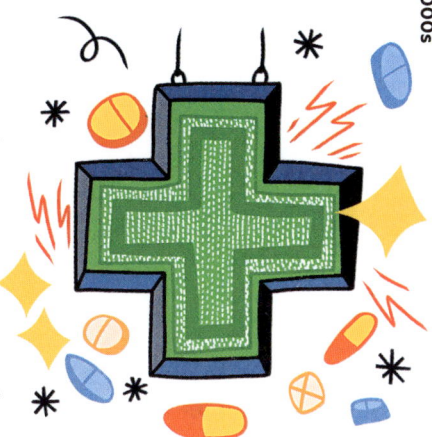

SO, THEY WERE YOUNG ARTISTS, BUT WHAT WAS PARTICULARLY BRITISH ABOUT THEIR WORK?

The peak of the YBAs' popularity came in the era of 'Cool Britannia' in the 1990s: a period of economic prosperity and deep pride in the international successes of UK's cultural output, including 'Britpop' bands, filmmakers and fashion designers.

WHAT WAS THE ROYAL PHARMACEUTICAL SOCIETY'S BEEF WITH DAMIEN HIRST?

Many of Hirst's artworks featured real medicine and medical equipment, but he really upset the RPS when he opened a restaurant and bar called *Pharmacy* in 1998 (where you could sip on a Formalin Martini and wee into a glass-case urinal filled with surgical swabs and heart medication), which was found to be breaking the rules of the 1968 Medicines Act with its misleading name.

WHAT COULD YOU PICK UP FROM THE SHOP?

Created in 1993, Tracey Emin and Sarah Lucas set up The Shop as a studio, shop and party venue, where you could buy the artists' work, put out a cigarette on an ashtray of Hirst's face and throw a coin into a fish pond full of fish called Ken (Livingstone).

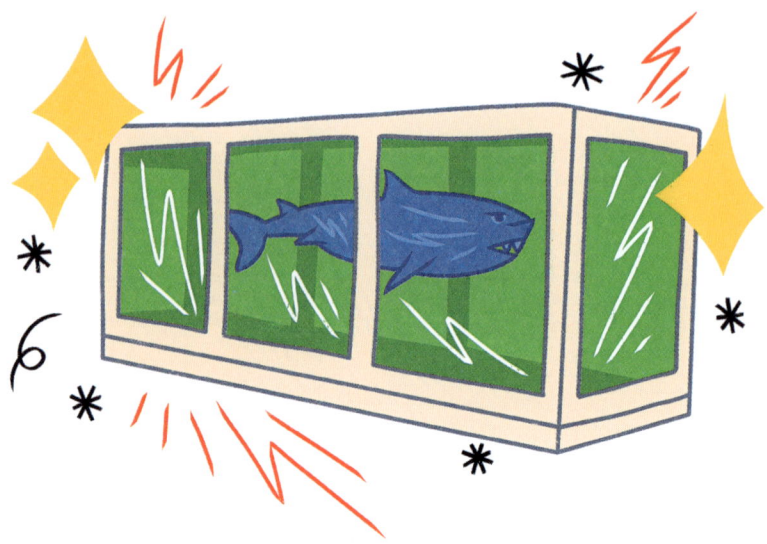

WHAT'S IT GOT TO DO WITH THE PRICE OF FISH?

Hirst's *The Physical Impossibility of Death in the Mind of Someone Living* (that shark in that formaldehyde tank) is an iconic YBA artwork, but within two years, the shark began to rot and needed replacing – the owner didn't bat an eyelid at the $100,000+ cost, given that he had already shelled out around eight million dollars to buy it.

WHY IS CHARLES SAATCHI SO IMPORTANT TO THE YBAS' LEGACY?

Having seen the YBAs' work at the Goldsmiths graduate show, advertising giant Saatchi became their biggest collector, regularly exhibiting their work, and in 1997 his Sensation exhibition cemented the rebellious whippersnappers as modern classics.

WHAT WAS 'FREEZE'?

Curated by Hirst, it was a three-part pop-up exhibition held in an empty office building in London's Surrey Docks in 1988, and at which Saatchi first bought work by Hirst.

IS 'FREEZE' THE SAME AS 'FRIEZE'?

Nope: the mega art fair Frieze (first held in 2003) developed from the 1991 art magazine of the same name, referring not to Hirst's exhibition but to a type of architectural decoration.

3 KEY ARTISTS

Rachel Whiteread (b.1963)

English sculptor and first woman to win the Turner Prize; known for her casts of rooms and buildings.

Gillian Wearing (b.1963)

English artist, really into wearing masks and best known for her *Signs That Say What You Want Them to Say and Not Signs That Say What Someone Else Wants You to Say* series in which strangers were photographed holding up placards revealing their deepest thoughts.

Chris Ofili (b.1968)

British painter, first Black winner of the Turner Prize, caused a stink with his elephant-dung paintings.

3 KEY ARTWORKS

Marcus Harvey, *Myra* (1995)

Perhaps the most controversial YBA artwork, Harvey recreated child-murderer Myra Hindley's police mugshot using hundreds of casts of children's hands... oof.

Sarah Lucas, *Self-Portrait with Fried Eggs* (1996)

Known for her works in which foodstuffs, machinery and stuffed tights represent the female body (kebab vagina anyone?), *Fried Eggs* is probably Lucas's most famous femininity-parodying self-portrait.

Tracey Emin, *My Bed* (1998)

Made following a period of not leaving her bed due to depression, and inspired by the bed as a place of conception as well as death, Emin's *My Bed* contains condoms, blood-stained underwear, booze, cigarettes and a pair of slippers among other trash.

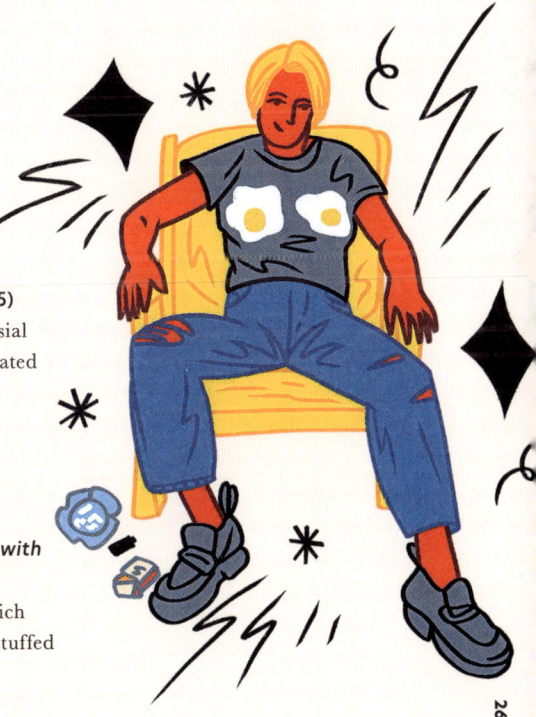

INDEX

Thank yous

Is it possible to thank everyone you need to in a sentence?

No.

I'd like to thank Daisy at PFD for seeing the potential in this book and in me; Grace and Kiron at Bloomsbury for helping this first-time author through the chaos; Rona, for knowing exactly what this book needed at every stage; and Bess and Alexandra for bringing it to life. A big cheers to the people whose academic encouragement set me up to be able to do this: Mr Tom Christy and my teachers at Chenderit School; and Professors Jane Garnett and Gervase Rosser. There would be no me without my friends – Eulalia, thank you for helping me to celebrate this win. Maddy, Lucy, Ani, Giddy Aunt Improv, and the Articulation team, just because. Thank you to my family, especially my mum, for everything. And Xander, I love you and the life we are building together, which makes this all possible.

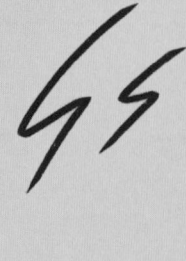

About the author

Verity Babbs is an art historian, presenter, and comedian from Northamptonshire. She studied History of Art at the University of Oxford and has written for *the Guardian*, *RA Magazine*, and *Artnet News*. Verity founded and hosts 'Art Laughs' live art-themed comedy events, which have been held around the UK including at the National Gallery and the Edinburgh Festival Fringe. She has worked as a presenter for major arts institutions including Tate and London Art Fair. She has appeared on BBC News and BBC Radio 4, and was named as one of BBC History Extra's '30 Under 30' in 2024. This is her debut book, inspired by her series of '1 Sentence Answer' videos she began sharing online in 2022.

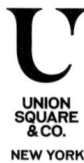

UNION SQUARE & CO.

NEW YORK

UNION SQUARE & CO. and the distinctive Union Square & Co. logo are trademarks of Hachette Book Group, Inc.

Text © 2025 Verity Babbs
Illustrations © 2025 Alexandra Ramirez

All rights reserved. No part of this publication may be reproduced, stored in a retrieval system, or transmitted in any form or by any means (including electronic, mechanical, photocopying, recording, or otherwise) without prior written permission from the publisher.

All trademarks are the property of their respective owners, are used for editorial purposes only, and the publisher makes no claim of ownership and shall acquire no right, title, or interest in such trademarks by virtue of this publication.

Original edition published in the UK in 2025 by Bloomsbury Publishing. This 2025 hardcover edition is published by Union Square & Co.

ISBN 978-1-4549-6553-4 (hardcover)
ISBN 978-1-4549-6554-1 (e-book)

Union Square & Co. books may be purchased in bulk for business, educational, or promotional use. For more information, please contact your local bookseller or the Hachette Book Group's Special Markets department at special.markets@hbgusa.com.

Printed in Dubai

2 4 6 8 10 9 7 5 3 1

unionsquareandco.com

Cover design by Kaylie Pendleton and Hello Daly
Interior design by Hello Daly

Back cover image © 2025 Alexandra Ramirez